Ciderland

Explore everything;
keep the best

John Evelyn
1620–1706

Ciderland

JAMES CROWDEN

BIRLINN

First published in 2008 by
Birlinn Limited
West Newington House
10 Newington Road
Edinburgh
EH9 1QS

www.birlinn.co.uk

ISBN13: 978 1 84158 627 4
ISBN10: 1 84158 627 7

British Library Cataloguing-in-Publication Data
A catalogue record for this book is available from
the British Library

Designed and typeset by Mark Blackadder

Printed and bound by Bell & Bain Ltd, Glasgow

Contents

To
Carol Trewin

Acknowledgements

This book has been a voyage of discovery and it has been an enormous privilege to have had the time to interview some of the country's leading cidermakers. They are not just dedicated enthusiasts; they have given every second of their spare time to learning about and improving their craft. It is an art; but the science sometimes helps them to understand what is happening, or not happening. Without these people there would be no book and no exceptional cider to drink. So thank you, cidermakers.

And a word about perry, too, because it deserves a book on its own. The confidence and skill of those craft perrymakers and their dogged determination to find out what it is the perry pear is trying to give them is astounding.

Pears for heirs. Get planting now. I feel that the traditions of artisan perry and cider are really beginning to take off. And the public is now at last ready to explore the lanes and byways in the west of England on pilgrimage to seek out these producers.

My thanks to Claire Davies for wonderful photography and a real ability to put the cidermakers at their ease; and to Chris Chapman and Bill Bradshaw for their photographs. My thanks to Liz Copas for allowing me to use little bits from her book *Somerset Pomona* about Long Ashton and the classification of Somerset Cider apples; to the Museum of Cider in Hereford for allowing me to use their archive; and to David Prysor-Jones for lending me his copy of Worlidge and Thomas Andrew Knight; to Julian Temperley, who employed me for 12 seasons pressing apples, as well as Andrew Lea, Simon Russell, Nick Bradstock and Peter Mitchell for answering technical queries on cider-making.

I am also very grateful to the staff of the British Library for helping with research into Ralph Austen; Hazel Forsyth at the Museum of London for discussing early bottle glass and Scudamore's flute; the staff at the Royal Society Library for allowing me to research the early letters and registers of the Royal Society; Richard Watkins for finding old rare cider books and for compiling the index; Tom Stevenson, Bob and Sam Lindo of Camel Valley wines; Alistair Peebles of the Devon Wine School for reading the text on Sparkling cider/*méthode champenoise* with a critical eye; the Comité Interprofessionnel du Vin de Champagne; CIVC in London; Derek Pritchard; Liam Steevenson; Prof. James Turner of Berkeley, California to use quotes about Ralph Austen; Ian Atherton of Keele University for information on John Scudamore; Dr Serena Marks of Glasgow University for her work on cider and health; *The Hereford Times*; Rupert Best for allowing us to photograph his orchards in Dorset; David Jones and Sue Morgan at Sink Green Farm, Rotherwas for putting me up when 'researching' in Herefordshire.

Thanks are due also to Carol Trewin for endless proof-reading and sub-editing; my father once again for helping to test-drive the various ciders and perries; Michael Raffael for suggesting to Birlinn that I should do the book; to Hugh Andrew and Susan Sutterby for commissioning; Alison Moss and Andrew Simmons for editing and Mark Blackadder for design.

James Crowden,
August 2008

Glossary

abv Alcohol by volume; this gives the strength of the cider, usually between 6 and 8 per cent if fermented naturally without added sugar. Some ciders can be above 8.5 per cent but they are taxed as apple wine.

acetification Cider becomes vinegary. Although it can affect any cider stored in contact with warm air, the problem is more common with scrumpy made with rotten fruit in unclean barrels. The cause is aerobic bacteria *acetobacter* and *acetomonas*. These bacteria metabolise alcohol as well as sugars and are not killed during fermentation, which is why they appear afterwards.

alcohol Ethanol which is derived from the fermentation process where yeasts turn the natural sugars in the apple juice into alchohol and carbon dioxide. There are other higher alcohols called fusel alcohols.

angel's share The proportion of spirit lost in the maturation of cider brandy while in oak barrels in bond. This can be 2 per cent a year. See **maturation**.

apple A fruit that has evolved from the native crab apple and the sweeter apples that have migrated from the Tien Shan in Central Asia.

apple engine In the old days a horse used to walk round a solid granite trough in which the apple was crushed. Then *ingenios* were invented with men turning wheels and cogs, and the apple was crushed between teeth or rollers. Now a high-speed mill does the job, fed by an elevator.

aroma compounds These are the compounds that give cider its fruity flavour and taste. They are fusel or higher alcohols and esters, as well as fatty acids, aldehydes and ketones. Some are in the apples and others are created during fermentation.

artisan cider and perry making This has been taken up by the Three Counties cider and perry makers, who are very active, and the Artisan Perry Makers, who are linked into the UK Slow Food Movement and already have a presidium for their product.

asparagine An amino acid, $C_4H_8N_2O_3$, which is found in cider-apple juice along with aspartic and glutamic acids. These acids provide essential nitrogen for the fermentation. This enables the yeast to provide its own protein and hence multiply. Asparagine is also found in asparagus, hence its name.

barrel A wooden cask usually made from oak or chestnut and bound with metal hoops. Usually one barrel contains about 36 gallons. They are made and repaired by coopers.

bitter-sharp A term used for cider apples that are high in acidity and tannin, such as Kingston Black, Porter's Perfection, Lambrook Pippin, Stembridge Clusters and Lorna Doone.

bitter-sweet A term used for cider apples that are high in sugars and high in tannins, such as Tremlett's Bitter, Dabinett, Chisel Jersey, Yarlington Mill, Ellis Bitter, Bulmer's Norman, Michelin, Brown Snout, Vilberie, and Major.

bond This is the bonded warehouse where spirits are kept while they mature. The duty is paid on each barrel as it is removed from bond. This is the demesne of Customs and Excise, now known as HM Revenue and Customs. Bonds are notoriously well built and all the windows are barred. Certain bonds have a cool, damp atmosphere like a cave, which is just what you want – even temperature and a secure environment.

bottle-conditioned cider Also called the Normandy method, this is where the natural fermentation is halted by the process of keeving and there is a residual sweetness left in the cider when it is bottled. See **keeving**. Bottle-conditioned cider contains yeast and is cloudy. It is also naturally sparkling, but not as sparkling as bottle-fermented cider. The process takes three to five months to mature. This is the *cidre bouché* of Normandy and varies between 4 and 5 per cent abv. This is not to be confused with bottles of artificially sweetened and carbonated cider.

bottle-fermented sparkling cider The time-consuming process known in the wine trade as *méthode champenoise* or *methode traditionelle* involves the first fermentation outside the bottle and then a secondary fermentation inside the bottle. Strong dark bottle glass has to be used. A little champagne yeast is added with the correct quantity of sugar. Too much and the bottle explodes; too little and there is no sparkle. The bottle is crown capped and allowed to ferment on its own. When fermentation is complete the bottles are stacked on a bottle rack or pupitre and riddled (given a quarter turn each day) over several weeks; this gets the residual yeast sediment into the neck of the bottle. Next comes the *degorgement* or disgorgement, where the neck of the bottle is frozen, uncapped and the sediment pops out as a solid plug. The bottle is then topped up and cork inserted, wired down and the bottle labelled. The whole process can take eighteen months to two years and leaves a clear sparkling cider or perry. It can be kept for up to two years. Its average strength is between 8 and 8.5 per cent abv.

butt These large wooden casks can hold anything from 108 to 140 gallons. They are usually reckoned to be the same as two hogsheads.

carbonation Carbon dioxide is introduced to a bottled cider to give it fizz and sparkle: not to be confused with the natural sparkling methods of bottle-conditioned and bottle-fermented cider.

chaptalisation Named after Jean-Antoine Chaptal, Comte de Chanteloup (1756–1832). He was a chemist and politician in Paris and an interesting man in Napoleon's government, in charge of midwiferey as well as gunpowder. He saw the advantages in adding sugar to grape juice before fermentation in the wines of northern France when there was a poor year. In France the technique is still used but is heavily regulated. In Engand cider makers have also used this technique to raise alcohol levels by 1 or 2 degrees; it is a technique widely used by the industrial cider makers, who take cider up to 14 per cent abv by using glucose syrup and bring it down again when it suits them, which is a completely different ethic altogether. Some regulation of this practice might well be long overdue.

chapeau brun The brown cap, this is the flying lees that forms a cap on top of the cider during the keeving process, which keep the air out. It consists of pectin and calcium.

cheese Refers to a neat layered mound of chopped cider apple and straw which is built *in situ* within the press. Now cheese cloths are used, which used to be made of horsehair then hessian, now nylon. The old use of the word 'cheese' is for anything that is wrapped up. In large farms the cheeses are built on small trolleys and wheeled in and then out of the press. They weigh about a ton. In Somerset, 'cheese' can also refer to Cheddar which is also wrapped in cheese cloths. The process of a wrapping and pressing is of course very similar, though the pressures and time scale are different. Cider and cheese always go together.

cider A strong alcoholic drink made from cider apples. In the West Country this traditionally refers to a drink made from cider apples with high tannin content to aid flavour and preservation.

cider brandy Distilled liquor of cider aged in oak. The word brandy comes from the Dutch meaning burnt wine. The terms apple brandy and cider brandy have been used since 1676.

ciderkin Term used for small cider made from the second pressing. Often drunk at harvest as it was less potent for those wielding a scythe.

Ciderland A seventeenth-century term for the western counties that made cider – Cornwall, Devon, Dorset, Somerset, Gloucestershire, Worcestershire and Herefordshire. The term is used by John Phillips in his poem 'Cyder' (1708).

cider shoe This was about twelve inches high, usually made of copper or brass and was used for mulling cider by shoving the toe into the ashes of an open fire.

cider sickness This is a milky haze that occurs in warm weather and has the smell of rotten banana skins. The problem happens if the cider is not acidic enough and is stored sweet. It can be prevented if the fermentation is completed by adding yeast and nutrients.

citric acid Found in small quantities in apple juice and at a greater concentration in perry pear juice. It is sometimes added to a final blend of cider to correct a deficiency in natural acid.

concentrate Usually apple or pear concentrate, this is the residual liquid left after the fruit juice has been heated up (usually under a vaccuum) and evaporated. It usually has a caramelised flavour like toffee apples and gives the colour and flavour to mass-produced cider. It can either be foreign or home made.

costrel: A small wooden cask that could be tied around the waist and taken out into the fields by farm workers. (See **firkin**.)

cyser Cider strengthened with honey before fermentation. It was common in medieval times. Also refers to apple-flavoured mead.

Devonshire colic This was an eighteenth-century term for lead poisoning caused by a reaction between the cider and the lead used to repair the bases of presses and in runnels. Also some unscrupulous cider makers used lead acetate to sweeten cider to make it keep better. The Romans used this in their export wine with disastrous consequences.

feints The generic term for the fractions of cider brandy distillation which are put aside to be redistilled. They are the tops and tails of the fraction that you really want.

fermentation The natural sugars in the apple juice are turned into alcohol by wild or introduced yeasts. At the beginning there is a lot of frothing and this normally escapes from the barrels and carries with it unwanted apple debris. The frothing is caused by carbon dioxide. There may be as many as 10 million yeast cells per single millilitre of juice. So it is a vigorous chain reaction. This often continues till all the sugar has been converted, and can be tracked by using a hydrometer to monitor the specific gravity, which will fall as the fermentation progresses. Once the fermentation has stopped you can rack the cider into another barrel and then filter and bottle.

fining Clarifying cider which has too many solids in suspension. Various compounds can be used, such as bentonite, gelatin, chilin, casein and albumen as well as isinglass. Fining agents either have a positive or negative charge, depending on which you need. Fining of ales has been going on for centuries.

firkin Small wooden barrel carried into the fields by farm labourers holding about half a gallon. Also called a **costrel**.

graft The ancient and skilled act of grafting or securing a new graft or scion onto a rootstock.

gribble Young tree that has grown from a pip from pomace thrown from last year's pressing.

hogshead A barrel that holds between 54 and 64 gallons. A Herefordshire hogshead was deemed to be much larger, sometimes 110 gallons, hence the wider doorways in Herefordshire houses giving access to the cider cellar.

Jaisy Old Somerset term for apple now corrupted into 'Jersey' in Chisel Jersey. The term means bitter-sweet cider apples in south Somerset.

keeving or Normandy method An ancient method of making cider which allows some of the natural sweetness to remain, whereby after initial maceration, enzymes and chalk are used to trigger the formation of the *chapeau brun*, which also traps nutrients from the juice. The trick is to carefully rack off the middle clear section of the cider.

kler cidre A liquid obtainable from France which has the pectin esterase enzyme and calcium chloride available together for use in the keeving or *defecation* process to make Normandy cider. It helps in the formation of the *chapeau brun*.

lactic acid Known as milk acid. It is found in sour milk and yogurt but in cider making it is formed during the malolactic fermentation when the harsher malic acid is converted into the so-called buttery notes of Chardonnay. This secondary fermentation is caused by lactic acid bacteria, not yeast.

low wines The alcohol produced during the first distillation, with a strength of approximately 25 per cent abv. This is redistilled or, in the case of a Coffey still, recycled.

maceration This occurs when the cider apples or perry pears are milled and then left in their own juice in an open trough overnight to oxidise: it also softens the tannins. They are sometimes left for 24 hours. This was common practice in Normandy, the Channel Islands and Devon for making a sweeter cider. Perry makers also use this technique.

malic acid A natural acid occurring in apples, hence its name. It is what makes green apples taste sharp. It is an essential part of the cider-making process as it adds acidity, which controls bacterial infections. It is also turned into lactic acid in the malolactic fermentation, which softens the cider.

malolactic fermentation This occurs naturally and is sometimes called secondary fermentation, although this is not strictly true as it differs markedly from the first fermentation. It normally occurs in late spring or early summer, when the air temperatures rise above 15°C. Instead of sugars being converted into alcohol by yeasts, the sharp malic acid is turned by lactic acid bacteria into lactic acid, which is milder

and softer, and carbon dioxide. It improves the cider and takes out the rough edges. It also gives the cider a natural sparkle. The acidity can fall by as much as 50 per cent.

Malus pumila The domestic sweet apple, which was introduced by the Romans and which is in turn descended from ***Malus sieversii***.

Malus sieversii The apple from which British apples are descended, found in the Tien Shan mountains in Kazakhstan. Recent work by Barrie Juniper at Oxford has shed new light on this remarkable DNA journey.

Malus sylvestris The common crab apple that is indigenous to Britain. It provides good rootstock and you can make very good cider as well as crab apple jelly from it. It often grows in hedgerows.

Malus sylvestyris mitis A sub-species of crab apple formed from the descendants of cultivated apple, for example, an apple from a tree grown from a core thrown out of a passing train or car window.

maturation The process of allowing cider and perry to mature at their own pace in oak barrels. It is also a key part of the distillation process and happens within a bonded warehouse. Some spirit is lost but the remainder improves and is smoothed out.

méthode champenoise See **bottle-fermented cider**.

mouse A technical term used in cider tasting for a cider that has deteriorated and has a stale, musty, oxidised flavour, sometimes reminiscent of popcorn or a mouse cage. Primarily caused by unwanted contamination with certain wild strains of lactic acid bacteria. Can also refer to a small animal running round the cider house.

mulling A way of using spices, sugar and lemon juice to make a warm and heartening winter drink: usually involves cloves, mace, nutmeg and cinnamon in a muslin bag. In the old days a red hot poker would be thrust into the cider.

Normandy method: See **keeving**.

orchard Derived from Old English *ortgeard*. These days orchards are classified as either standard orchards with tall, mature, well-spaced trees, half standards or bush orchards, which are on dwarf root stock. Bush orchards crop much more heavily and are planted much closer together. They also require much more maintenance and spraying. Traditional orchards will have about 30 trees to the acre compared to 300 for bush orchards.

PGI Protected Geographical Indication is a European designation designed to protect a product that comes from a particular area, thus safeguarding the integrity of regional food and drink. So far only the Three Counties of Herefordshire, Worcestershire and Gloucestershire have taken this up and registered their cider and perry, which has to be made entirely with fruit from the Three Counties. An alternative but slightly different EU designation is PDO (Protected Designation of Origin). To qualify, the fruit must come from a particular county and the product be a minimum 85 per cent pure juice, with the process to be agreed in advance with the Three Counties Presidium.

pasteurisation This is the process of heating up a product and keeping it at a certain temperature for a set amount of time to destroy harmful bacteria that might either spoil it or cause it to re-ferment. For instance, in the case of cider, 63°C for 20 minutes gives 55 pasteurisation units. The higher the temperature of pasteurisation, the more the flavour is affected. There is also flash pasteurisation, which is useful when filling bag-in-the-box cartons with cider or apple juice.

pear cider A new term that has crept into the industrial cider language over the last two years. Although the NACM has approved its use the definition is relatively meaningless and is in many ways counter-productive. A drink is either cider or perry, it cannot be both. Pear cider is almost always made from imported pear concentrate, not perry pears. Pear cider is an industrialised drink not to be confused with the ancient and very skilled craft of perry making.

pectin This is naturally present within the apple and the skin. It is often left in the pomace after pressing, where it is extracted to make pectin commercially, and it is then used as a setting agent in the jam and jelly-making process, and in many other products. Its chemical properties are also used in the keeving process. It is a most useful by-product of cider making.

perry An alcoholic drink made from perry pears. Perry is really an aperitif for a summer's day and can have a floral hedgerow nose like elderflower. Unlike cider, it tends to have some residual sweetness, as it contains some unfermented sugars, which makes it very palatable. The centre for perry making is the Three Counties of Worcestershire, Herefordshire and Gloucestershire, but many other counties did make it historically. There is now a revival in perry making in Somerset, Devon and Dorset. Not to be confused with pear cider at any cost.

perry pears These are pears used to make perry and are mostly to be found in the Three Counties of Gloucestershire, Herefordshire and Worcestershire. The pears are unpredictable and very varied in shape, colour and seasonality. They are odd to say the least, often hard as bullets and can go soft overnight.

pipe A large wooden vessel synonymous with a butt holding about 110 gallons. These were often used for transporting cider, sherry, port or wine in ships and barges. Often used by cider makers once the port or sherry has been drunk. The residual flavours are very useful.

polyphenols A technical term for the compounds found in tannins which give cider apples their distinct characteristics and set them aside from dessert apples.

pomace Term used for the milled or pulped cider apple as well as the layers of spent apple after it has been pressed. Often fed to farm animals.

possett An Elizabethan drink or pudding made with cider, sugar, cream, eggs and spices.

press A mechanical device for pressing apples. Some were beam presses exactly like those used by the Romans for pressing grapes and olive oil. Later there were single-thread wooden presses to be followed by double metal thread presses. Sometimes there were capstan presses. Now there are hydraulic presses, belt presses and centrifugal presses.

pruning An important part of the orchard work. Good pruning lets in light and air, which cuts down disease; it also leads to greater fruiting and more blossom. Ideally trees should be pruned every year, but it is more often every other year.

puncheon A wooden vessel holding 84 gallons.

pupitre The French term for the bottle rack used in *méthode champenoise*.

quinic acid One of the acids found in cider apples and also obtained from cinchona bark and coffee beans.

racking A simple method of pumping or, better still, siphoning cider from a barrel to take it off its lees – the residue left after fermentation has ceased. The trick is not to disturb the lees. Cider may benefit from racking several times, particularly if you are after residual sweetness.

ropiness A term used for cider that has gone slimey and has an oil-like texture. This is caused by unwanted strains of lactic acid bacteria. It can be cured by gelatin fining.

scratter Mill for cutting up apples while crushing, sometimes driven by a horse. Sometimes known as an *ingenio*, these efficient devices were first used on plantations in Cuba in the seventeenth century to crush the sugar cane.

scrumpy Traditionally cider made with any old cider apples, or apples that have been scrumped or stolen. It is a slightly derogatory term today when compared with high-quality farmhouse ciders. It is a natural, unfiltered cider produced without access to modern production techniques, such as introduced yeasts, sulphur dioxide, filtering or bottling. It can be very good indeed; on the other hand, if it has been hanging around in plastic bottles or unclean barrels, it can be awful and vinegary.

sharps Cider apples that are generally high in acidity but low in sugars and tannins: they are also good as dual-purpose apples.

sodium metabisulphite This is an inorganic compound and source of sulphur dioxide (sulphites), widely used in the food and drinks industry as a steriliser, antioxidant and preservative. It is often used to clean cider-making equipment before use and is introduced into bottled cider to help preserve it. It is also used to knock out natural yeasts at the beginning of a controlled fermentation.

specific gravity This is usually measured with a hydrometer and refers to the density of the liquid. The denser the apple juice, i.e. the more sugar it has in it, the higher the hydrometer will float. Conversely the more alcohol in the cider after fermentation, the lower the hydrometer will float. Water has an SG of 1000 so the measurement of specific gravity is an important way of monitoring the cider's progress. Fifteen per cent sugar corresponds to a specific gravity of 1070 and a total potential alcohol of around 8.5 per cent, which is right on the legal limit for cider; 10 per cent sugars have an SG of 1045 and a potential alcohol of 6 per cent. Most ciders are between these levels.

sweet A term for a cider apple that is high in sugars but low in tannins.

sugar This occurs naturally in apple juice as glucose, fructose and sucrose and is a vital part of cider making, because it is the sugars that are converted into alcohol during the fermentation process. The sunnier the weather the more sugar, the sweeter the apple juice, the more alcohol in the cider.

sulphur This has been used since Roman times to fumigate barrels and keep cider-making and wine-making equipment clean. Some cider makers still use sulphur candles. Usually the term covers sulphur dioxide, which is produced when sulphur is burnt or it is produced when sodium metabisulphite is added to water. Many bottled ciders contain sulphites these days to stop them re-fermenting in the bottle, a potentially dangerous situation on a supermarket shelf. Sulphur has been a great asset to cider makers and still is but its excessive use can be detrimental to the taste of final product.

syllabub A light frothy pudding made with cider, cream and lemon peel. Like posset, it was all the rage in the sixteenth and seventeenth centuries.

tannin A term that covers a whole range of nonvolatile phenolic substances found in cider apples, which provide depth, complexity and body to cider as well as the astringent feel in the mouth. There are a dozen or more of these phenols in apples, such as chlorogenic acid, phloridzin, epicatechin and the procyanidins. These procyanidins are capable of tanning animal hides, hence the name. Tannins are also present in tea, oak bark, red wine and pomegranates. They are in a sense the apple's natural defence mechanism against mould and bacteria. It is the high levels of tannin in cider apples that clearly defines the difference between dessert-apple cider and cider made in the West of England. Tannin also helps to preserve the cider once it is made: without tannins cider will not keep long at all unless preservatives are added.

thiamin or thiamine Vitamin B1, a nitrogen-containing vitamin that helps yeast in the fermentation and the final conversion with enzymes of pyruvate to ethanol.

tun A large wooden barrel which holds 2 pipes or 220–240 gallons, used for transporting wines and cider by boat; hence the term tunnage or tonnage as a term of lading in shipping.

tundish Old type of wooden funnel used for filling barrels, usually made from the end of a small barrel.

vat These are made of vertical oak staves held together with iron or wire hoops and can hold anything from 5,000 to 60,000 gallons. Often lined with beeswax.

verjuice Sharp green juice from fresh crab and cider apples, used in possetts and syllabubs. Drawings for verjuice presses exist and indicate they were not as big as normal cider presses. Each home could have one, even in towns.

wassail The act of drinking a toast to the cider god in the orchard, accompanied by the letting off of firearms and shotguns, and the consumption of liquor. Wassail cups and bowls are much prized. Some villages in Somerset, such as Drayton and Carhampton, still have intact wassail songs. Most celebrate this on the eve of Twelfth Night (5/6 January), while others choose the old New Year (17 January).

white cider Large manufacturers of cider make this on an industrial scale. With the addition of water and glucose it is fermented out to about 15 per cent and then brought down to around 7.5 per cent. It is cheap and easy to make. It has some apple content but doesn't really deserve the accolade of the name 'cider'. The colour is removed by adsorption with the charcoal, i.e. carbon: like rough acetic scrumpy, it has given cider a bad name. Best drunk in bus shelters!

yeasts These are important organisms for the cider maker, for without yeast there is no fermentation. Cider will ferment of its own accord with wild yeasts but there is no telling in which direction it will eventually go. With judicious use of sulphites to clean the barrels, or stainless steel vats, wild yeasts can be used successfully. There are many types of wild yeasts and most cider makers use trial and error when starting out to see what works best for them. Some notable wild yeasts found in the apple juice are *Kloeckera apiculata*, *Saccharromycodes ludgwigii* and *Candida sp*, and these will kickstart the fermentation, but the ones that you want to take over, are more likely to be the genus *Saccharomyces*, such as *S cerevisiae* and *S bayanus*. These are found on the cider-making machinery. They can also be added deliberately. Alternatively you can knock out the wild yeasts with sodium metabisulphite and introduce your own yeast to suit your apples. Yeasts can lead to various cider disorders such as film yeasts, snowflake infection, hydrogen sulphide formation and the musty/acetic taint often associated with wild yeasts.

Introduction

'Their orchards might well be styled as
temples and apple trees their idols of worship.'
William Marshall, 1796

With names such as Kingston Black, Yarlington Mill, Foxwhelp, Redstreak, Pig's Snout, Sheep's Nose, Slack-Ma-Girdle, Hangdown, Long Tom and Hoary Morning, cider apples have a long and interesting history. But these apples are a fraction of the hundreds of varieties used in cider making and are very different from the 'normal' eating apples you find in the supermarket. For a start, cider apples are often smaller, and if you bite into them they taste sour or astringent, more like wild crab apples. But it is their precious juice, which is often surprisingly high in natural sugars, that is so crucial to the cider making process. For once fermented with yeasts in large vats or wooden barrels called hogsheads, butts and pipes, this juice eventually gives us the rich, deep colour and taste of farmhouse cider for which the West Country is justly famous.

And then there are the small, hard, quirky perry pears with strange and wonderful names such as Ducksbarn, Brown Bess, Hellen's Early, Gregg's Pitt, Hendre Huffcap, Dead Boy, Holmer, Blakeney Red, Brandy, Butt, Coppy, Taynton Squash, Oldfield, Winnal's Longdon and Moorcroft, alias Stinking Bishop, which is used for rind-washing one of Charles Martell's more famous cheeses of the same name. These perry pears, like the cider apples, are also steeped in history and mythology. It is often said in folklore that you can only make good perry if

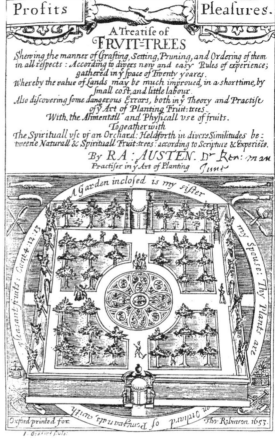

you are within sight of May Hill, which is near Newent. There is a certain amount of truth in this, as the heartland of the perry-making area covers most of Gloucestershire, Herefordshire and parts of Worcestershire.

To visit a traditional cider farm in spring and to stroll through the orchards when row upon row of apple trees are in full blossom is one of the finest experiences of the whole year, a sight that will stay with you for the rest of your life. There is something magical about orchards and cider farms; something that keeps drawing you back time and time again; something ethereal that you can't quite put your finger on. Some orchards are well organised with long lines of regimented trees, while others appear haphazard and dotted with wizened giants, which suddenly burst into blossom with the power of

Stravinsky's 'Rite of Spring', the sheer force and intensity taking you by surprise. Old perry pear trees are often like this. These magnificent giants can be 60 feet high and more than 300 years old, and still produce fruit. They are reminders of a bygone age and a clue to the prosperity and beauty that once must have graced our western counties.

It is these natural hidden rhythms that remind us of a time when the pace of life was less intense. There is also a sense that we have, however briefly, arrived in the Garden of Eden, particularly when there are sheep grazing among the trees with lambs at foot.

The planting of large-scale orchards in the seventeenth century following the bloody Civil War laid the foundations of the cider world we see today. That this was happening predominantly in the west of England is no surprise, because the monasteries

Above left. Two hundred-year old perry pear tree at Weston's, Much Marcle.
Above right. Frontispiece from *A Treatise on Fruit Trees and The Spiritual Use of an Orchard*, by Ralph Austen, 1653.

there had once held cider in great esteem and built great tithe barns that housed large cider presses and ranks of wooden barrels. The new land-owning families, who had taken their place at the helm of rural England, saw it as their duty to provide their own Garden of Eden, a spiritual paradise on their doorstep, which provided not only cider but rural employment and helped the economy in times of crisis. Great tomes and treatises were written on the subject. These aristocratic improvers had an almost religious zeal, which still hangs in the air today. So marked was the improvement that the whole of the West Country, from Cornwall to Herefordshire via Devon, Dorset, Somerset and Gloucestershire was simply referred to as 'Ciderland'.

During the Commonwealth period 1650-60 many writers saw cider and orchards as a sure way to improve the rural economy. The combination of beauty and productivity was so seductive that many of the early writers and poets made a direct link between orchards and earthly paradise. Even the new Puritan politics approved of cider.

The real heyday of cider was therefore during the seventeenth and eighteenth centuries. It seems that a bout of very severe weather in the early 1600s knocked out many of the vineyards, particularly in Gloucestershire. The production of cider was the obvious alternative and some of the best minds in the country became obsessed with it. Men like Lord Scudamore, Ralph Austen, John Beale, Samuel Hartlib, Sir Kenelm Digby and William Harvey (he who discovered how blood circulates). They saw cider as the national drink, as a symbol of Englishness and independence from Europe and Catholic France. Cider was to rival wine in their affections and because of the English weather, cider orchards would be far more productive and economic than English vineyards would ever be; and they still are.

Today cider and perry are experiencing a renaissance. There is a grass-roots reawakening, which is very heartening to see, and I hope to reveal some of the enthusiasm that I have encountered talking to people whose lives revolve around cider apples and perry pears.

My journey through Ciderland has taken me from Andy Atkinson's Cornish orchards at Duloe, three miles inland from Looe, right up to Ivor and Susie Dunkerton at Pembridge, six miles west of Leominster in Herefordshire. And in between I have visited countless cider farms and perry orchards interviewing and researching, probing and recording, finding out what makes these cider and perry makers tick, what it is that they are after, and why they have dedicated their lives to producing what is after all a very labour-intensive drink.

Here the comparison with cheese is a very valid one. For years we became accustomed to the bland, industrialised, block cheddar, but now we have access to top-quality unpasteurised mature farm-house cheddar, as well as many other artisan cheeses, such as Stinking Bishop and Dorset Blue Vinny. Over the last 30 years there has been a quiet revolution in the countryside and cider is very much a part of this. The pendulum is swinging very much in favour of the small- to medium-sized cider makers who have access to top-quality fruit. The public is quite rightly keen to explore new tastes and to learn about what is, after all, their heritage, particularly if they live in the West Country. Within their cider they want the deep complexities of taste that tannin gives, as it does in good claret; they want character and they want a real human story to go with it. And this book provides those stories, encompassing a very wide range of cider makers. Some only make 1,500 gallons a year, if that; others, well established, such as Sheppy's and Burrow Hill, make around 100,000 gallons a year; while at the top end, Westons of Much Marcle make 3.5 million gallons a year or, as they put it, 28 million pints.

The diversity of producers is enormous. There are well-established family cider makers as well as ex-dairy farmers, haulage contractors, TV producers, rock-band roadies, environmental policy directors, agricultural engineers, radar specialists, barristers, sheep farmers, distillers, bio-chemists, medical students and commodity traders, indy band sound engineers, surf gear saleswomen, vegetable merchants, motorcyclists and photographers. All have somehow been inspired to enter the world of cider and perry. They are what make Ciderland exciting and vibrant today.

HISTORY AND CULTURE

To fully understand cider making, you have to first understand the importance of a well-kept orchard made up of a mixed variety of apple trees. Once the delicate blossom has been fertilised and the fruit has set then the trees are safe from the ravages of late frosts. One night's heavy frost in early or mid May can wipe out half an orchard and with it the farm's profits. In Devon, the nights around 21 May were always called 'Frankan' nights, as some farmers were said to do a deal with the devil if he kept the frosts away.

Over the next few months the apples will grow almost imperceptibly and then in September their growth intensifies and the apples colour up until they are ripe and blushing and ready to be picked. In the autumn it is worth returning to the same orchards you visited in spring to see the trees richly laden with fruit. Here you see nature at its most bountiful. But what also has a deep effect on the senses are the long mounds of apples piled up in the farmyards, giving off the intoxicating mellow scent of mature fruit. It is from this ripe fruit that orangey-brown apple juice will flow as the apples are pressed out. In the past this was done with tall wooden cider presses, but these days they have been superseded by hydraulic presses or belt presses. However, the principle is just the same as it was a thousand years ago. You have a crusher or scratter that chops the apples up (see pp. 18–19), a press and a long series of wooden barrels or vats.

One thing that is certain is that cider farms in the West Country are still places of worship and pilgrimage despite the modern moves in technology. These farms have a devoted following and enjoy an almost mythical status in people's imagination. To some they represent the true spirit of the land, bastions against industrialisation, bureaucracy and mediocrity. There is a heady whiff of independence and nonconformity which many find attractive.

In fact, cider and perry are so deeply embedded in the psychology and mystique of the West Country that it is very difficult to disentangle the tradition from the landscape itself. For hundreds of

years cider orchards have played a vital part in the rural economy. The vast scale of this orcharding, even in the late nineteenth century, is perhaps difficult for us to comprehend today. Every spring in the West Country there would have been more than 120,000 acres of orchard in blossom. In those heady days almost every farm had its own orchard and at harvest time there were also mobile cider makers. Some even pressed the fruit in the orchard itself. Sadly, through the ages many apple and pear varieties have become extinct, but a few have recently been rediscovered in remote spots and safely guarded. Many trees were simply cut down to make way for houses without ever being identified.

But cider making is quite complex. A cider apple is not just a cider apple. There are bitter-sweets, bitter-sharps, sweets and sharps depending on the amount of sugar, tannin and malic acid in them. It is the differences in these levels that the cider maker is really interested in, as it will often define the way he makes the cider and the taste of the end product.

Some apples, such as Tom Putt and Crimson King, are dual purpose and can be used for cider and cooking. The sharpness of cider apples, often associated with cooking apples like Bramleys, comes from the acidity of malic acid, not to be confused with the astringency, which comes from tannins. Tannins hold the key to good cider. They help preserve the cider to the following summer, they are nature's antioxidants and they are responsible for the rich rounded flavours which can sometimes make the taste of West Country cider as deep and complex as a fine Bordeaux.

A good orchard may well have between ten and twenty different varieties of cider apples and that is why one farmer's cider will taste totally different from another's. And then there are the influences of

Opposite. Nineteenth-century horse-drawn cider press, Burrow Hill, Somerset.
Above. Arthur and Harold Stephens with their circular cider press at New Barn Farm, Bere Ferrers, Devon. Sadly, Arthur (on the left) died two days after the photo was taken. (Photograph © Chris Chapman, 2004.)

the soils and the different situations of the orchards, micro climates and the weather patterns. In some ways tasting and blending high-quality cider each year is just as exciting as wine tasting, and cider *terroir* is on your doorstep.

In the past the skill of individual cider makers was always held to be the social barometer and farmers either had good standing in the community or not. The reputation of their cider also had a marked effect on their ability to attract the best farm workers. Some sheep shearers on the Dorset/Somerset border would drive into a farm and taste the cider and if it wasn't any good they would drive on out again, their philosophy being that if the farmer couldn't make decent cider, his sheep would be in poor condition and difficult to shear. And he would be left till last on the list.

Cider was a common denominator. It was drunk by royalty at one end of the social scale and by farm workers at the other. It was on the tables of the Oxford Colleges, in every pub and every farmhouse kitchen. It had a value way beyond its economic worth, and even sometimes replaced wine at communion. For centuries cider paid the rent and was used to pay the wages on the farms. Many nineteenth-century teetotal campaigners saw the consumption of cider in the workplace as deleterious to people's lives.

In 1887 a Cider Truck Act was introduced which prohibited the payment of wages in cider, but this had little effect and even as late as 1940 there were advertisements on the front page of Somerset newspapers attracting farm workers with a promise of 'good house and cider'.

One cider maker I knew quite well in the late 1960s was Horace Lancaster of aptly named Felldownhead, near Milton Abbot, whose cider farm nestled above the Tamar Valley on the Devon side. He used to quote an age-old aphorism as he came out of the dark barns rubbing his hands: 'Bread is the Staff of Life, but Cider is life itself'. Horace's cider was very good indeed and although he had an enviable local trade he also had the foresight to send cider on up to Aberdeen by lorry, where it quenched the thirst of oil rig workers on shore leave. North Sea Cider.

Quality farmhouse cider will always travel and be in demand and luckily the art of making it has survived through to the present day. No doubt it has benefited from modern advances in science, which have revealed the complex processes that take place during fermentation, but many would maintain it is still an art, not a science.

But how very different this farmhouse cider is from the mass-produced, computer-controlled cider processes which have been on stream for many years. In the big cider factories today they simply press a few buttons and stand back. Uniformity, consistency and profit have taken precedence over subtlety, depth and character. As one large-scale cider maker said to me: 'it is not what we put in that's the secret but what we take out'. This cider is made largely from apple concentrate, a trend that began in the 1960s. Looking back, although apparently leading to greater efficiency, the sustained use of concentrate was in fact a national calamity, particularly as the large companies diluted the juice down so that their cider is made with about 30 per cent juice rather than the pure 100 per cent favoured by farmhouse cider. The resulting drink is carbonated and has colourings and flavours added to make it seem like the real thing.

True, some of the 'traditional farmhouse' ciders can be unpredictable and in some cases very acetic and clearly undrinkable, but the new generation of cider makers who have emerged in the last 30 years can be justifiably proud of their cider and perry. Even a few of the large manufacturers such as Gaymers have started making 'orchard reserve' ciders, and this can only be a positive thing. Supermarkets have begun to understand that there is a niche market for good cider and that the public is keen to experiment with new tastes and flavours, as we once did with New World wine and real ale. Cider is the new temptation, and its place is once more back on the dining table at home or in the restaurant where it belongs, not just in the old cider houses – but it was the old cider houses and farmhouse cider makers who kept the real tradition alive. They are the forgotten heroes.

What is intriguing is that the history of cider and perry has had a distinct visual impact on our

landscape. Of the 120,000 acres of orchard in the West Country mentioned earlier, fewer than 20,000 acres now remain and half of those acres are in Herefordshire. Which means that over the last century the loss of orchards has been at a rate of roughly 1,000 acres a year. Some quite rightly regard the loss of this great natural resource as a tragedy, but because it happened gradually it almost went unnoticed. In 1990 the grass-roots environmental organisation Common Ground decided to raise awareness and began arranging events that were educational and fun. Common Ground started by taking fruit and apples and even cider making into Covent Garden. It was incredibly popular and caught the nation's imagination. In 1991 there were more than 50 events; in 2000 there were about 600 events in the weeks either side of 'Apple Day' on 21 October. The Big Apple event in Much Marcle and Putley is a very fine example and has been going on for at least 20 years. Cider orchards today fall into three broad categories: standard orchards, half standards and the much more prolific bush orchards. Standard orchards have tall, well-spaced mature trees

under which cows and sheep can graze contentedly. This is the idyllic orchard, low yielding, often organic but long-lived and multipurpose. 'Pears for heirs' is the old saying. The famous Holme Lacy perry pear tree on the banks of the Wye, which was in its prime around 1790, covered an area of three-quarters of an acre and yielded between five and seven tons of fruit. The original tree has long gone but its branches keeled over and rooted and survive today. Many of these older orchards are wildlife reserves in their own right and hosts to many species of bird, butterfly, moth, flowers, grasses and insects.

The second variety of orchard is the half standard, which is made up of the same trees but on smaller more manageable rootstock. They can be planted closer together and increase the overall yield per acre.

Then there are the bush orchards, which were specially developed at the Long Ashton Research Station in the 1970s. These can yield twenty-five tons to the acre as opposed to the five to ten tons per acre for the standard trees. What is very inter-

Above. Liquid lunch: Ye Olde Cider Bar, Newton Abbot, Devon.

esting is that the bush orchards, which are now 30 years old, with vigorous growth and pruning, now look more like half standards and are still cropping very heavily.

What is perhaps the most fascinating aspect of orchards is the evolution of certain varieties through natural selection and the propagation by man, with the use of selective grafting. In Gloucestershire alone there are more than 100 different varieties of perry pear with more than 200 names.

All cider fruit is descended, in one way or other, from two types of apple: the native wild crab apple, otherwise known as *malus sylvestris*, 'apple of the woods', and *malus pumila*, the Paradise Apple. The crab apple is that small, brightly coloured, bitter little green and yellow number that inhabits our hedgerows and oak woods and is indigenous to these islands. The Paradise Apple is the common eating apple that you find in gardens today. It probably came from Central Asia and Kazakhstan via Armenia in the Middle Ages. Interestingly, the Paradise Apple is recorded in a list of trees at Hotel St Pol in Paris in 1398. It then spread to Normandy and Rouen markets and was first recorded in England in 1629. Rootstocks often sound like motorways, with names like M9, MM106, M25 and M26. Most of these were developed at the East Malling Research Station in Kent. If you want to see a wide range of these apples you only have to go to The National Fruit Collection at Brogdale near Faversham, also in Kent, which has more than 2,300 different varieties of apple, 550 of pear, 350 of plum and 220 of cherry.

But it is the Romans who are usually credited with bringing larger sweeter, redder apples over to Britain to remind them of home. The juice of the crab would have been a little too harsh for their refined taste. But the native crab apple had one very useful characteristic, which the Romans would have exploited. It makes very good rootstock. It is more than likely that grafts from sweet Roman apples were brought over in boats, the grafts, like small twigs, shoved into wet lumps of clay so that they arrived healthy and not dried out. Then they would have been grafted on to native crab rootstock. Roman literature is full of poets and writers talking about orchards and the art of grafting and pruning – poets such as Ovid, Virgil, Pliny and Columella. It was these classical authors who later inspired cider makers in the seventeenth century. So in a sense the

Above. Men pressing perry pears at The Hellens, Much Marcle, once the home of Charles Radcliffe Cooke, MP for Hereford and Cider. (Photograph courtesy of The Hellens)

sweet Roman eating apple and the small bitter wild crab became joined at the hip, rather as the Romano-British people did. And we should be grateful to the early fruit traders and horticulturalists who decided to settle here and experiment with their orchards.

In the so-called Dark Ages apple growing would still have flourished. This was the mystical age of King Arthur, Merlin, Guinevere and Avalon – the Isle of Apples – which according to Arthurian legend was an island surrounded by a lake, famous for its beautiful apples. The location of Avalon is popularly considered to be Glastonbury, a natural island in the low-lying wetlands of the Somerset Levels, and even today there are many good cider orchards around Glastonbury and the Pennards.

On the European continent in AD 800 Charlemagne decreed that all crown lands in cities and towns in his empire should be planted with herbs and fruit, i.e. apples and pears. He also ordered that skilled brewers (the Sicetores) be kept on his estates to prepare ale, pommé (pomacium), perry and all the liquors liable to be used as drinks. The Anglo-Saxons were also not averse to wine and cider. An eleventh-century Anglo-Saxon document gives the preparation of orchards as one of the duties expected of a bailiff and he had the task of grafting in springtime. The earliest reference to wine in England is for a vineyard in Mere, Somerset, granted to Glastonbury by King Edwy, Alfred's grandson, who came to the throne in 955. Seven other Somerset vineyards are mentioned in the Domesday Book of 1086. Orchards and vineyards often lay alongside each other.

The Normans brought with them their own cider-apple culture. From AD 1100 Norman French bishops and abbots had control of the monasteries and were keen to extend their orchard practices. They introduced new varieties of cider apples high in tannins from the Normandy orchards. Above all they brought heavy-duty equipment for making cider. No doubt these were derived from Roman technology. The Romans had large beam presses and circular granite troughs with large granite mill wheels powered by slaves or horses, originally developed for crushing olives. The invention of the single wooden screw press was a major step forward and the medieval monasteries had the upper hand when it came to cider making.

These monasteries not only had large orchards

Above. Weston's perry pear orchard, Much Marcle.

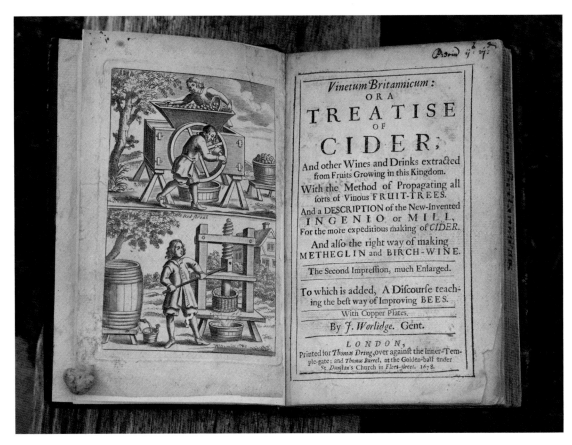

Vinetum Britannicum:
OR A
TREATISE
OF
CIDER;
And other Wines and Drinks extracted
from Fruits Growing in this Kingdom.
With the Method of Propagating all
sorts of Vinous FRUIT-TREES.
And a DESCRIPTION of the New-Invented
INGENIO or MILL,
For the more expeditious making of CIDER.
And also the right way of making
METHEGLIN and BIRCH-WINE.

The Second Impression, much Enlarged.

To which is added, A Discourse teach-
ing the best way of Improving BEES.
With Copper Plates.

By J. Worlidge. Gent.

LONDON,
Printed for Thomas Dring, over against the Inner-Tem-
ple-gate: and Thomas Burrel, at the Golden-ball under
St. Dunstan's Church in Fleet-street. 1678.

but they had the capital to build large presses, and in their dark but cool tithe barns they could store the cider in oak barrels. Some monks took the vow of abstinence but others preferred to be close to nature, tend the fruit trees and even try their hand at distilling. Monks were often buried in orchards to be nearer God. It is often in the monasteries that the earliest written records of cider making are to be found.

In 1230 cider presses in Somerset are listed in a Royal Charter as a source of income for Jocelin, Bishop of Bath. In 1235, the Bishop of Winchester's bailiff purchased 129 apple and pear trees for an orchard at Rimpton outside Yeovil. Interestingly, the island of Jersey was in the diocese of Winchester and by 1212 Jersey cider was a source of income for Battle Abbey. These cross-channel links were important, not just as sources of cider but for the cider apples themselves and the grafts to propagate

new varieties here. For more than 400 years there were close links with French monasteries and the Basque region of Spain, which is still a strong cider area. Who knows what they distilled behind the abbey walls and what wonderful experiments they must have got up to. Even after the dissolution of the monasteries, cider would have been a common drink alongside wine.

By the time of the Restoration cider making was being taken very seriously indeed by the eminent horticulturalists of the day. In addition to being a prolific writer and diarist, John Evelyn (1620–1706) was also a keen gardener, and a founder member of the Royal Society. Evelyn studied at Balliol College, Oxford and the Middle Temple and even took anatomy lessons in Padua. He is credited with introducing the first olive oil salad dressing to England.

Evelyn's book *Sylva* of 1664, a treatise on

Above. Worlidge's *Vinetum Brittanicum* or *A Treatise on Cider*, 1678.

growing timber, was the first publication to emerge from the Royal Society. *Sylva* was put together after a lecture by Evelyn in 1662 and has at the back an important addendum called 'Pomona' about the cultivation of cider orchards and fruit trees. This was written with the help of Revd John Beale, a man who, although brought up in Herefordshire, became vicar of Yeovil and was on good terms with Lord Scudamore of Holme Lacy and the Phelips family of Montacute. Of real interest to the present-day cider maker are the Aphorisms which accompany the text: notes and conjectures from a wide variety of sources including Beale himself, Sir Paul Neile, John Newburgh, Doctor Smith and Captain Sylas Taylor. They discuss the many aspects of orchards, the making of cider and perry, as well as a fine description of bottle-fermented sparkling cider (see section on *méthode champenoise*, p.23).

John Worlidge (1640–1700) lived in Petersfield, Hampshire. He was a keen observer of nature and his *Treatise on Cider*, otherwise known as *Vinetum Britannicum*, was first published in 1676 and was very well received. It was dedicated to Elias Ashmole of the Royal Society (after whom the Ashmolean Museum in Oxford is named). The second edition of 1678 also includes a 42-page discourse on bees. The book runs to 242 pages and is an extension of John Evelyn's 'Pomona' of 1664.

Worlidge constantly refers to the Classics, notably Virgil's *Georgics*, and makes notes on the finer points of planting an orchard, grafting and pruning, as well as the making of cider and perry. He also discusses the bottling of cider and the bottle-fermented process, even the distillation of cider into cider brandy. It is a classic book, which, alas, has been out of print for far too long. Worlidge also wrote *Systema Horticulturae* in 1677 on gardening and *Systema Agriculturae* in 1699. He deserves to be better known.

John Philips (1676–1709), the 'Cyder poet', was born in Bampton, Oxfordshire, in the same year that John Worlidge published his *Treatise on Cider*. A bright lad, he went to Winchester and then Christ Church, Oxford, as a classical scholar. He is chiefly remembered for his 'Cyder Poem', which was first published in 1708 and was very popular, running to

many editions. It was written in the style of Virgil's *Georgics*, and captured the mood of the time. If read carefully it is a very closely observed piece of writing extolling the virtues of grafting and well-made cider which can pass as wine. He died of tuberculosis a year later, in Hereford, when he was only 33. He is buried in Hereford Cathedral, and there is also a plaque to him in Westminster Abbey between those to Chaucer and Drayton.

Let every Tree in every Garden own
The Redstreak as supream; whose pulpous fruit
With Gold irradiate and Vermilion shines …

… Heav'n's sweetest blessing, Hail
Be thou the copious Matter of my song
And thy choice Nectar, on which always waits
Laughter, and Sport, and care beguiling Wit,
And Friendship, chief Delight of Human Life.

Two extracts from Philips' 'Cyder Poem'

Another great pioneer was Thomas Andrew Knight (1759–1838), born at Wormsley Grange, Herefordshire. His father had inherited great wealth and the family estate comprised 10,000 acres. Knight spent some time at Balliol College and at Elton Hall, following which he constructed a greenhouse and developed a walled garden for his plant experiments.

In 1786 he began grafting and breeding fruit trees including apple, sweet cherry, plum, nectarine and pear. He also crossed cultivars of strawberry, potato, cabbage and peas. At one time he had 20,000 apple seedlings. In 1797 he published his *Treatise on the Culture of the Apple and Pear*, which went through four editions to 1818. This covered cider and perry making and was a seminal work for cider makers.

He was also the author of *Pomona Herefordiencis* (1809), which contains many fine hand-coloured illustrations of fruit. This was the standard work until the Woolhope Naturalists' Field Club produced their own edition towards the end of the nineteenth century. This great illustrated book, *Herefordshire Pomona*, was published in seven parts over the years 1876 to 1885. The Pomona Committee was led by Dr Robert Hogg as the

technical editor and Dr H. G. Bull as the general editor. The artists were two ladies, Alice Blanche Ellis, and Bull's daughter, Edith Elizabeth. Each year they painstakingly painted cider apples and perry pears from the autumn exhibitions.

The reason for producing such a lavish book was that members of the club 'became strongly impressed with the necessity of some great effort to restore Herefordshire to its true fruit-growing supremacy; to call the attention of the growers to the best varieties of fruit for the table and the press; to improve the methods followed in the manufacture of Cider and Perry, and the quality of these products; and thus to improve in every way the marketable value of its orchard products'. *Herefordshire Pomona* became a classic of late Victorian natural history. Only 600 copies were ever printed. A copy can be seen at the Museum of Cider, Hereford. The Woolhope Naturalists' Field Club was founded in 1851 and continues to this day. Its headquarters and club library are in the Woolhope Room in Hereford Library. Woolhope is a well-esteemed village in Herefordshire between Fownhope and Putley. One

of the club's key members was Revd Charles Henry Bulmer, whose son Percy started the Bulmer's cider business in 1887.

And so began the age of the large-scale producers – companies that became household names. In Somerset back in the early 1820s a certain Revd Thomas Cornish planted orchards and started to make cider at Heathfield outside Taunton. By the 1840s he was supplying Queen Victoria, William Cavendish, the Carlton Club, Lord Rivers, the Duke of Bedford and the Bishop of Bath and Wells – no mean feat for a country parson. The cider went far afield to Dundee, Cumberland, Yorkshire and Carlisle. This was high-quality cider and no doubt its popularity came with the rise of the middle classes in Queen Victoria's reign. The business was carried on by the Spurway family, but in 1911 their cider maker, Arthur Moore, famously went to work for an extra shilling a week for a cider firm at Norton Fitzwarren. This became Taunton Cider, which expanded into the largest cider maker in Somerset for many years until it was swallowed up by Matthew Clark of Shepton Mallet.

Above. (left) Black (or Monmouthshire) Foxwhelp; **(right)** Moorcroft, alias Stinking Bishop
or Malvern Hill Pear derived from a farm called Moorcroft in the parish of Colwall near the Malvern Hills.
From Hogg's *Hereford Pomona,* 1885. (Reproduced by permission of the Royal Botanic Garden, Edinburgh)

In 1891 the Whiteway family moved to Whimple in Devon and thus began another cider dynasty. Coates at Nailsea and Showerings at Shepton Mallet were both large companies, Showerings producing the very successful sparkling perry called Babycham. Other firms such as Inchs, Henleys, Horrells, Symons of Totnes (not to be confused with the Herefordshire, Stoke Lacey Symonds), Hills, Clapps, Langs, all came and all went and many more in between times, such as Roger's Sunshine Cider Works outside Chard. One of the works' deliverymen, who I met in 2000, Mr Sherston, lived to be 104. Indeed the health benefits of cider in moderation are only just beginning to be understood.

In the last 15 years there have been some significant changes in the cider world. In 1995 Taunton Cider was bought out by Matthew Clark of Shepton Mallet, who had previously bought Coates and Showerings. And in 2003 Bulmers was taken over by the brewers Scottish and Newcastle and is now part of Heineken. So the big two industrial cider companies have both had changes at the top. Matthew Clark was absorbed by Constellation Brands; its cider wing is now known as Gaymers, an old Norfolk cider maker, which is a slight anomaly for Somerset cider drinkers. The two other large-scale producers that are still family-run businesses are Thatchers of Sandford in Somerset and Westons of Much Marcle in Herefordshire.

This book, however, is concerned far more with the small-scale high-quality end of the cider industry which is again thankfully gaining pace, due largely to the efforts of the artisan cider makers. What really matters to these cider and perry connoisseurs is searching out old cider-apple trees and perry pears, saving them from extinction, learning the skills of grafting and pruning or experimenting with single-variety ciders. Some do this on their own farms; others, as is now common in Dorset, belong to cider clubs, many taking a real pride in their own county and its traditions. Suffice it to say, cider making has turned a corner and a new golden age beckons. What concerns me is how the cider tastes and whether the producer has got the very best from the fruit that nature has provided.

MAKING CIDER

To understand some of the complexity of cider making, it is necessary to understand the role of tannin. Cider apples are commonly grouped into four classes: bitter-sweet, bitter-sharp, sweet and sharp. This research work was originally undertaken in the 1890s by Sir Robert Neville Grenville (1847–1936) and Frederick James Lloyd (1852–1922) who founded the National Fruit and Cider Institute in 1903 at Long Ashton just outside Bristol. This later became the Long Ashton Research Station or LARS. Long Ashton became famous for juice analysis on cider apples and perry pears, and experimenting and improving ways in which cider and perry could be made, both in the factory and on the farm. Many key research papers and reference books were written, which are valuable to this day. The Long Ashton book on perry pears from 1963 is a classic and is still used for identification and reference.

Tannins are the complex phenolic compounds often found in tea, red wine and oak. Traditionally oak bark was used for tanning of hides, hence the name. Tannins are also found in fruits and berries such as pomegranates, persimmons, cranberries, blueberries and whortleberries and strawberries.

Tannins produce an astringent or drying sensation within the mouth, which is what happens when you bite into a high-tannin cider apple. This is not to be confused with sourness, which is the opposite of sweetness and is to do with sugar levels. The tannins restrict oxidisation and therefore not only give the cider more depth, body and colour but actually help to preserve the cider from oxidisation. Tannins also have a pronounced health benefit. One particular tannin, a procyanidin, has been shown to suppress the peptide that causes hardening of the arteries. Tannins are also antibacterial.

What is fascinating is the way in which many of the cider apples have evolved within each county, depending on the variations in their tannin, acid and sugar levels. Some are peculiar to certain villages and cannot be found elsewhere.

Apple classification:

	Acid	*Tannin*
sweet	below 0.45%	below 0.2%
bitter-sweet	below 0.45%	above 0.2%
bitter-sharp	above 0.45%	above 0.2%
sharp	above 0.45%	below 0.2%

Almost 90 per cent of cider-apple juice is water. The remaining 10 per cent is made up of sugars, which give it the sweetness, and certain organic acids such as malic acid and quinic acid, which give the juice its sharpness. The tannins and phenols give it the astringency and bitterness. Here are also amino acids like aspartic acid, glumatic acid and asparagine. These provide soluble nitrogen, which is important during fermentation. Apple juice also contains natural aroma compounds, such as esters and alcohols, which give the apple juice its distinctive, rich appley smell. There are also Vitamin B compounds such as thiamine, which are important. Pectin is also found in the apple skins, extracted and widely used for jam making and helping jellies to set. The juice from bitter-sweets, bitter-sharps, sharps and sweets will have different profiles of acidity and tannins and this is what makes harvesting apples at the right time important.

Harvest: This depends on the orchards, whether they are bush, half standard or standard, the age of the trees, the varieties, the weather and how the owner wants to pick the fruit. Many large orchards are under contract to large cider makers and they will almost certainly use either tractor-mounted machines, which sweep the apples up and deposit them into a trailer with a small conveyor belt, or smaller self-propelled, hand-operated machines, which can be used under low trees. Sometimes trees have to be shaken, but there is a great danger in picking up apples too early or too late. It may well require several sweeps of the orchard, so grass length is critical. What also matters is how bruised the fruit gets and whether the trees and the fruit are diseased.

Excessive handling by machinery can affect fruit quality and that in the end affects the quality of the cider. Mud, moles, leaves, twigs, shotgun cartridges and binder twine don't help either.

Many purists simply pick up the apples by hand and store them in sacks. Hand picking is slow and at times tedious, particularly if the weather is bad, but on a fine day it can be very exhilarating, particularly if you are part of a large apple-picking gang. Hand-picked apples will often keep in good condition in the sacks longer than machine-harvested fruit, and reach a more optimum point in their maturity before being pressed.

Apple storage: What is interesting is how apples change during the season. They invariably start off green then take on hues of yellow, red,

Above left. Mike Johnson machine-harvesting near Ross-on-Wye.
Above right. Ben Gray with his son, bagging up apples, Devon.

14

orange, even purple. What is happening on the skin tends to be an indicator of what is happening under the skin. A green apple is often still immature and the starches have only just begun to change into the sugars, and it is those natural sugars, such as sucrose, fructose and glucose, that are so important to the whole operation. If there has been a good summer with lots of sunshine then the sugars will be high. Sugar levels can vary from 10 per cent to 17 per cent. An apple is deemed to be ripe when it falls off the tree of its own accord. But that does not mean it is necessarily ready for pressing. A rough guide is to keep them for another three to four weeks. Old farms used to have apple lofts and in Herefordshire some farms still use the old hop-drying lofts to store the apples. Ideally the apples have to be kept out of the rain, but they are not averse to fresh air. The apples are allowed to sweat, and they dehydrate, which concentrates the juices and raises the ratio of sugar levels. Other more subtle changes take place and this is where the art of cider making kicks in – knowing when to press and which apples to mix together. This is where the small- to medium-scale producer wins out. By storing the apples in the appropriate conditions before pressing them, the aroma compounds such as the esters and alcohols, the acids and tannins and sugars are allowed to change and mature subtly. And each variety will follow its own path.

In the South Hams in the seventeenth and eighteenth centuries, people would lay the apples out in the sun to raise the sugar levels like the Sauternes grapes. There may even have been a touch of the noble rot in the misty valleys. Some old farmers will only press the apples when they are almost black. But there is a fine line between fantastic aroma and rottenness.

Washing: This is usually an essential way to get the apples to flow into the mill. Apples float, perry pears do not. Many large and even medium-sized cider makers have their own systems, where apples are tipped and then hosed into channels and then systematically washed. This not only cleans them, it prevents all sorts of stray debris getting into the mill. Sometimes in a ton there can be 10 per cent debris and this is not an advantage. Also rotten fruit will

decompose as it moves along. Small-scale producers who hand pick fruit may not want to remove the wild yeasts on the skin of the apple and so washing is unnecessary. The greater care you take at this stage the less likely you are to have trouble with your fermentation.

Milling: Assuming the apples are in good condition the next thing is to find a way of crushing or chopping them up efficiently without losing the juice. In the old days this was done by a variety of methods. In Wales they have been known to use a circular stone running backwards and forwards in something like a dugout canoe. This might be 'stone age' technology but no doubt it was very efficient, as was the next step up, a circular granite trough for the horse to go round and round, crushing the apples with a vertical mill wheel set within a wooden frame and revolving around a central post. In France these circular horse mills are known as *le tour*, and the trough *l'auge*: hence the Pays d'Auge in the Calvados region. These horse-driven crushers were popular in the Channel Islands, Devon and Cornwall, the Forest of Dean and Herefordshire. And it is quite a sight to see one in action. The secret is to get an old but reliable horse – young horses get frustrated and often go too fast – and not put too much apple in the trough. When the apple is properly crushed it is lifted out with a wooden shovel on to the press. Horses were also used to power mills indirectly with bevel gears and even pulleys.

In Somerset and Dorset these circular horse mills were rare as the indigenous stone is limestone or chalk, neither of which is suitable. Cider juice is very corrosive and it would dissolve the stone very quickly. In these counties cider makers devised the scratter, to scrat, or chop, the apple up. These usually consisted of two granite rollers or apple-wood cogs. The teeth chewed the apple up. These scratters or *ingenio*, were apparently based on seventeenth-century sugar-cane grinders from Cuba. They were powered by a big wheel, which was turned by a man or a boy, and was always very hard work. One or two have been adapted to work from a Fordson's pulley belt drive or a small Lister diesel engine.

Modern machinery consists of stainless steel drums into which are fitted sharpened blades or centrifugal mills. These are high speed and efficient. The apple must be well milled to release the juice. The resulting semi-liquid pulp is called pomace and this is used to build the layers of the 'cheese'. In some methods of production where keeving takes place the pomace is left to macerate and stays in large vessels open to the air overnight. This is a process often used in perry making. The oxidisation that takes place naturally helps the process, particularly in the Normandy method, to increase soluable pectin levels, encouraging the retention of residual sweetness.

Pressing: This is the fun bit, because the apple juice pours off the press out of the cheese, and is transferred or pumped into long lines of old wooden barrels. But first you have to build the cheese. Most old presses are wooden and can be at least 20 feet high. The bed of the press is usually made from oak or elm, and the threads can be single or double and traditionally were made of wood. These are now rare, although there is one still operating at Hamptonne in Jersey with a horse mill alongside. The wooden threads have been replaced with wrought iron, cast iron, or even steel threads like those found on the backs of tipping lorries. Even with a hydraulic press a cheese has to be made and this consists of about a dozen layers of pomace, which are made by folding in cloths and separating the layers with lattice boards usually made from ash, oak or chestnut. Traditionally, long straw was used to bind the pomace into layers and some people still make cider this way. Straw was replaced by cloths made from horsehair or hessian, but these are now made from nylon netting, and have to be washed out regularly to be kept clean. The layers must be even and the cheese kept vertical. Each cheese can hold as much as a ton, and on some of the very large Devon presses it was said that the cheese could hold two tons of apple. Making a large cheese with straw is a skilled business.

When the pressing starts the pressure must be

Opposite. Tim Chichester milling apples with his ten-year-old horse Giles, near Honiton, Devon.

applied evenly and steadily so that the cheese does not slew. The pressure is exerted by screwing down the top board with a large nut, which is levered with a wooden pole, or in some cases a windlass is used. A ton of pomace will yield about 150 gallons of juice. Some people reckon that the hydraulic presses, which can give 150 tons pressure, are too heavy and the resultant juice has too much of the squashed pip in it. Some used to make a separate barrel with the juice that simply flowed freely from the cheese under its own pressure. If organic straw is used in making the cheese the juice will have a unique flavour and wild yeasts.

One thing is certain, different apples behave differently at different points in the season and each apple will have its optimum period for pressing. For almost a 100 years the hydraulic pack presses have been used and they are very efficient, but they are labour intensive and building cheeses and their deconstruction can be monotonous over a prolonged period. When I worked at Burrow Hill we would make at least a dozen in an eight-hour shift. The dry pomace at the end of the pressing was turned out into a trailer and fed to sheep and cattle, which loved it, as did the pheasants and peacocks.

Many medium-scale cider makers have continuous belt presses, which are made in Germany or Austria. These are not cheap but they rely on a circuit of rollers and belts that slowly squeeze the pomace like a sophisticated mangle. Some say the juice is different and has more solids in suspension and that the pomace is not quite as dry but they are semi-automated and one person can run them by pressing a few buttons.

Fermentation: This is the crucial step that relies on a biochemical chain reaction. The key

Above (left and right). Kevin Minchew and his favourite scratter, near Tewkesbury, Gloucestershire.

ingredients are the yeast organisms, which can be a whole range of wild yeasts or a carefully chosen introduced dried wine or champagne yeast from a packet. This is where the real transformation takes place, where the natural sugars are turned into alcohol and the apple juice into cider. The alcohol is ethanol, but higher alcohols called fusel alcohols can occur. Temperature and acidity levels are now important: the higher the temperature, the faster the reaction. The acidity level must be high enough to prevent rogue bacterial infections taking hold, but at the same time not so high they give the cider a sharp edge.

As far as sugar levels are concerned 15 per cent sugar corresponds to a specific gravity of 1070 and a total potential alcohol of around 8.5 per cent, which is right o the legal limit for cider; 10 per cent sugars have an specific gravity of 1045 and a

potential alcohol of 6 per cent. Most ciders are between these two levels. (The specific gravity of water is of course 1000.)

If the temperatures are too low fermentations can be stopped in their tracks and have to be re-started, or allowed to start again when the weather warms up. The secret of blending before fermentation is to get the right levels of acidity, sugar and tannin to allow the natural process to take hold. Some cider makers add malic acid in powdered form to raise the levels of acidity; some add sugars at this stage.

The real divide is between those who rely on natural yeasts that are on the orchard floor, or on the machinery in the barn, or on the cheese cloths, or on the surface of the apples … and those that use an introduced yeast. Each farm will have its own cocktail of wild yeasts. The skill of the cider maker

Above left. Kevin Minchew (Gloucestershire) and the Little Throbber, with spaniel.
Above right. Kevin's pomace.

is in being able to control these wild yeasts and allowing the one that you want to dominate. This can be done by a small but judicious use of sodium metabisulphite, which breaks down to give off sulphur dioxide to kill off some of the unwanted yeasts, particularly ones hanging around in old barrels. This is where hygiene plays a role. Sulphur has been used since Roman times in winemaking and was well documented in the seventeenth century by John Worlidge. The trick is to add just enough, otherwise it will dominate the flavour and be counter-productive. Many large-scale makers cannot take the risk of using natural yeasts so they knock them out with a hefty dose of sodium metabisulphite right at the start after pressing and then a day or so later introduce their own yeasts, which will in all probability be a dried wine yeast. Usually yeast from one vat will be used to kick-start the next vat. This gives guaranteed but uniform fermentation, which is fine if you want your cider to taste the same day in day out, for years on end.

One of the problems with wild yeasts is that some of the weaker species are killed off as the alcohol level rises. You are never quite sure which one will dominate. Fermentation is an active process and the yeasts need nutrients, and if there are not enough nutrients the fermentation will also stop. The vitamin thiamine is sometimes used and ammonium sulphate or phosphate are added in small quantities.

What is really happening during fermentation is that the sugars are being converted into alcohol and carbon dioxide and it is the creation of the carbon dioxide that powers the frothing. It is the same carbon dioxide which gives the small bubbles in champagne, but that is deliberately induced by secondary fermentation within a bottle not a barrel, a process commonly known as *méthode champenoise*. Some cider will, however, come out of the barrel with a small natural sparkle, and that is often what the cider maker is looking for.

When the fermentation has stopped, all the available sugars will have been converted into alcohol: in cider this usually means that the cider has been fermented to dryness, i.e. it has no residual sweetness left. These ciders can be around 7–8.5 per cent abv and very dry indeed. Some cider makers use a process called keeving to stop the fermentation when it is about two thirds of the way through, and this is done using chalk and enzymes. A thick brown surface forms on the cider, which is called the flying lees or *chapeau brun*, and then the cider is carefully siphoned off from the middle section of the barrel. Known as Normandy-style ciders, they are very popular as they retain their natural sweetness and have a real appley flavour. Cider used to be made this way in Devon right up to the Second World War.

One way to stop, or at least slow, the fermentation down naturally is to rack and rack until all the yeast-rich sediment has been left behind and the cider stops fermenting.

What sometimes happens naturally when the weather warms up is a second or malolactic fermentation. This is quite common if the natural yeasts are not knocked out by doses of sulphur dioxide. This second fermentation is really the conversion of malic acid to lactic acid, which is softer and the by-product of carbon dioxide. This fermentation is caused not by yeasts but by bacteria. The acidity can fall by as much as 50 per cent and it creates that almost buttery taste often found in Chardonnay, plus the natural sparkling from carbon dioxide.

A secondary yeast fermentation can be induced within a strong bottle with a little champagne yeast and sugar, and this is the bottle-fermented cider method pioneered in England before Dom Pérignon (1638–1715) was even born. Lord Scudamore was definitely bottling cider by 1632 and in 1653 Ralph Austen, author of *A Treatise on Fruit Trees* (1653), was adding sugar to cider and bottling it in Oxford. Revd John Beale was also experimenting. What Dom Pérignon did was refine the process as far as wine was concerned and this then allowed the French champagne makers, in true

Opposite top. Kevin Minchew building a cheese on a Forest of Dean stone, Gloucestershire.
Opposite bottom. Liz Montague using an Austrian press at Heron Valley in the South Hams, Devon.

nineteenth-century Republican style, to claim all the glory. The real heroes of the *méthode champenoise* to my way of thinking are the early cider boys, the aristocrats who could afford to play around with the new tough, dark glass bottles, which were invented in England around 1628 (see section on *méthode champenoise*, p.23).

Storage, fining, filtration, pasteurisation and carbonation: Once the cider is made there are several options: it can be stored as draught in its original oak barrels, pipes or vats and drunk at leisure, or it can be racked off and filtered and fined. Some cider needs to be stabilised and clarified to keep it in best condition and there are a number of ways to do this. There are sheet filters, powder filters, cross flow filters, ultra filtration, microfiltration and sterile filtration. Cider can then be bottled, carbonated, coloured, blended, canned or pasteurised.

Carbonation is the introduction of carbon dioxide under pressure to give the cider fizz and sparkle. It also enhances the flavour slightly. Low levels of carbonation are often acceptable but excessive carbonation is counter-productive. Counter-pressure bottle fillers are used and more sulphur dioxide is added at this stage to maintain the stability of the cider, which is why some ciders taste of sulphur. Even organic products can use sulphur. The label normally says 'contains sulphites'. The best carbonation is of course by natural means but this requires the bottle-fermented or bottle-conditioned method, which is expensive and time consuming but truly wonderful when it works well.

Above left. Bottling line at Cornish Orchards, near Liskeard.
Above right. Andy Atkinson using a hydrometer, Cornish Orchards.

MAKING PERRY

In many ways this is similar to cider making because it uses the same equipment, but it is much more skilled. Perry pear trees are totally different to the cider apple trees. They tend to be scattered and are often tall, ancient trees: pickers are dependent on the small pears falling to the ground. Some new orchards are on dwarf rootstock but the majority of pears are still hand picked from old orchards. Perry pears often don't even look like pears; they can be round, elliptical or even square. In fact they are very odd beasts to say the least, but the flavours and aromas that they contain are well worth the effort of picking them up. Perry pears can be rock hard one minute and soft as butter the next, so timing is vital. Unlike cider apples they don't float, so handling them in any quantity is much more difficult.

Some varieties require processing immediately, others require weeks of resting. Pears rot from the inside so it is difficult to spot when they are on the turn. Another major difference is that you have to macerate them after milling, leaving them open to the air in a trough overnight, and sometimes for 24 hours. Perry pears also contain considerable quantities of sorbitol, a sugar alcohol, which is unfermentable and this is why perry that is fermented out will still be sweet. Perry pears are much higher in citric acid than cider apples and this can be converted anaerobically to acetic acid by lactic acid bacteria. Perry pears are higher in acetaldehydes.

As a result, perry is much more unpredictable and volatile than cider. It oxidises much more easily and can take bad ways more easily, but if made well can be superb. It also lends itself to bottle fermentation to produce a sparkling perry, and this can have a delightful elderflower nose to it.

Perry should not just be regarded as a white wine substitute. It is a fine drink in its own right and is best drunk as an aperitif rather than an accompaniment to a meal. Its flavours are often very subtle. Some of the sweeter perrys, such as Oldfield, make an interesting substitute for a dessert wine. Keeping perry is also more difficult than cider, and temperature is important. Knowing when to bottle is vital.

As Tom Oliver of Oliver's Cider and Perry (see Coppy and the Proclaimers) says: 'Cider is a hard master but perry is a beautiful but fickle mistress.'

SPARKLING CIDER AND THE EVOLUTION OF MÉTHODE CHAMPENOISE

Many people who make sparkling bottle-fermented cider today may not realise it but they are treading in the footsteps of some very illustrious seventeenth-century Englishmen, who experimented not only with making dark, strong bottle glass, but also with the skilled secondary fermentation of cider and perry within those bottles. This method of perking up cider with a bit more sugar and yeast to give a healthy sparkle is today known in the wine trade by another name: *méthode champenoise,* or outside the Champagne region 'Traditional Method'. These intelligent and eccentric English-men knew they were onto something special. Men such as Admiral Robert Mansell, James Howell, Lord John Scudamore, Sir Kenelm Digby, John Beale, Ralph Austen, Sir Paul Neile and Captain Silas Taylor, all played their part in experimenting with the new invention: bottle-fermented sparkling cider. And they documented this from as early as 1632, six years before Dom Pérignon was born and 97 years before the foundation of the first champagne house.

Many people assume that the French invented champagne because that is the story that has been perpetuated down the centuries, and to their credit the French have made an extraordinarily vibrant and lucrative industry in the Champagne region of northern France. But to make champagne, which is after all simply sparkling wine, you first need tough, dark bottle glass that will withstand the pressures of a secondary fermentation, and you need to know exactly what you are doing. This particular subject has until now only been seen through a glass darkly.

The French Benedictine monk, Dom Pierre Pérignon (1638–1715), who worked as cellarmaster for fifty years at the Abbey of Hautvilliers in the Marne valley just north of Epernay, is often credited with the invention of champagne, but at that time

the production of sparkling wine was very problematic, and the fragile woodfired bottles were forever exploding. Dom Pérignon's task was to *stop* wine sparkling too much and to tone it down so that it did not break expensive glass bottles. What Dom Pérignon did was to adapt viticulture by cutting vines back and to improve the still wines of the Champagne region by blending certain grapes before pressing, throwing out any that were bad or oversized. He wanted a wine that would complete its fermentation safely in one cycle and not re-ferment in the spring. The King of France only allowed champagne to travel out of France in bottles legally in 1728. It was to be at least a century after Dom Pérignon died that the French laid the invention of champagne at his feet, and there it has stayed.

In his 1998 *World Encyclopaedia of Champagne and Sparkling Wine*, Tom Stevenson brought to light certain references that have altered our view of champagne history. He makes a very eloquent and plausible case that the English invented not just the method of making sparkling wine with the addition of extra sugar after the first fermentation, but also that they also invented a means of successfully containing it within new, strong, dark, English bottles. Stevenson quotes from a paper read by Christopher Merrett (1614–95) to the Royal Society on 17 December 1662, six years before Dom Pérignon arrived in Hautvilliers: 'Our wine coopers of late times use vast quantities of sugar and molasses to make all sorts of wines to make them drink brisk and sparkling and to give them spirit as also to mend their bad tracts [i.e. to cover up their blemishes].'

But Merret was only the messenger. He mentions sugar, molasses and coopers, i.e. barrels and sparkling wine in his paper, but does not mention bottles directly. For that we have to turn to the cider makers. The French will no doubt defend their rights to the *méthode champenoise* to the last cork and rigorously prevent anyone using the Champagne name outside a very tightly controlled region. But however ingenious they may be, they cannot claim to have invented the *méthode champenoise* itself, and for one very simple reason: they did not have the new, strong English bottles. The French even had a name for these bottles – *verre anglais* – a term that was in common usage for many years. It

Above. Barrels of perry at Ocle Pychard, Herefordshire.
Opposite. Paul Stephens inspecting bottles of perry in his bottle rack, Newton Court.

is the invention and manufacture of these glass bottles that is the key to the process as much as the addition of extra sugar.

The real history of the development of *méthode champenoise* is therefore much more interesting and complex than it might at first appear and relies not so much on the vintners of London but on the anonymous glass blowers and the aristocratic cidermen of the West Country, and there is plenty of hard evidence that these men were the real heroes who pioneered the process.

One person who drew attention to the role of these early cider makers was Roger French in his important book *The History and Virtues of Cyder* (1982), which gives an excellent background to the cider world of seventeenth-century England and puts the political and medical importance of cider and orcharding in context. The evidence comes from books, letters, various discourses and even domestic accounts.

John Evelyn's *Sylva,* a treatise on growing timber, was read to the newly formed Royal Society on 15 October 1662 (though only published in 1664). It includes a section called *Pomona,* which consists of aphorisms not just concerning cider production but also regarding bottling cider and the addition of sugar.

One of the leading lights in the Royal Society was John Beale, a Herefordshire man, who came from Yarkhill, where the Brown Snout cider apple was later found. He studied at King's College, Cambridge and became a clergyman, scientist and garden designer. He visited Paris in the 1630s and saw Lord Scudamore there and corresponded with the scientist Samuel Hartlib. He also became Vicar of Yeovil and later chaplain to Charles II. His father, Thomas Beale, had worked closely with Lord Scudamore of Holme Lacy. He was also a relative of the Phelips family of Montacute House who had given him the living of Sock Dennis in 1638. The Phelips family also had interests in glass making and were connected to Sir Robert Mansell. So it was a small world indeed.

In 1656 Beale published an eloquent *Treatise on Cider and Orchards* which mentions not only the various soils of Herefordshire and the need to be very selective with your fruit, but also the complex mysteries of fermentation. His '57 Aphorisms on Cider' were read to the Royal Society on 10 December 1662, one week before Christopher Merret's paper.

> *Bottleing is the next improver and proper for Cider; some put two or three Raisins into every Bottle, which is to seek aid from the wine. Here in Somersetshire I have seen as much as a Walnut of Sugar, not without cause, used for this Country Cider.*

A walnut of sugar is equivalent to about 20gms of sugar, which is the amount used these days for a 75cl bottle of sparkling wine or cider to give an impressive secondary fermentation. So John Beale and Edward Phelips were spot on. This in a few simple words helps to establish the process that later came to be known as *méthode champenoise.*

Beale also advises that 'The time of drawing Cider into bottles is best in March it being then clarified by the winter, and free from the heat of the sun' – i.e. when the first fermentation is finished.

Further advice about bottling cider comes from Sir Paul Neile (1613–1686), an active member of the Royal Society famous for his optic glasses and astro-

nomical telescopes. His 'Discourse on Cider' was read to the Royal Society on 8 July 1663.

> When it is bottled it must not be perfectly fine; for if it be so, it will not fret in the bottle, which gives it a fine quickness, and will make it a mantle and sparkle in the glass when you pour it out.
>
> And if it be too thick when it is bottled, then when it hath stood some time in the bottles, it will ferment so much that it may possibly either drive out the corks, or break the bottles, or at least be of that sort (which some call Potgun-drink) that when you open the bottle it will fly about the house, and be so windy and cutting that it will be inconvenient to drink; For the right temper of the bottle cider is, that it mantle a little and sparkle when it is put into the glass, but if it froth and fly it is bottled too soon.

The skill is judging exactly when to bottle it, neither too soon nor too late. The interesting thing is that the addition of sugar is often only used when the cider needs it. The fact of secondary fermentation when the warm weather comes in the spring is well known, and the cider can be helped on its way. The secret is to leave just a little bit of yeast in the bottle to help the secondary fermentation:

> If it be too fine when they bottle it for if so it will not fret in the bottle at all. Then there is a remedy . . . In case you be put to the necessity of using it, that you open every bottle after it hath been bottled a week or so, and put into each bottle a little piece of white sugar about the bigness of a nutmeg, and this will set it into a little fermentation, and give it that briskness which other wise it would have wanted.

So as with wine they were seeking to improve the beverage. These men were clearly on the right lines, and the production of cheap sugar from the West Indies was no doubt a great help.

One other interesting fact was recorded by Neile:

A gentleman of Hereford who last autumn that by accident had not provided cask enough for cider he had made and having six or seven hogsheads for which he had no cask, he sent to Worcester, Gloucester and even to Bristol, to buy some, but all in vain; and the gentleman being then dispatching a Barque for London with cider and having ne'er at hand a conveniency of getting glass bottles, and did so, and filled seven or eight hampers with the clearest of this cider… The barque had a tedious passage and was delayed at least seven weeks before it came to London. The cider in the cask had wrought so much that it was much harder than it should have been. But the other, which was in bottles, and escaped breaking, was excellent good beyond any cider that I had tasted out of Herefordshire …

Another experienced contributor to John Evelyn's *Pomona* was Captain Silas Taylor, (1624–1678)who had several observations of his own which he read to the Royal Society on 22 July 1663, a fortnight after Sir Paul Neile's paper: 'The cider made and sold here in London in bottles may have that windiness with it as bottle beer hath . . . and with how many bubbles and bladders of wind it doth work . . . it clears itself by that operation of all such injurious qualities.'

Taylor was born in Shropshire and studied at Oxford before taking part in the Civil War on the Parliamentarian side. He was later responsible for the sequestration of Royalist lands around Hereford, which included the estate of none other than Lord John Scudamore. Taylor showed great leniency to the Scudamores and even supported them behind the scenes politically. Taylor also leaves us with a fine description of Herefordshire Redstreak cider which may well have been Lord Scudamore's own:

I have tasted of it three years old, very pleasant, though dangerously strong. The colour of it, when fine, is of sparkling yellow, like Canary, of

a good full body, and oyly: the taste, like the flavour of perfume of excellent Peaches, very grateful to the Palate and Stomach.

Maybe it was no coincidence that Silas Taylor was asked to give a paper at the Royal Society.

More importantly, Taylor also notes that after bottling the cider it is advisable

to lay it in a repository of cool springing water, two or three foot or more deep. This makes it drink quick and lively, it comes into the glass not pale or troubled, but bright yellow, with a speedy vanishing nittiness (as the vintners call it) which evaporates with a sparkling and whizzing noise.

This is, without doubt, a description of bottle-fermented sparkling cider (i.e. cider that has undergone a long secondary fermentation) and it is his words which confirm the effectiveness of the method.

But even this is just the beginning of the real story. Politics often have their part to play too, and even the enlightened vigour of the Royal Society and the Restoration aristocracy could not ignore the work of one man, Ralph Austen, a Parliamentarian who set up a cider works in Oxford on a corner plot of some size where New Inn Hall St joined Queen Street, very close to where Silas Taylor had once studied. Austen was in Oxford from 1646 until his death in 1676, at which he left a fully equipped cider house (possibly the first in the land) containing seven hogsheads of cider and 528 bottles.

Austen was an ardent Puritan and proctor of the University and very strict on the Royalist dons in some of the colleges. Austen wrote several books, the most well known being *A Treatise on Fruit Trees – The Spiritual Use of an Orchard* which was published in 1653 and 1657 and in which he mentions bottling cider:

Cider maybe kept perfect good many yeares if being settled it be drawn out into a bottle and well stopped with corks and hard wax melted thereon, and bound down with pack thread and then sunk down into a well or Poole, or buried in the ground, or sand laid in a cellar. Put into each bottle a lump or two of hard sugar or sugar bruised.

And there you have it: cider, sugar, corks and bottles, all dating from the early 1650s.

Austen also worked with Robert Boyle, the natural philosopher and chemist (1627–1691) and together they came to the same conclusion, that

Cider is more conducing to health and long-life then Beere and Ale (though they are also good liquors, especially for some persons) for cider is a cleare Liquor without dregs, and does not onely not leave any dreggs in the body, of its own substance, but it hath the property to cleanse the body, & carry downe superfluities and hurtful humours in the body, which other liquors and meats have engendered, and left in the body, which are the seas of many distempers and diseases.

Austen was also approached by Isaac Newton to supply grafts of cider trees for some of the Cambridge colleges. So the history of science and cider are deeply entwined.

Some of the best minds in the country were therefore involved with orchards, but Ralph Austen, English eccentric to the last, also saw heaven on earth in the form of orchards, hence the use of the word 'spiritual' in the title of his book. He believed that trees spoke to us in their own language and it was our duty to listen, 'for as trees (in a Metaphorical sense) are Bookes, so likewise in the same sense they have a *Voyce* and speak plainely to us and teach us many good lessons'.

Another factor in early seventeenth-century England was the change in climate. The winter of 1607–1608 known as the 'Great Winter' and the 'Mini Ice Age', during which trees died of frost and ships were stranded a mile or two out in a frozen North Sea. During these years many of the vines which survived from the medieval period into the Elizabethan period were knocked out, which is why there was such a great interest in cider and perry. In addition, the Navigation Act of 1651 affected the imports of French and German wine. The Civil War did not help matters either, but the Parliamentarians were just as keen on orchards as the Royalists. Both sides saw orchards as means to economic prosperity and strived to make cider a national drink. So in a sense cider and cider apples brought the two sides together, healing some of the great rifts that had torn the country apart.

The cider clock can actually be turned back even further to 1632, a full ten years before the Civil War. The place is Holme Lacy just outside Hereford near the banks of the Wye, the country house of Lord John Scudamore, a man well known in cider circles. Scudamore is credited with discovering Scudamore's Crab, alias the famous Redstreak, which alas no longer exists. Lord Scudamore was keen on God, cattle and cider, and turned this rural craft into an aristocratic art form. John Beale states that Scudamore turned cider from 'an unreguarded Windy drinke fit only for clownes and day labourers into a drink for kings, princes and lords'.

By chance the steward's accounts for Scudamore's estate still exist for the years 1631–32. The interesting entries are under household furniture on St Mary Day 1632, and a well documented trip to London.

Paid Jeffrey Cook for carrying 6 hogsheads of sydar to London		1 6 6
Pd Jeffrey Cook for bringing downe from London a dozen and a half of bottles		0 4 6
pd Henry Prosser for makeing 6 stooles		0 1 0
thrid [thread] and incle for them		0 6
[incle is a type of linen tape or yarn]		
Pd Wilcox for 2 dozen and half quart bottles		0 7 6
1 dozen and a half pint bottles		0 3 9
6 dozen corkes		3 0
a basket corde and porters carryge		1 3
a watering pot		3 6
a great knife to cut bread		1 6
a new lock for sydar house doore		0 1 0

This sounds very like the sort of kit you might need if you are experimenting with bottling cider. Scudamore was known to have 'rare contrived

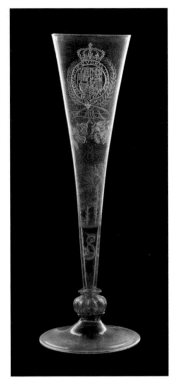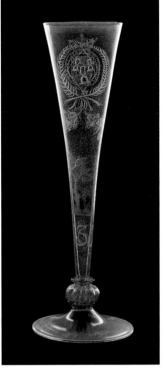

sellers in his park for keeping cider with spring water running into them'. He also had a lake and an ice house. Stooles may well refer to racks to keep the bottles off the ground – John Beale reckoned Scudamore's cider was best kept a year before drinking. Scudamore also had tall thin elegant soda glass flutes with his arms and the Royal arms, i.e. 'champagne' glasses. One very fine example still exists in the Museum of London, with engravings of the Redstreak apple tree carved on it. Standing at 14 inches high it is a slender and very elegant glass. More than anything else it shows how important cider was to him

In 1635 Scudamore became Charles I's ambassador to the court of the French king, Louis XIII. So these cider enthusiasts were right at the top end of the social pecking order, highly clever and inventive men, who were also perfectionists and well travelled on the continent. When he came back from France, Scudamore once more took up his

cidermaking experiments, as these 1639 accounts show:

Gathering grafts for London	*8d per diem 7 days*
Mending the cider mill	*1s per diem*
Apple gathering	*6d per diem*
A cooper	*1s per diem*
A common labourer	*6d per diem*
Making a hogshead	*5s*
Apples and cider sent to London	
	2,600 at 6s the 100 £5.16s
Pears carried to London. 6 bottles of cider.	

These '6 bottles of cider' could well have been supplied for a special event, and no doubt would have been used in conjunction with Scudamore's flute, assuming that he had it then.

The accounts often refer to wine, sugar and burnt wine, which is brandy. It was common to take wine with sugar, and half a pound of sugar cost only

Left and middle. The 'Chesterfield' flute. © Museum of London/Garton Collection of English Glass
(Donated to the Museum of London in memory of Sir Richard Garton, G.B.E., by his daughters and grandchildren).
Right. Wine bottle, c.1650, with seal and string lip. © Museum of London.

10d. Cider apples themselves would not feature on the accounts as he owned the orchards. Interestingly, today there is a perry pear tree by the river Wye which is descended from one that stood there during Scudamore's lifetime.

The excerpt quoted above is the earliest account yet found of bottled conditioned/fermented cider, though who knows what another secret experimenter, Sir Kenelm Digby, might have been up to at the same time? In a court case in 1661 against John Colnett four glass makers, John Vinion, Robert Ward, Edward Percival and William Sadler who had been employed by Digby to make bottles, all asserted that he had invented bottle glass and that 'it has been near 30 years hence', i.e. 1632–3,. This is exactly the same time that Lord Scudamore was ordering bottles from London.

Digby and Scudamore knew each other well, both having been in Paris at the same time. Scudamore had studied at Magdalen College Oxford, and Sir Kenelm at Gloucester Hall. They had both travelled very widely in Europe and had a facility for languages. They were also Royalists. As surveyor of the Navy, he also knew Admiral Sir Robert Mansell, but more importantly was on familiar terms with James Howell, the manager of Mansell's glass works in Broad Street, London as early as 1618. James Howell was a very interesting man, an author who had travelled widely on glass business in Europe persuading skilled glass makers to come to England. Sir Kenelm also set up a small glass house under license from Mansell, which produced bottles unlike anything that had been seen before. They were of thick dark strong glass with a round onion-shaped lower body and a long tapering neck with a thin pronounced collar at the top called a string rim, which could be used for tying down a cork. In addition they also had a significant indentation in the bottom for increased strength.

Eleanor Godfrey, author of an excellent book called *The Development of English Glassmaking 1560–1640*, reckons that Sir Kenelm Digby was the inventor of bottle glass and thinks it a possibility that his glass works were at Newnham on Severn, close to the coalfields of the Forest of Dean and within easy access to tidal waters. It was the proximity of coal that was the economic factor, as the cost of transporting it to London was prohibitive. And in this matter the British were ahead of the French. As early as 1615 James I had prohibited the use of charcoal for glass making because it was using valuable timber that he needed for sale to the Navy in order to bolster his income. Sir Kenelm's monopoly on glass making came to an abrupt halt in 1642, when he was imprisoned as a Royalist and a Catholic. Mansell's monopoloy came to an end in the same year.

But even Digby's invention did not come out of the ether. Robert Mansell allowed Sir William Clavell to have an earlier glass works at Smedmore in Purbeck which was eventually closed down due to yet another court case. The change from charcoal to coal left plenty of room for early experiments. The cliff coal and oil shale burnt with many 'dark vapours' and it was the impurities of iron and manganese that gave the glass its strength. Early fragments of dark bottle glass have been picked up in Purbeck and these may well go back to 1617–18. Other glass works were set up briefly in Pembrokeshire, Newnham on Severn and then more successfully in Newcastle upon Tyne, where there was plentiful sea coal.

The story of the invention of bottle glass is very murky indeed and no doubt much of the research was undertaken in great secrecy.

Curiously enough Christopher Merret, who gave the paper at the Royal Society, which Tom Stevenson brought to public attention, was also at Gresham's College in the 1640s, so he would have known Sir Kenelm and would have been familiar with some of his experiments. It was an intriguing time and many of these ventures were eclipsed by the Civil War and the struggle between King and Parliament. How much bottled cider was stored down wells and only recovered many years later?

Strong dark bottle glass obviously took quite a while to develop. First there was the invention, probably by accident, between the years 1618 and 1628, and then a long process of perfecting the shape of the bottle. It took someone with Sir Kenelm Digby's understanding of chemistry and fermentation, as well as the shape and form of scientific glassware to perfect the bottle design, not so much for production as to satisfy his own curiosity. He also received the regional monopoly of sealing wax in Wales and the Welsh borders, which was very useful if you were sealing the tops of bottled cider.

It may well be that the real inventors will always remain anonymous, as they were working for others in the actual glassworks. Great secrecy was needed particularly if a patent or monopoly was being infringed. James Howell may well have conveyed to Sir Kenelm certain knowledge about glassmaking, and they may have perfected the bottle in secret, as was Sir Kenelm's style.

We shall perhaps never know if Lord Scudamore was putting sugar into his cider bottles at Holme Lacy in 1632. My hunch is that he probably was. He had the time, the money and the interest. There was plenty of sugar to be had. But his appointment to Paris in 1635 put his experiments on hold. In 1643, when he was captured at Hereford, he was sent to London as a prisoner and all his belongings were seized by Parliament and later sold. Like many after the Civil War he kept his head down, and persevered with tree propagation.

One thing that is certain is that Ralph Austen produced the first dated and published reference in 1653 to what later came to be called *méthode champenoise*, saying also that cider stored this way keeps 'a good many yeares'. This could take us back to around 1643, just after Sir Kenelm's monopoly comes 'out of the closet', so to speak. Ralph Austen also deserves more credit for his work as a writer, nurseryman and cider maker than perhaps John Evelyn was prepared to give him at the time.

Sadly Austen died in debt. The aristocrats on the other hand were not making bottle fermented sparkling cider out of financial necessity, but as a useful and delightful experiment to impress their peers. For Lord Scudamore it was a political gesture to bring cider to court, which he did as early as 1627, giving *rondlettes* (small barrels holding around eighteen gallons) of cider to Sir Thomas Edmondes, the Duke of Buckingham, the Earl of Worcester, Sir

Opposite. Tim Chichester's horse Giles taking a well earned rest.

Roger Palmer and William Laud. All these men were keen amateurs, yet their experiments bore rich fruit indeed.

My suspicion is that the vinters of London, who were well documented by Christopher Merret, learnt a few tricks of the trade from the aristocratic cider makers of Herefordshire. In the 1660s, in their wine cellars by the Thames, vintners started to bottle up the still Champagne wine that came into London in barrels and sold it on as sparkling 'champagne' wine and made a small fortune. And in turn the Champagne vintners in France started doing the same thing with their own wine in France once they had acquired these new, strong, dark bottles and made an even larger fortune.

What is equally interesting is the description of bottling cider in John Worlidge's 'Treatise on Cider' of 1676. Here he describes how one should 'add a small quantity of loaf sugar, more or less according to how much you require', in order to give 'new life to the cider', and that the 'laying of bottles sideway is to be commended not only for preserving the Corks

moist, but that the air that remains in the bottle is on the side of the bottle, where it can neither expire or new be admitted…. Some place their bottles on a frame, with their noses downward.'

This 'frame' is without doubt a bottle rack or *pupitre*. Worlidge also mentions that some lay their bottles with 'their necks facing downwards, and that if there is any lees, it is in the first glass'. It only takes a small step to use salt and ice from the ice house to have *dégorgement,* but this was not invented till the early nineteenth century in France. Worlidge also discusses at length placing bottles on the ground, in sand, in cisterns and in little vaults in the sides of wells near the bottom. These cidermakers under-stood all to well the need to keep a cool, even temperature similar to that of a damp cave to ensure that their cider would keep for many years and hopefully improve in flavour and complexity whilst lying on its lees.

In summary, the history of '*méthode champenoise*' should in fact be told in reverse. The real heroes are not so much Dom Pérignon and the French, or

Above. Half-moon orchard, Melplash, Dorset.

even the vintners who later took the method to extraordinary heights, but the dogged experiments and writings of these much earlier men – men such as Lord Scudamore and Sir Kenelm Digby, Admiral Robert Mansell and James Howell, Ralph Austen, John Beale, Sir Paul Neile and Captain Silas Taylor, as well as Christopher Merret, who kept an ever watchful eye on the vintners. It is perhaps fitting that the Royal Society should be host to their detailed papers and aphorisms which were read there in the early 1660s, all of which bear witness to their scientific observations and endeavours.

So next time you open a bottle of sparkling cider, perry or even, dare I say it, champagne, hold the glass up and hopefully you can see history in the bubbles. And if you are very lucky, the sparkling cider, perry or champagne will, to quote the enigmatic Silas Taylor 'drink quick and lively, as it comes into the glass not pale or troubled, but bright yellow, with a speedy vanishing nittiness (as the vintners call it) which evaporates with a sparkling and whizzing noise'.

TASTING CIDER AND PERRY

This is perhaps the most difficult part of the book to write because everyone's tastes are so different. Henry Williamson, the author of *Tarka the Otter*, commented: 'Cider is a difficult drink, even when it is really cider: one pint can make you feel fine, but two, perhaps three pints can entirely throw your world out of orbit, into a dimensionless space.' This quote brings sharply into focus the fact that you are drinking an alcoholic drink and not lemonade. Some cider and perry is deceptively strong and it can creep up on you.

That said, the range of tastes and depths of flavours can be incredible. Some people may not have ever had a pint of 'real' cider in their lives and so the experience can be even more illuminating. The cider makers described in this book cover the full range from small-scale farm-produced cider, even horse-drawn cider, right up through hogsheads and pipes to large oak vats, barrels and shiny stainless steel. The colour of cider can be pale straw right through the

Above. Half-moon orchard, Melplash, Dorset.

spectrum of browns, oranges even reds. If it is green, leave well alone. If it is industrial cider the chances are it is sweetened and heavily carbonated. The fact of the matter is that natural cider, unless keeved, should be bone dry, and this is where the maximum flavour can be found. Artificial sweeteners, excessive carbonation, preservatives, heavy-duty pasteurisation, chilling and microscopic filtration can often mask the real flavours that nature has provided.

The first thing to do with cider is to look at it and smell it. Cider can range from being cloudy to crystal clear, but if you can't see your fingers round the other side of the glass when you hold it up to the light there is usually something wrong. The image of cider has suffered from badly made and badly kept farmhouse cider for far too long. That rough pint, which put you off drinking cider when you were a student, has done no one any favours. Neither perhaps has the very clean, consistently bland, cider made by some of the larger companies.

The main point to keep in mind is that cider is apple juice that has been fermented, sometimes twice. It is the control of these fermentations that make, the cider taste the way it does. So when you open a bottle of cider, or are given a pint from a barrel at a cider farm, be aware of what sort of cider it is you are actually tasting. Hopefully you will know where it has come from and who made it and even what sorts of apples are in it, as well as which orchards they came from. Some makers put a vast amount of information on the label. This is very useful indeed. Others only have the minimum. In an ideal world, the labels should tell you how much alcohol is in there, whether sulphur has been used and whether it has been carbonated, whether it has been bottle conditioned and whether it is organic, what preservatives it contains and whether it has been pasteurised or chill filtered. What it probably won't tell you is whether apple concentrate has been used or what the juice content is in the final product, as manufacturers are not obliged to include this information.

Now for the smell: this can be fantastic, particularly with perries. It can be a smokey effervescence almost like elderflower in blossom. Cider can have a rich smell of ripe apples but it doesn't necessarily have to. Does wine always smell of grapes? Smell it like a wine, savour it, try and work out what is in there. Sometimes it will smell of oak, or if it has been in rum casks or old whisky casks or even sherry casks it will smell of the predominant spirit. Oak can be old or it can be new; it can be Allier or Limousin, or Hungarian. However, any whiff of farmyard, vinegar or excessive sulphur can be off-putting. There is something called 'mouse', which is just that – a flavour of caged mouse – and is caused by harmful bacteria, the cider being stale and musty. The most common problems are oxidisation and acetification, that vinegary smell.

Assuming the cider is well made, take a sip and let it roll around your mouth. This is where the tannins will make their presence felt. There will be a bit of drying of the mouth. Too much is unpleasant, but lack of tannin will make the cider taste thin and weak. You need body, you need full, rounded flavours, dark tones, complexity, warmth and a long finish that keeps on going. Complex fruitiness, with a long, constantly evolving flavour is what you are after. Then swallow and swallow again.

With perries you may want a lightness of touch and an explosion of hedgerow blossom that fills your head like a good champagne. Let the natural flavours come though – that is the real skill of the perry maker. Subtlety and sunlight.

The real fun and skill is in slowly building up your own repertoire of tastes and a discerning palate. Don't just doggedly stick with the one cider or perry that you like most: go out there and experiment. Have your own tastings, buy single varieties and blend your own, talk to the cider makers, learn from them. Who knows, you may even make some cider yourself. It's not that difficult.

At the end of a glass or bottle of cider I always ask myself, would I buy that again? Would I drive fifty miles to get another bottle or two? If the answer is 'yes' then the cider maker or perry maker has done his or her job well. It is above all else a voyage of discovery.

Opposite. Kevin Minchew with a glass of his bottle-fermented perry, Gloucestershire.

CIDER AND HEALTH

From the earliest times cider has been seen as beneficial to health, and was drunk particularly on long sea voyages to protect against scurvy, as this early quotation from Francis Bacon illustrates:

> *Cider and perry are notable beverages in sea voyages … A wonderful refreshing drink … an assured remedy for sicknesse taken at sea.*
>
> Francis Bacon,
> *New Atlantis* 1626

Not forgetting of course that there was land scurvy and that in times past vegetables, and thus vitamin C, were often in short supply in the countryside, particularly towards the end of winter in the so-called hungry gap.

Cider was also perceived to have a beneficial effect on a wide range of other maladies:

> *Cider, generous strong sufficiently heady … excites and cleanses the stomach, strengthens the digestion and infallibly frees the kidney and bladder from breeding the gravel stone …*
>
> John Evelyn, 'Pomona', 1664

And another quotation, this time from a Parliamentarian living in Hereford:

> *Cider does relax the belly … aid concoction, depress Vapours, resist Melancholy, Spleen, Pleurisy, Strangury, and being sweetened with sugar abate inveterate colds …*
>
> Captain Sylas Taylor,
> Evelyn's 'Pomona', 1664

All were keen to promote cider's health-giving properties and its aid to longevity.

> *The constant use of this liquor, either simple or diluted, Hath been found by long experience to avail much to health and long life; preserving the drinkers of it in their full strength and vigour even to very old age.*
>
> John Worlidge, 1678

Recently in Chard, Somerset, Frank Sherston reached the age of 104. He was born in 1897 and died in 2001, and for many years he worked for the Roger's Sunshine Cider Works delivering bottled cider. Another local hero in Stoke Abbot, Dorset, is Jim Webber, who on Christmas Eve 2007 celebrated his one hundred and fifth birthday in the village hall. For many years he also made cider on his farm in the village. Keeping active is no doubt part of the equation, as well as taking a well-earned pint of cider at the end of the day.

The health effects were, however, not just perceived to be in the drink but in the orchards, which clear the air. This quotation is from Herefordshire:

Orchards being the Pride of our County ... do not only sweeten but also purify the Ambient Air (which is conceived conduces so much to the constant health and Long Lives, for which our county has always been always famous).

John Beale, 1652

More scientific approaches to the benefits of cider have been made in recent years, but the conclusions are pretty much the same. Scientists have been looking mostly at the high levels of tannins and polyphenols which appear naturally in certain cider apples. The beneficial effects of these tannins are carried over into the cider and these act as antioxidants, which prevent disease by quenching harmful free radicals. This could reduce the risk of heart disease, cancer and strokes. Cider has been proved to be as good for this as red wine in certain cases, but the proportions of juice, the way in which the cider is made and the timing of the apple harvest are all important factors.

Recent research work carried out at the Institute of Food Research, Norwich, and by scientists at Brewing Research International, in Surrey, confirms that high levels of antioxidants do exist in cider. This research was taken further at Glasgow University by Dr Serena Marks, who looked in greater depth at the role of individual apples and the fluctuations that can occur with varying methods of making cider.

Dr Marks studied the phenolic levels of 19 varieties of English cider apple, 35 varieties of cider and 1 variety of dessert apple to analyse how and why levels differ and to understand the effects that the cider-making process has on the final phenolic content of cider. She concluded that: 'Unit for unit the top cider had levels of phenolics comparable to red wine. The cider with the highest levels of phenolics had 18 times more phenolics than clear apple juice and 7 times more phenolics than cloudy apple juice.'

This implies that the true cider apple, high in tannins, has the most beneficial effects on the system. The key issue is that the choice of cider apples is important and the way in which the cider is made is crucial. The secret is to make pure juice cider with the cider apples high in tannins, i.e. the West Country way.

The beneficial effects are of course only apparent when the daily recommended intake is not exceeded. Alcohol also has the ability to relax the system, which has its own benefits. Alcohol in moderate quantities is also known to reduce incidence of heart disease by increasing the amount of good cholesterol in the blood.

Research in 2004 underaken at Cornell University by food scientists led by Professor Chang Lee indicates that polyphenols in apples can protect the brain from the type of damage that triggers neurodegenerative diseases as such as Alzheimer's and Parkinson's.

So if you want to live a long life and avoid scurvy, melancholy, pleurisy, strangury and the kidney stone, as well as the possibility of Alzheimer's and Parkinson's disease, simply drink a pint of well-made, tannin-rich cider a day and take long walks. Cider vinegar and honey is not bad either, for arthritis that is.

The recommended daily intake of cider is between two and three units per day for women, and for men, between three and four units. An average cider has about 2.5 units per pint. Some 'real' ciders are around 8 per cent abv naturally and others are diluted down to around 4.5 per cent abv.

PART ONE: *The Cidermakers*

CHAPTER I
Alchemy and Cider Philosophy
SOMERSET

Julian Temperley,
Burrow Hill and the Somerset Cider Brandy Company,
Pass Vale Farm, Kingsbury Episcopi, Somerset

One of the chief delights about visiting cider farms is the journey to find them, which often requires driving down narrow rural lanes. One of my favourite views is from the top of Burrow Hill, near Kingsbury Episcopi in South Somerset. There is a sycamore with a swing, a bench and a triangulation point. In winter when the rivers burst their banks the grazing land below is flooded and the levels and moors shimmer and glimmer, the 'silver meadows'. Beyond Muchelney Abbey you can glimpse the town of Langport and to the north east, Glastonbury Tor itself – Avalon, the Isle of Apples.

In this ancient landscape the church and monasteries held sway for many centuries. They not only started draining the levels, they laid the foundations of the Somerset cider tradition. The warm damp climate of the low-lying land is ideal for apples and the alluvial soils are rich and fertile. It is not uncommon to see orchards and lines of fruit trees dotted along the riverbanks.

If you look south from Burrow Hill in May, you can see blossom right to the foot of Ham Hill, some five miles away. In Kingsbury Episcopi there are 18 orchard owners and in autumn the air is heavy with the smell of cider. Just across the narrow lane you look down on to Pass Vale farm, a

higgledy-piggledy set of farm buildings, steeply angled roofs, some red tiled, some green corrugated iron, and for a moment you might be forgiven for thinking you were in France. This archetypal cider farm exudes old world charm, but a surprising degree of sophistication lurks beneath the surface. This is the home of Julian and Diana Temperley.

Walking into their farmyard is a great experience. Twenty years ago there were sheep, chickens, Vietnamese potbellied pigs, sheep dogs, peacocks, ponies, old tractors, hippies, a battered blue Volvo estate car, acres of wooden barrels, apples, half-timbered Normandy barns, orchard boxes, gypsy caravans, a walnut tree or two, a strong whiff of cider and an air of genteel shabbiness that belied the serious nature of the undertaking. Farm workers had unusual names such as Pigeon Biter, Buzzard, Brownsey, Footy, Noddy (aka Nathaniel of Wessex), as well as Shaney, Carl, Jason and Dickey, Bird's Eye, Kinger and Pridey alias Nathaniel. Old wellies, torn sweaters and an anarchic sense of old liberal views pervaded the farmhouse kitchen. What has changed? Very little in fact. Those farm workers have moved on but the scene is pretty much the same, except that the old hydraulic presses are no longer used and instead there is a highly efficient

Opposite. View towards Ham hill – the bush orchard.

gleaming automatic belt press. At the far end of the farmyard, looking as if it they have dropped down from outer space are 'Josephine' and 'Fifi', the large polished copper cider brandy stills (see below).

Over the last 35 years Julian Temperley has taken the cider world to another level. His dynamic, individual style, laced with enthusiasm and a scruffy punchiness, has helped to put high-quality cider and cider brandy back on the map. Julian is one of Somerset's most colourful cider-makers: you get brains and brawn in equal measure, as well as a strong cider philosophy. For him *terroir* doesn't just mean the lie of the land, it implies the intense and individual relationship with the trees in the orchard, the fruit, the soil and the climate. *Terroir*, as Julian explains, can change even within a single orchard as the soils change.

The Burrow Hill story is a complex and intriguing one. Diana, Julian's wife, patiently makes tea and coffee for visitors while Julian holds forth. During the Second World War Julian's father helped develop magnetic mines and homing torpedoes, so from an early age experimentation with hazardous substances was in Julian's blood! The cider-making came about almost by accident. After working on a farm in Kenya, Julian returned

to his native Somerset and in the early 1970s was at Pass Vale Farm, a beautiful area on the edge of grade one soils, with South Petherton on one side and the Somerset Levels and Moors on the other.

At his kitchen table beside the apple wood dresser Julian waxes lyrical about cider history and shows how fate can play a large part in cider-makers' lives. 'When I bought the farm there was a large wooden press and some cider in the corner of the barn: we could just as easily have ended up sheep farmers as apple farmers. Cider has been made on the farm for at least 150 years and gradually it has taken over everything. You fall into cider by mistake. I don't think cider is a logical thing … We had nine acres of orchard and we now have 150 acres.'

For 15 years Julian just made large quantities of cider, much of which was sold at Glastonbury Festival, but he soon got bored, decided to push the boundaries further and founded the Somerset Cider Brandy Company in 1986, an astute move. Since then Julian has gone from strength to strength with his adventures in the distilling world culminating in the recent release of his 15-year-old cider brandy, appropriately enough called Alchemy, and another called Shipwreck.

Above left. The cider barn.
Above right. High tide in the orchard.

With Julian you get quantity and quality. Back in the 1960s, the cider world was very different, as he explains. It was either rough-and-ready farm cider known as scrumpy, which varied from refreshing to undrinkable, or the more refined bottled and draught cider made along industrial lines by large firms such as Coates, Taunton Cider, Bulmers or Whiteways. At around this time one or two of these firms slowly slid into the use of apple concentrate, either from abroad or from their own apple juice concentrate on site. This made economic sense; they could make cider all the year round when it suited them and save on the cost of vast storage tanks. But the resulting cider was different. It contained less cider-apple juice, tasted sweeter, had preservatives added and was heavily carbonated.

Somewhere in the middle, between these two extremes, there survived, against all the odds, a narrow band of high-quality farmhouse cider, which was treated like wine and graced the dinner tables of gentlemen-farmers. They took pride in their cider and in their cider-making expertise, much of which was handed down though the generations. It is from this tradition that the modern high-quality cider world has evolved, and Julian is very much at the forefront.

Today Somerset has more working cider farms than any other county in England, and their orchards give the landscape a very particular feel and rich diverse habitat.

Sadly, since the Second World War many farmers in the south-west have abandoned cider-making altogether and instead sell their cider apples to the large companies. Twenty years ago many farmers were guaranteed a price of around £120 a ton and orchards were on 30-year contracts. This was a boom time and orchards provided a significant part of the farm income, but the inexorable rise of imported foreign apple concentrate has put paid to that. Today the price of apples has fallen to about £90 a ton, delivered in, which is a reduction of about two thirds in real terms.

Some farmers simply turned their backs on commercial apple growing. Their eighteenth-century farmhouses have been sold off, their barns have been converted and their orchards ripped out. In retrospect they may have been a bit too hasty, for cider is now going through a major revival, driven mainly at the quality end by the smaller and medium-scale cidermakers.

As Julian proudly says: 'Kingsbury Episcopi is one of the three vintage areas in Somerset which were recognised by Long Ashton Research Station, the other two being Baltonsborough and Wedmore.'

Vintage areas are important. It comes down to soils, climate, outlook and inclination, but above all

to cider apples and varieties that grow well in that area.

'In France, in the Calvados region they have a maximum tonnage per hectare of twenty-five tons, which is about ten tons to the acre and they think it poor form if you grow more than that ... In Somerset a big orchard used to be ten acres and in Hereford it used to be forty acres.'

Julian now has 150 acres. Of these, 73 acres are at Over Stratton, a village a few miles away on the other side of South Petherton. These are some of the largest orchards in Somerset. 'We need clay, we need loam over clay. Over Stratton is more likely to be too light, too sandy; we are looking for heavy soil. Cider needs to go back to that world of *terroir*.' The orchards at Over Stratton were originally planted for Showerings, the makers of Babycham.

As for cider-apple varieties, Julian is keen on the local 'Jersey' apples, a term which comes from *jaisy* rather than the island of Jersey. 'All cider apples with the suffix "Jersey" originated in South Somerset. So it is Yarlington Mill, Dabinett, Stembridge Jersey, Harry Masters Jersey, Coat Jersey, Chisel Jersey. Any Jersey apple comes from South Somerset. They are the heavy-tannin, bitter-sweet apples. Kingston Black is almost certainly from Kingston St Mary near Taunton. Dabinett is from Mid Lambrook ... but the origin is very important. Dabinett is the biggest, most important apple. Dabinetts should be green and red with a little bit of yellow, and they should be ripe, not too much leaf. In the past a lot of these trees actually came from the hedgerows. *Jaisy* therefore just means bitter-sweet apples, a generic word for cider apples.'

Julian has about 20 acres of bush orchard, planted when his first daughter was born. Alice Temperley is now a very fashionable dress designer and is arguably even better known in London than her father. And then there are 130 acres of standard orchard. Julian likes old standard orchards; he grazes his sheep underneath them.

He also buys in cider apples from other growers. One of his main suppliers is Montgomery's in North Cadbury (the same family that makes the award-winning cheddar cheese).

Here, excellent cider and excellent cheddar cheese come from the same soil, so to speak: a very fortuitous link in Slow Food terms. The Slow Food Movement began in 1989 to counteract the disappearance of local food traditions and create awareness of where food comes from. Both Jamie Montgomery and Julian Temperley believe that the way forward is the artisan approach, where *terroir* is a vital ingredient in producing a top-quality product. North Cadbury is next to South Cadbury, which has an earthwork castle reputed to be Camelot – so Arthur creeps in again. Certainly a two-year-old truckle of Montgomery cheese, a fresh loaf of granary bread and a flagon or two of Julian's best cider would have been much appreciated at the round table.

Cider philosophy fascinates Julian. Twenty years ago he agrees that all the cidermakers were chasing the same market, but now there is a definable difference. There is a new generation of people drinking cider and cider has gone decidedly up-market over the last ten years. If the smaller makers are to have a role, they should be seen to have a different philosophy to the larger makers. That is a fundamental difference.

As Julian says: 'We have to have a different philosophy, we have to make cider out of apples, there is a difference. We have to be small cidermakers, as opposed to making cider in an industrial way with apple concentrate. We are artisan producers and we have to be seen as artisan producers. Cider doesn't have to be at the bottom

Above. Sheep grazing in orchards form an integral part of the agricultural year on a cider farm.

end of the market; indeed, if cidermakers aim for that market then they are missing a trick.'

For the moment Julian has enough orchards. Compared to 20 years ago, cider apples are incredibly cheap. 'We are now looking at a period of over-production. Bush orchards are lasting far longer than anyone imagined, and they are producing far more.'

The earliest apples used at Burrow Hill are Morgan Sweet, then Bulmer's Norman, Tremlett's Bitter and Taylors; in the middle of the season, Michelin, Yarlington Mill and Harry Masters Jersey; then Stoke Red, Kingston Black, Vilberie, Chisel Jersey, Stembridge Jersey, the latest being Black Dabinett. Julian uses more than 40 varieties of cider apple in all, including Burrow Hill Early and Royal Somerset. As he says: 'The art and the craft of cider-making has to be blending the cider apples. When we used to press cider for a local farmer, Frank Yandle, he wanted a blend of apples with every colour of the rainbow in it, and as long as every colour of the rainbow was going up the elevator he was happy. And that was actually the art and craft of cidermaking. And as a rule of thumb that was a bloody good thing.'

The old school of cidermaking was that you left the apples for a long time to mature until they were almost rotting. Some say that the industrial sector finishes pressing far too early: 'It is easy to harvest apples in October but it is a bugger to harvest them in late November.'

In 2006 Julian finished pressing ten days before Christmas, some years it has been even closer than that. In 1990 there were seven weeks of shift work and the presses were going from 6 a.m. till 10 p.m. And that is hard manual work. The major companies with their sophisticated automatic pressing machinery usually finish by the beginning of November. But to Julian what is really important is the apple quality, and apples at the end of November can be very good indeed.

'If you go to France they like to keep their apples in lofts and artificially dehydrate them: maybe they are colder and dryer in the autumn than we are, but as the season goes on the apples sweat and loose water, it is true that the specific gravity goes up as the percentage of sugar rises.'

It is, after all, the natural sugars that you are looking for, because during fermentation it is the sugars that are turned into alcohol. The more sugar, the more alcohol and the more alcohol the better your cider will keep. Not only that but the apples are easier to press when they are well and truly ripe. You also get more juice and better quality juice.

As far as Julian is concerned, 'One of the greatest errors of cidermaking is to press apples too early. I would have thought our late-November, early-December apples are our best apples. We are about 30 per cent bitter-sharps. There is a great shortage of bitter sharp apples. But the blending of apples is the essential thing, for us tannin makes Somerset cider. If you want quality you have to have tannins. They give you the colour, the mouth feel, the texture, the depth, the quality.'

The philosophy of apples and cidermaking goes much further afield than Somerset. Ciderland shares its traditions with northern France, Normandy, Brittany and some of Spain. Indeed it could easily be argued that the cider traditions of using high tannin cider apples along the western Atlantic seaboard of the British Isles, which includes Ireland and Wales, is closer to the European continental tradition than it is to the cidermaking of the eastern counties of Kent, Sussex, Norfolk and Suffolk. Certainly the tannin is very important and a defining criteria for good cider in the West Country.

As Julian says: 'In the cider world you have varieties and you have regions in exactly the same way you have with cheeses.' This is the way that cider must progress, not just the county identity, which often already exists, but the specific region, which may be a group of villages or a vintage area.

The one factor that has without doubt distorted this image is the wide-scale use of apple concentrate by the large companies, and this can be in two forms. The first is imported apple concentrate, which comes in bulk from various countries in Eastern Europe, Turkey and China and is derived from dessert apples. It is apple juice that has been subjected to intense heat; this drives off the interesting volatile fractions, which give you the subtle

The knowledge slowly filtered northward into the monasteries, and then across the English Channel into the cider-making counties of western England. With the dissolution of the monasteries by Henry VIII in 1538–9 all this knowledge suddenly came onto the open market.

In Somerset a will that survives dated 1560 shows that Robert Gibbes of Sherbourne, the last prior of Montacute Priory, leaves his *stillatorie* and *lymbeck* to his nephew, a parson. This is clear evidence of distilling and it is interesting that the still, a highly valuable item, should be in the hands of the prior.

Over the next 200 years cider brandy was distilled annually, but this decreased with the availability of cheap, smuggled French brandy. The final nail in the coffin was the Excise Act of 1823, which required all distilleries to be registered and for a duty to be levied on every gallon of spirit that was distilled. The distilling of cider brandy from that time in the West Country almost certainly went underground.

Reintroducing the art of distilling cider has always been the goal of several cidermakers. Bertrand Bulmer started the ball rolling in 1984 with his King Offa distillery at the Museum of Cider in Hereford. And it wasn't long before Julian Temperley followed in his footsteps. Distilling began at Brympton D'Evercy in 1987 and then moved to Thorney in 1989, when Julian formed the Somerset Cider Brandy Company. He imported two elderly French calvados stills on the back of an old lorry from Normandy. One was called Josephine and the other Fifi. Both were made between the wars by Gazagne of Paris. They are now almost part of the family, and Julian pats the old girls affectionately from time to time.

Josephine is matronly and reliable, and Fifi, as her name implies, is small, fast and pretty. Rumour has it she was named after the French au pair who was working on the farm at the time of their arrival. Josephine and Fifi are Coffey stills named after Aeneas Coffey, who invented this type of still in 1831. They are 'continuous' stills, and once set up can work long hours with an uninterrupted flow of cider going in at one end and 70 per cent cider brandy coming out at the other end.

Aeneas Coffey (1780–1851) was an Irish excise man born in Calais but working in Dublin. His Coffey stills were much faster than the pot stills, which could only distil one batch of cider at a time. His system of using two pot stills back to back is ingenious. In one column with the boiler the cider is heated and the alcohol forced off as vapour. It then rises and enters a series of bubble plates or baffles with small copper mushrooms, and this allows the vaporised alcohol from the cider to condense and re-vaporise in a series of fractions. There are six sections with two bubble plates, so each plate represents a separate distillation. The vapour rises, hits the mushrooms and condenses out on each plate and goes on again, like a ladder. The process continues up through the first column, goes across in a narrow pipe and into the second column where it condenses, the heat of the distillate warming the incoming cold cider: heat exchange at its best and simplest.

What this system enables you to do very neatly is to drive off the fractions that you don't want and to keep the ones you do want, and the spirit gets stronger and stronger as it rises through the system. Ideally the cider brandy spirit comes off at just above 78°C and condenses at 68–72 per cent abv. It is a colourless liquid, and the strength is regularly checked with a hydrometer. Accurate logs and diaries are always kept and regularly inspected by Customs and Excise. There are 64 locks and seals on each still.

It is hot work and the distiller has to be ever watchful in case the device overheats or becomes empty. Nobody wants weak spirit. Julian's distiller is called Tim Edwards, and he has been working with Josephine and Fifi for eight years. As Tim explained to me 'the feints, which are the tail ends, go into a jar and the low wines are mixed in and re-distilled'. The lighter fractions such as methanol, which he doesn't want, are allowed to escape into the atmosphere.

Opposite. Tim Edwards hard at work with Josephine while Fifi looks on.

The stills are fired up with gas and every morning Tim lights the burners with a rolled-up newspaper. The *Daily Telegraph* for Josephine and *News of the World* for Fifi. In a 12-hour day Tim can distil up to 12,000 litres of cider. It takes ten litres of cider to make one litre of spirit a day. So he is distilling roughly 1,200 litres of spirit. He is referring of course to the cider: 'They like to get their teeth into it, they love it when the cider strength is up around 7 per cent.'

For distilling, the cider has to be made organically, without sodium meta-bisulphite, otherwise the sulphur will react with the copper and you will get green distillate, i.e. copper sulphate.

What the stills really don't like are sudden changes in temperature. Draughts are not welcome. Even fresh cold cider is not to their liking. 'The old girls like it quiet and gentle, they're sensitive little souls really.' Once the clear spirit comes off it is pumped into a wooden barrel and then whisked down to the bond, where it starts its maturation.

This is when distiller's skill becomes really crucial. It all hinges on the barrels. Some spirit is released immediately as *eau de vie*, but the majority is aged for three, five, ten or even fifteen years.

As Tim says, the three-year-old is young but has a bit of fire to it; it has got the apple still in it. The five-year-old is more oakey, less apple. The ten-year-old is smoother still, but it is losing the apple. The 15-year-old, called Alchemy, is 'idyllic.'

Tim uses three-year-old cider brandy for cooking. 'It is wonderful with roast pheasant, making a nice stuffing with fresh bacon, apples, chilli and ginger. You get that lovely appley flavour coming through. My whole take is that if you can, use the very best you can get. Most people would use three-year-old, but Valentina Harris always uses five-year-old, Rick Stein made custard out of ten-year-old and Michael Caines uses fifteen-year-old in a chicken dish.'

Good maturation of any spirit is required in the cool, even temperature of the bonded

Above. For many years this bus lived at Taunton cricket ground and is now used every year at Glastonbury Festival to sell cider. **Opposite left.** The hydrometer encased in glass.

warehouse and the individual barrels. Barrels lose large amounts by evaporation through the oak, maybe as much as a third over ten years. If the spirit goes in at 70 per cent proof it will come out at between 50 and 55 per cent. In the trade the amount lost is called the 'angel's share'.

At the Somerset Cider Brandy Company, each barrel is marked with its date of purchase, its past history and how it has been conditioned. Some might be made from Limousin oak, others from Allier oak. Some may be conditioned with cider, others with port, sherry or Pomona.

Recently Julian has managed to get hold of a few of the barrels that were washed ashore from the *Napoli*, shipwrecked in January 2007 off Branscombe in Devon. The barrels were protected from the sea by a large shipment of bibles printed in Zulu. God moves in mysterious ways, or is it the Holy Spirit wanting to get in on the act? The oak barrels were destined for a vineyard in South Africa. Some ten-year-old cider brandy has recently been finished off in a few of these wonderful new Allier oak barrels. This single cask spirit is appropriately enough called Shipwreck.

CHAPTER 2

Hangdowns
and Longhorns

SOMERSET

David and Louisa Sheppy,
Sheppy's Cider, Bradford-on-Tone, Somerset

Nestling under the Blackdown hills in the Vale of Taunton near Bradford-on-Tone, Sheppy's Cider has been around for as long as anyone can remember. The red brick farm buildings on the main road between Taunton and Wellington are well-known landmarks. Sheppy's is without doubt one of the oldest cidermakers in Somerset and can trace a family history in cider back at least six generations, to John Shepson of Iwood near Congresbury in North Somerset. John's wife, Deborah Walter, had an ancestor who was none other than John Walter, who founded a newspaper called the *Daily Universal Register* in 1785. Three years later he changed its name to *The Times*.

John Shepson was born in 1788: his nickname apparently was 'Sheppy' and the nickname stuck. One of his sons, also John, was born in 1816 and when he died his will was in the name of John Sheppy otherwise 'Shepson'. The will stated that he had three hundred gallons of cider in his cellar and seven empty casks, which would imply that he was a cidermaker, a cider dealer and a cider drinker. The family was by this time living at Iwood Farm and an older brother, Thomas, also had the mill at Iwood. No doubt cidermaking went back much further, but this is the earliest actual documentation.

It is still cider country around Congresbury today.

John's son, James Sheppy, was born in 1852 and in 1897 he moved to Keynsham, near Bath. He farmed there for 20 years and in 1917 sold up, moved south and bought Three Bridges Farm at Broad Ford, otherwise known as Bradford-on-Tone.

Before too long he passed it on to his son Stanley. Stanley's wife, Edith Coate, was from Stathe. Her uncle was Redvers Coate, who set up the big cider works in Nailsea, aptly named Coates. 'Coates comes up from Somerset, where the cider apples grow', was the refrain. So there was cider on both sides of the family. Redvers had studied chemistry at Bristol University and then worked at Long Ashton Research Station under Professor Barker, who carried on the work of Sir Robert Neville Grenville and Frederick James Lloyd as head of department from 1904. It is interesting how many of the cidermakers before the Second World War owed their knowledge and skill to the wisdom and enthusiasm of Professor Barker and his laboratories.

Stanley was no exception, and like Redvers he learned all he could about cidermaking from Long Ashton: not just testing juice but the science of cidermaking, which involved bacteriology, plant

Opposite. One of David Sheppy's pedigree Longhorns, with the Quantocks in the background.

science, genetics, yeast, grafting and blending and storage of cider. The 1920s and 1930s were the heyday of Long Ashton and people came from far and wide to attend their courses, to use their laboratories and to find out how to improve their cider. Their tasting sessions were legendary.

When Stanley started at Three Bridges Farm there was only a five-acre orchard, which had been planted in the 1880s. The soil, a medium loam, was very good for Kingston Black. Stanley planted more trees and was soon winning prizes for his cider, receiving 200 in all. His greatest achievement was to win the overall Gold Medal, not once but twice, in 1932 and 1938, at the International Brewers Exhibition in Islington, London. Competition was stiff and there were more than 135 entries in various classes of cider. The winning cider came from a small two-and-a-half-acre orchard that had been planted after his son Richard was born in 1927. This orchard is still known today as 'Father's Orchard', and its apples make up the Gold Medal cider, which even in the 1930s was bottled. There were five varieties of cider apple: Hangdown, Dove, Yarlington Mill, Dabinett and Kingston Black – all good-quality vintage cider-apple varieties. The idea was to produce a very high-quality cider from a specific orchard. Other blends that Stanley developed were called Bullfinch and Goldfinch, which were lighter and sweeter. Lloyd George is said to have taken a liking to Stanley's Kingston Black.

Hangdown is otherwise known as Horners, or Pocket Apple, and is a mild-bitter sweet. It is not much used now because of the small size of the fruit; it was once very popular in North Devon as well. It is said to have originated from the Glastonbury area. Dove is also from the Glastonbury area, a late medium bitter-sweet, which is sometimes known as Pennard Dove, where it probably originated. There are a few other Dove apples – Improved Dove, Stone Dove and Late Dove.

Stanley also made 'champagne' cider, which was shipped up to London and sold for 30 shillings a case. Between the wars French champagne was in short supply and both cider and perry were carbonated and sold as an alternative.

Stanley died in 1948, leaving his son Richard

Opposite. Standard orchards are magnificent in fruit.

to take over. Richard was only 21 and so it was a steep learning curve. He had an enormous job on his hands and had to get the 250-acre farm back on its feet before concentrating on the cider. With the encouragement of Professor Barker at Long Ashton, Richard planted more orchards, some of which were standard orchards with experimental root stocks. Slowly the business blossomed. Ted Heath was presented with a flagon of Sheppy's cider when he visited Taunton in 1966 on the very day that Richard's son, David, was born. Richard and his wife Mary were delighted: an auspicious sign indeed.

After leaving school at 17, David started on the farm initially as a tractor driver. He learned the cider trade from the resident cellar man and went to agricultural college at Hadlow in Kent, with a fruit option: he learned a lot about top fruit, but there is no cider fruit in Kent. Following this, he went travelling for six months, working on farms and fruit-picking in Australia, before attending another course on farm management at Sparsholt in Hampshire, which he completed in 1989.

With his father at Three Bridges Farm he slowly developed other varieties of cider that were added to the portfolio, such as Oakwood, which was then bottled in three-pint glass flagons. And then came the single varieties. In 1998 they brought out Dabinett and Kingston Black, followed by Tremlett's Bitter a couple of years later, then Taylor's Sweet. But the Sheppys did not stop there. David started to sweeten cider with local Sedgemoor honey and produced an organic cider in 2003. The irony about the cider with honey is that it is taxed at three times the level of ordinary cider because the honey is an additive that does not feature in the Customs Regulations 162.

When David started he had 40 acres of orchard. There are now 55 acres, of which 18 are bush and the rest are standard. The bush orchards were planted in 1975–6 and are still the main cropping orchards: Dabinett, Michelin, Harry Master's Jersey, Chisel Jersey, then a block section of Tremlett's, Brown's, Taylor's, Porter's Perfection, Coate's Jersey, Yarlington Mill and Somerset Redstreak. As David says proudly: 'We still have

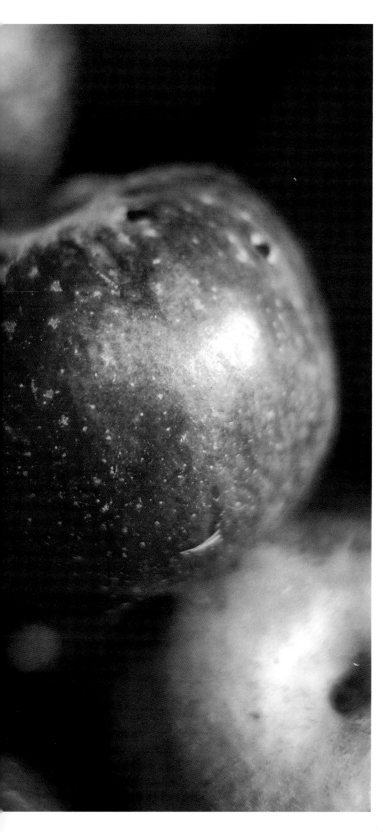

families called Tremlett and Dabinett who come and buy their ciders here. It must be in their blood.'

Cider apples are idiosyncratic; they have their own character even on the tree. As David says, 'The Redstreak comes out in blossom later than the Kingston Black, but it crops earlier. Porter's Perfection are the oddest one of all, they are nearly the first variety to come out in flower but the last apple to fall. Late December. Never go by the flowering date.'

Slowly over the years the farm in general has expanded and today the Sheppys have 350 acres, with 200 acres of arable crops and the rest is beef and sheep. One of David's hobbies is Longhorn cattle. 'A little passion of mine. It is easy to have a hobby without having to travel away from home.' And the Longhorn cattle look very good in the orchards. Their beef is on sale in their farm shop, so you get two bites of the apple, so to speak, as the pomace from cidermaking is fed back to the cattle. David has won many prizes for his cattle as well as his cider.

Wisely he married Louisa, a bright, sharp, sparkling lady who has done wonders for modernising the business on the marketing side. 'We are selling top-quality cider. Labels have to appeal to the modern market. In recent years people have begun to look for different styles of cider rather than the more commercial brands. Modern taste is for lighter, lower-tannin cider, like some of our single varieties. Our traditional Gold Medal is a heavy, still cider, which has always appealed to experienced traditional cider drinkers – you could call them connoisseurs. Hence, we market it in a wine presentation; it has a more limited, but avid following. It's all about different products for different markets.'

What is very refreshing is to see the standard orchards in blossom. One or two of the trees could be up to 120 years old. In Father's Orchard, planted in 1930, probably 60 per cent of the orchard is still there, 75 years old and still cropping well. In early spring, sheep and cattle are allowed to start grazing the standard orchards but are taken out by the middle of August to let the ground rest before the apple fall begins.

As to harvesting the apples, David uses a Somerset Fruit Machine, the Sabre, an excellent piece of equipment, one of the original Bulmer's prototypes. David doesn't want too much bruising, the cleaner the better. 'The Sabre actually picks up remarkably well in grass. The optimum length of grass to cushion the fall off the apple is about four inches. Any more and the apples get lost.'

Harvesting starts earlier and earlier these days. Weather and changes in the climate bring them on quicker. As David says, 'We were pressing some Michelin at the end of September last year, ridiculously early. Redstreak is our earliest variety, but they are still young trees. The main early ones are Tremlett's, Taylor's, Brown's, Michelin, a few Bulmer's Norman. We start in the last week in September. Our main month is now October but we hope to finish by the end of November. The best juice is now late October. November can be very wet. You damage the ground and you can lose a lot of apples. If they are ripe we press them as and when they come in.'

In the farm's museum, which is well worth visiting, you can see a variety of presses and cider equipment. There are old single-thread wooden screw presses, old pack presses with boards and cloths, and even old carbonating machines. Today Sheppy's use a state-of-the-art belt press from Austria. They make around 120,000 gallons of cider and still use natural yeast for fermentation. The most impressive sight is the wooden vats, which hold about 10,000 gallons each.

But where has the renewed interest in cider come from? Many of its suporters are wine drinkers who are looking for a new local drink that has an alcoholic strength in between wine and beer. Some are coming from the micro-breweries end of things, and the trend that Campaign for Real Ale (CAMRA) started has certainly had a good effect on cider by making people more aware of what it is they are actually drinking.

As Louisa says, 'A lot of our customers are experienced cider drinkers. We do tours on the tractors and trailers through the orchards and people are always interested in the family business. The museum gives them an insight into what used to happen. A lot of older people love it.'

Younger cider drinkers are often keen to know about the way the cider is made and are coming to it from the local food and drink angle. They are also keen to learn about the health benefits of drinking cider and apple juice. People are more conscious of what they are eating and drinking.

Louisa explains: 'Local food and drink is becoming a very big thing. We have just started trying to turn Wellington into a "food town". People come from miles around. Now is the right time. It is a social thing, people don't feel part of anything much these days, they like to buy into something that has roots and tradition behind it.'

Sheppy's is a very good example of a family cider farm that has kept its feet on the ground but has at the same time broadened its horizons without compromising on quality. The future is bright, and these bottled ciders go the length and breadth of the country.

CHAPTER 3
Lord Beaverbrook and the other Mr Churchill
SOMERSET

George Perry,
*Perry's Cider, Dowlish Wake,
Ilminster, Somerset*

There are few cidermakers in Somerset more respected than the Perrys of Dowlish Wake near Ilminster. Their cider farm with thatched ham stone barns nestles in the bottom of the valley beside the Dowlish Brook, which joins the River Isle near Ilminster. Dowlish Wake is famous, not just for Perry's Cider, but as the ancestral home of the Speke family who lived here from the fifteenth century. The church on the hill overlooking the cider farm is the last resting place of John Hanning Speke, the famous African explorer. In 1856 he discovered Lake Tanganyika with Sir Richard Burton and went on to give Lake Victoria its name and discover the source of the Nile. It is a peaceful location for an explorer: home at last to quench his thirst.

What is fascinating about Perry's is not just the diversity of the cider but the family history. Perry's was started in 1921 by William John Churchill, known as 'Bill'. He was a blacksmith, born in Dowlish Wake in 1885. By 1901 he was apprenticed to his father Joseph, who was a master blacksmith originally from Blackdown, a small hamlet in the Axe valley just over the border in Dorset. Blacksmithing was very much in the family, as two of Joseph's younger brothers also went into the trade. Frederick Churchill even worked with William in Dowlish Wake before becoming the blacksmith in the neighbouring village of Winsham. Cider and blacksmithing seem to go together. Shoeing horses was hot work at the best of times and so cider would have been an obvious and refreshing drink to quench that thirst. Horses were an important part of cidermaking, bringing the cartloads of apples into the farmyard. Some people even used horses for grinding up the apples in the circular granite troughs, but these, although common in Devon and Herefordshire, are not often found in Somerset. The blacksmith's was the hub of the village where all news was shared – no different from a cider house today.

William stayed in Dowlish Wake all his life except when he was called up for the First World War and served on the Western Front as a farrier. In the days after the war many self-employed people had to take on various jobs to make ends meet. In 1920 the landowner, Major Speke of Jordans, near Ashill, decided to sell Dowlish Wake Manor estate. William managed to buy Lot 9, a smallholding, which he called Churchill's. The smallholding, smithy, enclosed yard and the barn cost him £1,175, no mean sum in those days but a sound investment. William then began making cider in earnest. Interestingly, the sale catalogue shows that there were already three cider houses in the village with apple lofts. These were very important

because they allowed the apples to dry out and mature before being pressed. Having an apple loft also meant that gravity was on your side when feeding the scratter.

William carried on with both jobs. No doubt his smithy skills were very useful when setting up and repairing old cider-making machinery that involved cogs, long metal-threaded screws, handles, ratchets, spindles and rollers. In the Ordnance Survey map of 1889 Dowlish Wake is shown replete with orchards. It is an ideal place to start a commercial cider-making operation. The soil is clay, which tends to hold the water, so the trees are very rarely parched. William planted a cider orchard opposite the barn, which is still there today.

No doubt the cider was a draw for the local farmers and farm workers who needed repairs to carts and farm machinery. William also delivered his cider to local pubs and had a good arrangement with the Oakhill brewery. During the Second World War the brewery took all the cider he could

make. William married Alexene Humphries, who was a schoolteacher like her mother, and sometimes during the war when they were short-staffed she had to help shovelling pomace for the animals. Cows adore pomace and do very well on it. It has fibre and is nutritious. Imagine Somerset beef, pork or lamb finished on pomace.

William was quite a character, a hard-working man with a strong Somerset accent and dialect, and a fund of local stories. He struck up an unusual friendship with a neighbour who had bought a derelict farm in the next-door village of Cricket Malherbie. He gave the man a conducted tour of his cider works, after which they became the best of friends. This neighbour was the charismatic and energetic newspaper tycoon Lord Beaverbrook who, during the Second World War, was put in charge of aircraft production by the 'other' Mr Churchill. And while Lord Beaverbrook was overseeing the production of spitfires and bombers, William Churchill was overseeing the production

Above. The sixteenth-century thatched barn in Dowlish Wake.

of cider in Dowlish Wake, cider which eventually found its way into Winston's cellars – or was it the War Room? Lord Beaverbrook would often take his guests to see the cider farm and William was invited up to the big house where they would sit in the garden and chat. Cricket Malherbie Manor Farm was the first of many farms that Lord Beaverbrook bought and it was the start of his cheese and dairy empire, which is still running today as Cricketer Farm at Nether Stowey.

Lord Beaverbrook's farm manager, Sandy Copland, wrote a book about how the Cricketer estate was built up and leaves us with a good description of what it must have been like at Mr Churchill's cider works. 'His lordship was fascinated by the whole set-up. The huge fat wooden barrels with their girdle bands, the cider presses, the smell of apples as they were being pushed onto the conveyor belt leading to the cutters. The aroma of cider that hung in the air giving each intake of breath a special feeling of warmth and sunshine.'

William died in 1945 aged sixty-one, only two weeks after Alexene. The business was then kept going until his nephews came back from the war. Alexene's sister Maud had married a Perry and it was her two sons, Henry and Bert Perry, who took the business over. Before the war they had often worked with their uncle making cider, so it was a logical progression to keep the business in the family. Perrys have been in Dowlish Wake since the seventeenth century.

Both the Perry brothers were very lucky to survive the war. Henry had been sent on a troopship to Singapore but it turned around just in time, otherwise he would have been captured. He served in Ceylon, India and later Burma with the Royal Artillery, but rarely talked about it. Letters were sent to him in Burma by his Uncle William saying that cider apples had reached £20 a ton and that the demand for cider was higher than ever. How Henry must have longed for a cool pint of Somerset cider in the Burmese jungles. Bert was a commando with the Lovat Scouts and landed at D-Day on Sword Beach with Lord Lovat and the Highland Pipes going full blast. They also had a hand in relieving Pegasus Bridge.

It must have been a welcome respite for the two brothers to be cidermaking again. The business was now called Perry's Cider and it went from strength to strength. In 1950 they went hydraulic. An old wooden press, which had made cider for over 150 years, was relegated to the farm museum. William's blacksmithing tools, the bellows and old farm implements were slowly hoarded and then displayed. A visit to Perry's cider farm became an education in itself. The new hydraulic presses were bought from Stowe's of Bristol and Beare's of Newton Abbot, the same ones that are in use today.

Hydraulic presses run off water that is slowly pressurised, and are very powerful. The racks or slats are put in between each layer of pomace while the cheese is built up with about a dozen layers, and when complete is subjected to approximately 150 tons of pressure. The racks are made from ash or oak, or even wych elm. The ideal situation is to have two presses going at once. The main workers at Perry's are Walt Sumption, Dave Beeston, Godfrey and Gavin. Walt has been making cider here since 1957; Dave has been here since 1972. Visitors often stop to watch the process in action.

In the 1960s Perry's Cider had more than 100 apple suppliers from more than 50 villages. With most farms having a tractor and trailer it meant that cider apples could be brought a greater distance. The Perrys were still sending cider to pubs – the New Inn, Dowlish Wake; The Royal Oak and The Bell Inn, Ilminster; the Rose and Crown, Dinnington; the Castle Inn and a pub in Chard. 'Delivery was very labour-intensive. They had a car and trailer then with hogsheads on the back. It was nearly all dry cider unless there were a few barrels that were sweeter, then they mixed them to make a little bit of medium.'

Oak barrels are still important to the Perrys. They did not just have the hogsheads, holding 56 gallons; they had 28 gallons, 18s, 9s, and 4½s. There were also pipes holding 120–140 gallons each, still used for the vintage cider. As Marguerite Perry says with some feeling: 'We are well into barrels. It is so much easier now with a steam cleaner, but there are fewer coopers around. They do pop in from time to time. Yet another dying trade. They are mostly

older men. Barrels? We use them for years and years till they fall apart. We had some people from Portugal come a few years ago and he found one of his chestnut Fonseca barrels and that was pre-war from his family. Very taken up with it he was. So the barrel would have been over 60 years old.'

Henry Perry would also deliver the smaller barrels of cider to his customers. 'People often didn't have cars and you couldn't carry a barrel on a bicycle very easily. There were no fridges and people kept the barrel either in a cellar or in an outhouse. Then there were the stone jars, which had 'Perry's Cider – Dowlish Wake' written on the side. They were made in large batches first in Bristol and then up in Chesterfield. Sadly the banks foreclosed on the firm that made them even though they had full order books. When that firm closed it affected a lot of families in Chesterfield. Jars were used by many cider companies and this was in the age before plastic containers. There was quite a market for stoppers, corks, small wooden taps and spigots. All were re-usable. The corks came

from Benito Remous in Bristol.'

But in the 1960s the cider world was changing fast. With the mechanisation of agriculture there were far fewer men working on the land and because of National Service many of the young men had learned to drink lager in Germany, which was almost unknown before the war in country pubs. Many small and medium-sized family breweries were being bought out by the large national breweries and then closed down. One local example of this was in Chard, the company of Bratton, Mitchell and Toms at the top of town. Here they made cider on a large scale as well as brewing beer. In October and November the whole town of Chard smelt of cider and there were often apples rolling down the High Street. The words 'Autumn Gold' were painted on the brewery's roof, but even though the firm was bought out, the name continued for many years.

Slowly the whole nature of public houses changed. Pubs were no longer family-owned, they tended to be tied into a chain and the landlord had

Above left. William Churchill – the other Mr Churchill, blacksmith and cidermaker.
Above right. Mrs Perry senior, whose husband Henry Perry ran the cider farm for many years.

to stock what he was told to. In Somerset many pubs were going over to selling Taunton cider, which was itself owned by a string of breweries. Other West Country cider companies such as Whiteways, Coates and Showerings, also expanded but this again put pressure on many of the small and medium-sized cidermakers, who were squeezed out and went to the wall, just like the breweries. But not the Perrys.

After Burma and Normandy, Henry and Bert stuck to their guns. They realised that they had to be proactive and advertise to draw the tourists in, many of who came down to Devon and Cornwall by car. Being situated between the A30 and the A303 and only a mile and a half from Ilminster made it easy for tourists to stop off and fuel up with cider, either on the way down or on the way back to Dowlish Wake.

Bert died suddenly in 1967 and from that time Henry and his wife Marguerite ran the business alone. What also helped in a curious way was the national advertising campaign of Taunton Cider,

which certainly put Somerset Cider on the map. Taunton Cider, based at Norton Fitzwarren, was employing up to 400 people in the late 1970s. As Marguerite says: 'Taunton cider. Their advertising was very good for Somerset. Taunton cider was Somerset.'

In a curious twist of fate in the 1980s and 1990s several of the larger cider companies were bought out or amalgamated and everything was then concentrated in Shepton Mallet, in more ways than one. All those old Somerset-based cider companies are now under the name Gaymers, which is a Norfolk brand.

For small and medium-sized cider farms still in business in Somerset, using pure cider-apple juice from traditional varieties, this is in a sense good news, as the paths between the two kinds of cider-making have clearly diverged. The tradition of farmhouse cidermaking has come full circle. The future is high-quality, locally sourced and produced speciality cider.

What is fascinating about Henry Perry is that

Above. Perry's Dabinett was overall champion at the 2008 Bath & West Show.
Right. Somerset Redstreak, an early bitter-sweet.

like his uncle, William Churchill, he stuck to making the best cider he could with top-quality fruit and natural yeasts, fermented and aged in oak barrels. The museum was Henry's pride and joy and here you get a real feel for rural life as it was when he was growing up. As Marguerite says, 'Cider is not just the cider, it is a culture. That is how we market it.' And she should know.

Henry died in 1993. Hundreds of people turned up to the funeral: there was no room in the church and many had to stand outside. Marguerite continued running the cider farm with the help of her two sons, John and Andrew. All the family put their backs into it and lent a hand whenever they could. Henry had wisely encouraged his sons to get other jobs and qualifications. One is an accountant and the other an estate agent. Liz Perry, John's wife, often works behind the scenes and many changes have occurred not least in the bottling line. Marguerite, Mrs Perry senior, is still often to be seen serving customers and answering their questions.

Marketing is important, and to reach new customers farm shops have been very useful. 'People will go miles and miles. We say we are natural. We can keep going as long as people come down to the West Country. The villages have changed such a lot, people have visitors and hopefully they will still come down to a quaint little place.'

But there is nothing 'quaint' about Marguerite. A shrewd businesswoman, she has kept a firm hand on the tiller. 'We are very traditional; we have survived by being traditional and that is the way they will continue to do it now. We are sticking to cider apples, which have high tannins. People like to come here and see the orchards, it is genuine, we are what we are, and what they see, they get.'

But everything hinges, not just on the orchard, but on the skill of the cidermaker. As she says, 'People like Henry, his brother Bert and their uncle William Churchill, the blacksmith, they did not have any scientific knowledge but they just knew what they were doing, they just knew. They were intelligent to the very ends of their fingertips.'

Marguerite feels that the history of the

countryside has got to be revived. It has not been always recognised. Education about the countryside and nature is another important part of the cider farm. 'Some people can't understand that you are not making cider all the year round. You see they don't know that you get blossom in the spring and that apples grow on trees and those apples are harvested in the autumn. They just assume that because they can get apples all the year round in the supermarkets, we can as well.'

The cider travels quite widely. Bottling is good and pasteurising keeps it much better. 'People are drinking cider more like wine with their food. Because they are used to wine and like the taste of cider and it's English. We are in the speciality cider market.'

Perry's is still a family business. To help guarantee the supply of apples John planted a seventeen-acre bush orchard a mile or two down the road in Knowle St Giles and this is now cropping very well indeed. In the last year or two, George Perry, Henry's grandson, now in his mid-20s, has returned from university to run the business. As he says, he 'sort of fell into the business': he had always planned to work in London.

After studying land management at Reading University, George went round the world; saw vineyards in New Zealand, then across to Australia, Fiji, Thailand and Singapore. When he came back he had to earn some money to pay for his travels and ended up working on the farm. His father, John, is very happy that he is in the industry but never actively encouraged him. He has put up plenty of cheeses and he is often 'hands on', bottling and cleaning, although it is the marketing side that really interests him. Even as a young boy he was always over in the yard with his grandfather Henry, whom he remembers as being 'pretty passionate about cidermaking and very keen to keep the traditional Somerset cidermaking alive'. At school George did an A-level project on the disappearing orchards in Somerset. The family's five-acre orchard with more than twenty different varieties of apples is the only orchard left in Dowlish Wake.

Perry's were one of the first to get into single-

variety ciders in 1995 with Somerset Redstreak, which is an early bitter-sweet with soft tannins. Then they tried Dabinett, a late bitter-sweet, which originates from Mid Lambrook. Tremlett's Bitter followed, another early bitter-sweet, from Devon this time, and then Morgan Sweet, which is the earliest cider apple of them all, making a light, refreshing cider that can sparkle. Perry's are the only cidermakers bottling Morgan Sweet and the apple is often ready for pressing by early September, a full month ahead of the other apples.

Wild yeasts are still used to ferment the ciders. The apples have enough sugars and yeast to ferment of their own accord. Perry's can do this because they only ferment in small batches, with no containers bigger than 300 gallons. If one doesn't work it is not the end of the world, but with containers of 10,000 gallons or more it is a risky procedure. The cider spends between eight and ten months maturing in a barrel. Last year they made around 40,000 gallons, which is a lot of cider and a lot of barrels.

John spent ten years modernising the company and now it is George's turn. He is putting in a new bottling line and has changed the labels and bottles. Perry's have won Supreme Champion at the Royal Bath & West Show in 2003 and 2005, as well as a CAMRA award. George is very keen to move his cider into local outlets. 'There is such a good market within 40 miles, very few pubs and restaurants have got local cider in now and small bottles are the answer.'

George has also noticed his customers are more his age. He says, 'We are getting younger people coming in and buying packs of bottles. Bridging the gap. There has been a lot of talk in the cider industry about the generation that were brought up on mixed drinks and alcopops, who are now coming of age and are going over to trying ciders.'

George has converted the wagon shed and put in tea rooms, a food hall and visitor area. 'People from all over the world come to the cider works. It is nice to know where it all ends up. Word of mouth is the best way of advertising. That and the website.'

Perry's welcome about 50,000 visitors a year, which is remarkable for a small Somerset village.

10,000 GALLON'S
= 80,000 PINTS

IF YOU DRANK
4 PINT'S A DAY
IT WOULD TAKE YOU
54 YEARS
9 MONTHS
20 DAYS

while to fill them. As Martin says, the noise that a 10,000-gallon vat makes when it is fermenting is quite incredible. 'In the evenings, when everyone has left and the yard is quiet and you can hear them bubbling away, they do go quite rapid.'

This area of Somerset was always heavily into cider. On the road to Wedmore there used to be twenty-one cidermakers in a ten-mile stretch. Now there are only two, Rich's and Roger Wilkins. Many local farmers gave up making cider in the 1970s when decimalisation, duty and VAT came in on cider. At the same time Gordon Rich was expanding his business. He supplied virtually every pub in Bridgwater back then, delivering two or three times a week. 'It was nightmare keeping up with them,' Jan said. Today Rich's has extended its range – to Warminster, Frome, Taunton, Dulverton, Minehead.

Jan is one of the few cidermakers I know who goes out into an orchard and offers the farmer a price for the whole crop of cider apples on the spot, and then arranges for her hand pickers to go out there and gather the harvest in. At the age of 34, and the youngest daughter, she took over running the cider farm when her father died – a daunting task for a woman. And yet she has

managed magnificently. It is still very much a family firm, with Martin in charge of all the cider production.

Jan goes into orchards round about July and August. 'We walk round the orchard with the farmer and we say we will give you X amount for the whole orchard. They huff and puff a bit then after a while we come up with an agreement.' One problem today is getting people to pick. 'We used to have whole families out there, the same people we used for the vegetables; travelling people as well, all sorts. We were quite an employer then. We used to be up to 30 or 40 people when we were actually making – mothers, daughters, grandparents, all working. It used to be much more fun then. If you were out there in the morning there would be a frying-pan going. I used to have to do lots of shaking. That was physically horrible. Climbing the damn trees. Cider is the backbone of everything here. Cider just got bigger and bigger and took over more and more time.' Many of the orchards she goes to are small farmhouse orchards dating from the nineteenth century.

Jan and Martin planted a ten-acre standard orchard of their own in March 2000, the same year Jan's daughter Molly was born, so they will always

Above left. Lifetime's consumption.
Above right. Martin the Vat man.

be the same age. The apples are mostly bitter-sweets and some sharps. 'Some are called Bloody Butchers because of the red veins running through them. Bush orchards won't do well here because they are below sea level, the land is too damp and they don't like wet feet.' In the village up the road Martin reckons his front door is 13 feet below sea level. 'On Mark Church there is a line on up the wall. The sea is still two or three miles away at Burnham but if you go a mile and a quarter away at a point called Isle Port, back in time that was a port but it has silted up.'

This is the Somerset Levels and Moors, and as Martin says, 'All sorts of soils. If you go two miles inland it is all peat, and a mile down the road it is sandy, so we are a clayey-sandy mix, which is quite good.' Mark is the second longest village in Somerset and third longest in the country. The road just goes straight up through for several miles. 'The biggest problem here is wind, but it is not as cold as it should be in winter. Trees like to have dormant periods, a resting period. We do rely on cold weather to kill diseases, particularly for us as we don't spray anything. We plant a tree in the ground and leave it, we don't pamper it. And the picking season has got earlier.'

After they are picked off the ground the apples are pressed as soon as they come in. 'They do their resting out in the orchard. It was great in the old days with sacks, you could leave them and go back to them and use them when they were ready. Now when they come here they are ready to go.' Martin uses hydraulic presses, Beare's made in 1946. Prior to that Gordon was pressing by hand then eventually went to a Stowe press in the late 1960s. It was a slow process. 'One pressing took you all night. The old horsehair cloths were big, heavy, horrible things.'

Most of the picking is now done by machine and Martin has some good orchards around Street and Burrowbridge. 'Nice old ones. The orchards we like now are the ones that are spaced out with nice rows, easier to get in with machinery.'

Martin reckons that people nowadays drink with their eyes. 'A drink has to look good in the bottle and out of the bottle. It has now got to look

nice. But with apple juice it's the opposite, the bits are good for you. What is interesting is that people are coming back to cider when they are in their 30s and 40s because it is a local drink, which is great.'

Quite a few of Jan and Martin's customers come from the caravans at Brean and Burnham. 'In the summer the population increases tenfold. And the holidaymakers still prefer sweeter ciders more than the locals. The further up country, the sweeter they like it. There is still a macho image about cider with holidaymakers; they want the bottle to say dry but they want it to taste medium.' Even Martin's son, who is 19, has come back on to their type of cider and 'once they start drinking the real cider they don't go back'.

Rich's ciders are sweet, dry, medium, vintage, medium dry, a couple of single variety ones. 'There is a cider out there for everyone.'

Martin uses natural yeast unless it is extremely cold. 'So you are taking a bit of a gamble when you put the juice in the vat and let it do its own thing. Stainless steel will keep cider the same. They don't take anything away, but then again they don't add anything. If you get a cider in the oak vat and you think that its good, you whip it out into the stainless one. And it will stay like that. They are not actually that bad, I wouldn't want to have all stainless, but there is a place for them.'

Cidermaking for Martin is an art. 'I learnt from Gordon and other old boys who used to come in, just really sort of pick things up along the way. Curious tradition. Even now we get old boys coming in and telling us what we should be doing. And sometimes they talk sense and sometimes they don't. It is a continuous tradition, not like pressing buttons in a factory with a computer.'

In 2007 Martin experimented with two unusual single varieties, Lambrook Pippin and Yarlington Mill. 'There were quite a few in an orchard. It's a bit of fun. I like experimenting. It's nice to try different things. Sometimes there's so many varieties on a trailer you can't pick them out. In the old days they knew what they were doing, they had the right balance of varieties and they had their pollinators in there. You had what that particular farmer liked. Bit more tannin in there. Each farm would make a different cider and it would be this malolactic fermentation, they wouldn't be adding their yeasts. You could go to the same orchard and take half the apples to one farm, half to another and get them to make it and they wouldn't taste the same and so that's the fun bit. A lot of them in the old days, they liked to see a few that were overripe. Some were black. They were real men in those days.'

Martin is obviously keen to try things out and to learn. As far as I know he doesn't do any chemical analysis; it is all intuition. He probably makes 80,000 gallons a year and he has also started bottling, which is very useful for Jan's new shop.

This is definitely the way forward for many cider farms, diversifying into farm shops and restaurants. Jan has done both very successfully, with new buildings, opening the Cider Press restaurant and an extended shop with lots of local produce. Local people drop in to eat as well as visitors: one Sunday lunchtime she had 70 customers. 'Everything seems to be food-orientated with us at the moment with this restaurant opening, with all local suppliers, with all the cheese and the clotted cream and the baker up the road. So everybody is very excited because it is all helping other small producers, which is nice and so everybody gets a chance, because we get so busy during the holiday season. The cheddar cheese we get from a lovely chap called Bob Clapp. They make cheese at Baltonsborough, they used to be cidermakers once.'

The cider farms are becoming much more part of the local community, because small shops have had to close. If they can keep their heads above water – which may be difficult below sea level – then they are a real asset to the local community and will be valued as such.

As Martin says, habits have changed. 'In the old days when old boys came with their five-gallon barrels to be filled up, they had a good moan and put the world to rights. That doesn't happen now. Drink-driving changed it a lot. Now they have

smaller amounts but they will have cheese, chutney and wine as well.'

Martin supplies between 40 and 50 pubs locally. Volumes are going down, but it is more of a craft product, so the quality is up and the cider is slightly more expensive. 'Certainly people ask more questions about the cider now and it has stirred an interest, which is great, and we appreciate that. They realise what is on their doorstep. They realise how far their food has travelled.'

'We should do a wassail [a mid-winter custom, see p.xv]. It would be nice to do to get the fun back in the cider. Wassailing mug, two to three pints huge, you couldn't do that now, slurping out of it passing it round. It feels like we have had years and years of rules and regulations. I used to spend my day out in the yard and now so much time is taken up on the phone and filling in forms so some of the fun has gone. Let's have some fun again.' Martin has an infectious optimism which I am sure will stand him in good stead.

Above. Cider was often stored in stone jars to keep it cool.

Martin remembers the old days when Gordon was still alive and there was lots of storytelling in the old cellar. 'They used to have thirteen pipes: one to four were sweet, five to thirteen were dry. Every Saturday night, Saturdays and Wednesdays, a few of us used to get stuck in and put the world to rights. One chap from Weston, he was a dentist and he used to take people's teeth out. Everyone had names, like Mike the Brain, Larry the Lamb. It was an old-style cider club. Everyone will go back to a situation some years ago. It was an integral part of people's lives. Cider was the social part of your everyday life. cidermaking is a way of life not a job. In our cellar pipes nine and eleven were always best ones. Gordon was a great storyteller.'

With Martin and Jan you feel that they are part of a real, living tradition. 'Some barrels came from Harveys, Bristol Cream; some from 1936. Been used for so long. The Coates vats we think are 130 years old. There is a guy who has a book with vats in and all the names. A lot were named after World War Two planes like Spitfire. Gordon got them in the 1960s. We had a few that we couldn't stop leaking. In theory they should last 300 years.'

Location is important. 'People come down from the Midlands and call in on their way down to Cornwall or on their way back. We are only a mile and a half from Junction 22, so they haven't got far to come out of their way.'

Word of mouth also helps. 'When people come to Somerset they expect to stumble across cider farms found round every corner, well 50 years ago there was one. They now have bottles but many feel they haven't got the real thing unless they have got the rough plastic container. It is the farm cider thing.'

For Jan, losing her father Gordon suddenly was quite a shock. 'Nine years since I lost Dad and eleven years since I lost Mum. One thing has gone on to another and it is all in the right direction … Wonderful character, I still miss him dreadfully. Not an hour goes by when I don't think about him. Not an hour. People say, "What do you think your dad would say about what you are doing?" He would be really pleased. He always said, "You can do it, young 'n." I was one of three girls. I was the youngest. One's a JP now – they do their own thing, they never wanted the worry and the responsibility. I have always stayed at home and worked since I left college. Then Father and I used to walk the orchards, I used to go with him when he used to go buying the apples. I was always with him; we always had a very special bond. It just developed from there. I never really wanted to think about what would happen when he wasn't there. He was a young 74 when he died. He died suddenly.'

'I was 34 when I took over the business. He died in May. I had to walk in the orchards on my own, really awful, that was one of hardest times, going back round the orchards, things I can remember step by step, word for word what he said. "Careful of that variety, it can make the cider turn." I always thought he would be with me to remind me of all these things. So it was very, very hard. It was pretty much based on how many apples were there. Estimating how much is in the grass is hard. Whether it is five or ten tons or fifteen tons is

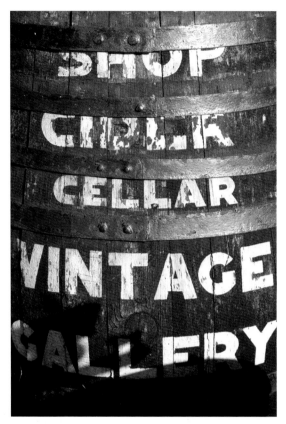

Jan does a lot of shows and at the Bath & West Show in 2004 she got her picture in *Hello* magazine, the *Daily Express* and *Daily Mail*. She persuaded Sophie, the Countess of Wessex, to pull a pint of cider and then drink it. As Jan says, 'She tried it. She got well stuck in.'

What Jan is doing at her farm should be an inspiration to others. 'What I am trying to create here is a little centre of Somerset, a taste of Somerset, all of its own, and when people come here they can get the feel of the lovely things we make here, and to try them and take them home and help other small producers. Being one myself. We have talked about having little units for crafts people to work in, developing in lots of different ways. You go up to Burnham-on-Sea you can't find anything that is locally produced. Cider farms are becoming the focus for villages again.' And this is really important. It is not just cider; it is the whole social and economic fabric of communities that are in their hands.

Jan got a lot of support from Julian Temperley when she took over. 'After I lost Dad, Julian was one of the people that didn't pooh-pooh the idea of a woman taking over in a man's world. I have got Martin. Russell has been here for 30-odd years. Russell came when he was 12 and he's still here. It is amazing, myself, Russell and Martin, we were all here after school as kids, all grown-up together. It all means a lot.

'I do enjoy getting feedback. I love Montacute, Bath & West, being out there — it's so important to really enjoy it. I love being out there.' She values every scrap of information. (Jan shoos a hen off the desk as she talks. This is a real farm.) 'All the research shows that people are moving away from gimmicks, they want authentic, original and real, see where it came from and are prepared to pay for it.

'The apple harvest used to be one of the most wonderful and colourful harvests of the whole year, when there would be hundreds out there.'

Her father Gordon would be proud of her. 'I know what he would say. He would say, "How much money have you spent young 'n?" That's what he'd say. He didn't like spending money. He was the old school.'

difficult, I must admit. I had actually learnt a lot more than I realised. People were glad to see me back. I don't think there is anyone else that buys them like we do down here. First year was tough but people were glad to see me back. Some of the places where we go it is the third generation, sixty to seventy years, particularly one orchard in Baltonsborough — Richard and Wilfred Dibble. Now I see his son Chris. We have a lot of apples round Baltonsborough, Butleigh: three at Butleigh, one on a slope.'

It would seem that in the cider world now there are more women taking the helm and running cider businesses. As Jan says, 'I was born in the house here, I have such a strong bond, it means more to me. The house is so alive again now with children running around the yard, up and down on their bikes. It went quiet for a while. I look at the walnut tree in the yard, so lovely when that is out — apparently that one was planted on top of a carthorse. Cider farmers always have walnut trees in Somerset. It must be a couple of centuries ago.'

CHAPTER 5
Land's End and Cheddar Cheese

SOMERSET

Roger Wilkins,
*Land's End Farm, Mudgley,
Wedmore, Somerset*

You might be forgiven for thinking that this cider farm is in Cornwall. It is down the end of a narrow, dead-end track on the edge of a hillside, and at one time the sea used to come in under the locals' noses, but only when it broke through the sea walls. In the distance is the distinctive sight of 'St Michael's Mount', only this is Somerset and the hill is Glastonbury Tor: the ruined church on top is called St Michael's and the Tor was once an island. Just down the road at Mere was the site of one of the earliest recorded Saxon vineyards given to Glastonbury Abbey by King Alfred's grandson, Edwy, in AD 955. Indeed this whole ridge, stretching from Wedmore to Wells, must at one time have been covered in fruit and orchards.

The owner of Land's End farm is famous throughout Somerset. Roger Wilkins' family came here in 1917 and many an individual has made the pilgrimage to his cider barn. You always get a very warm welcome. As Roger says, 'We are all one big family.' And that's just how cider farms used to be.

At one time there were seven dairy farms down this lane at Mudgley and that meant seven cider farms as well. Times have changed and many of the farmhouses have been converted and the land sold off or rented out. Roger's farm, unlike most cider farms these days, is also a cider house and the village parliament. Everybody gathers here

on a Sunday morning and in fact every weekday morning as the 'hard core' come down, lend a hand and help serve. Not only is there a cider press and countless barrels, there is a small farm shop, selling fruit and vegetables and countless jars of pickled onions. Roger also does a very good line in mature cheddar cheese, which is kept in the house, from Westcombe Dairy in Evercreech, one of the three artisan cheddars made in Somerset.

Roger knows the area like the back of his hand: he was born here, like his mother. She was born on Christmas Day 1917 in the house and Roger was born almost exactly 30 years later on 30 December 1947. As he explains, his family were farmers, mostly dairy. His grandmother made cheddar cheese, which is why Roger likes it so much. The views are very fine – Glastonbury Tor one way and Hinkley Point nuclear power station the other, and in between the peat moors.

Roger doesn't milk any more and he only keeps about 100 head of beef cattle. He owns 55 acres and rents another 100 acres. As he says, it works in quite well with cidermaking because he feeds the apple pomace to the beef cattle. 'We are not wasting anything at all. They go crazy for it.' The cattle normally go to Highbridge market from here. Roger bitterly regrets the closing of the cattle markets and the loss of the small slaughterhouses, for they were the backbone of the countryside. He feels, quite rightly, that the powers that be don't appreciate the realities of rural life. 'They haven't got a clue, half of them. Terrible. The simple thing is they just don't want us farmers at all. All they want is a holiday island but the trouble is they don't realise what work it is to look after the land and keep it clean.'

He feels passionately that there is something wrong somewhere. 'The land should be wanted more than ever now to produce more food but they just want to import all the time. It's a very dangerous policy, funny thing to talk about, but the truth don't hurt no man.'

Roger is plain-speaking and very likeable. Many people respect his opinions. He is a very good example of an unreformed cidermaker. Not for him single variety cider or fancy bottles or bottle fermentation. This is cider just straight as it comes out of the pipe – dry, medium or sweet. Tasters are usually half a pint, so by the time you have tried all three you have had your legal limit.

Roger's grandfather made cider here all his life and cider was being made when he came here, but back then they were only making 2,000–3,000 gallons a year, just to supply the family, the farm workers and one or two friends. 'If you didn't get cider, you didn't get no workers.'

Roger knows his ground and says that the soil here on the ridge is 'heavy, racy clay underneath, you get beautiful cider come off the soils'. He only has about five acres of orchard of his own, on the steep ground behind the farm, but he buys a lot from local farmers. He knows where to buy the apples and where not to buy them.

Roger learned the art of cidermaking from his grandfather. He was about 21 when his grandfather died. 'I used to help him before I left school because he was crippled bad with arthritis and he had educated me into the cider, but of course you've got to drink cider to know what cider is all about. It's no good making cider if you don't drink it. You've got to keep testing it …

'There are a lot of people making single variety

cider now but my grandfather always told me, he said, "me son, single variety cider is no good". He said, "Kingston Black is no good on its own, it's too heavy, you want some bitter-sharps to go in with it to break it down." Years ago there were no chemists or nothing but the old people knew what they were doing by blending and tasting. Hundreds of years of experience. I have got a few Morgan Sweets but not many. They only bear every other year. The next ones we come onto is the Bulmer's Normans, they are early. Then I got Tremlett's Bitter, Vilberie's, Yarlington Mill, Somerset Redstreak, Brown's Apple, I've got loads of them.'

Roger likes to have a good mix of apples. 'Yeah, the bitter-sweets and bitter-sharps and that. I do it all by taste. I don't test none of it, no scientific kits. It's real traditional farmhouse, all done by your own palate.'

When it comes to pressing, Roger uses a hydraulic Beare press from Newton Abbot. He makes around 600 gallons a day. The layers are built up using slats and cloths. It's a very efficient way to do it. 'That's old fashioned now, but that will do for me the rest of my life now anyway. I'm not gonna alter.'

Thirty years ago Roger made 50,000–60,000 gallons a year. Then it dropped off and he was down to about 10,000 gallons. But it started to climb back up again to about 15,000–18,000. Last year he made 26,000–28,000 gallons. So the tide has turned. More people are coming to the farm and buying it direct. Roger is clearly pleased that a lot of people drinking cider these days are in their 20s. And women are drinking cider again; something they would never have done 20 years ago. Roger has his own theory on this. 'A lot of it is they want a pure, natural drink. They have had all this chemical stuff like all these alcopops and lemonade: it's all colouring, neat alcohol. That's where they get the bad headaches from and that. They want something else.'

A lot less cider, though, is being drunk in pubs. In Roger's local pub, The Bird in Hand, 30 years ago they used to sell 50 gallons of cider a day. 'Now

Opposite. Roger Wilkins building a 'cheese'.

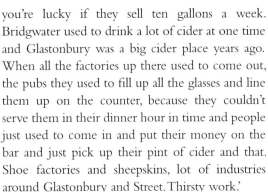

you're lucky if they sell ten gallons a week. Bridgwater used to drink a lot of cider at one time and Glastonbury was a big cider place years ago. When all the factories up there used to come out, the pubs they used to fill up all the glasses and line them up on the counter, because they couldn't serve them in their dinner hour in time and people just used to come in and put their money on the bar and just pick up their pint of cider and that. Shoe factories and sheepskins, lot of industries around Glastonbury and Street. Thirsty work.'

Drinking patterns have obviously changed and this is as much to do with the perception of cider as it is with social awareness. The cider hasn't changed on Roger's farm; it is just that people value it more for what it is. The cider sells itself. It is good value and excellent quality. It is made from local cider apples, and buying cider direct from the man who has made it is an experience all of its own. It is this direct link which is just as important as seeing the cider come out of the wooden tap.

It is the social aspect of the farm shop that is important as well. 'Farming is terrible, it's a hobby now, the farming, really. We have beef. We also sell

a bit of cheese, pickles and chutneys and that. We have a little farm shop. Saturdays and Sundays are very busy. It's like a meeting place, really. Nowhere like it in Somerset. Old tradition. I shan't alter it as long as I'm going. Hopefully I've got a few more years in me yet. We put the world right more than once in there.

'Years ago you got all the wheeling and dealing done in the farmers' cellars, you were in there, five or six of you, horses and carts, buying and selling, horses, cows and heifers, sit down, all over a jar or two of cider.'

Cider farms were great institutions. They were the hub of the rural community. It was where you learned what was going on. Now you have community centres that are shut up half the time and you can only get coffee and biscuits. What sort of place is that?

Roger uses just natural yeast that is in the skin of the apple. 'You won't get cider all the same, you get variation, every barrel is different. Each farm has its own yeast, same sort of apples, but the cider will be different. If you've got bad barrels, you have bad cider straight away. The juice was fine, just

depends on how people kept it.

'People come here from London, Liverpool, Leeds, Cornwall. Even though we are off the beaten track. Lot of people have been coming here more than 30 years now. You get all sorts.'

Roger also has a fine cider mug collection. 'Some are my grandfather's, but the majority of them I've bought myself. I've got two-handled ones, three-handled ones, single-handled ones. I've don't know how many I have got, 50 or 80, I expect. Different sorts. When they were haymaking and that lot, they'd come in and get the cider, and all the peat workers out on the Somerset Levels here on the moors, they used to take quart bottles out with them, put it down in the pit water to keep it cool and they would work from one end to the other and they had bottles buried all up through the turf bit.'

Not to be outdone by Michael Eavis on the other side of the Tor at Worthy Farm, Pilton, Roger has his own festival. The tickets are only £20 and for that you get a full weekend with Chris Jagger, Mick's brother. He plays the washboard and a few other things, guitar and mouth organ. Roger gets another band to play as well. Last year he had an Irish group from Bristol. 'They start off at eight o'clock then Chris takes over about ten o'clock, £20 for a hog roast and bread and cheese.' Last year Roger roasted a pig and served 400 beef burgers, 400 sausages from the local butcher, loads of bread and cheese and pickled onions, but they ran out of the pig, so he had two this year. 'Last year we had 450 people turn up. You weren't allowed more than 499.'

Roger has obviously got it sussed and it proves the point that if your cider is very good the world will beat a path to your door. Good bread, good cheddar cheese, good cider, good music and good company. What more can a man want? Apart from a pickled onion, of course.

Left. Hard-earned rest.
Right. Weighing-in sacks of apples.

CHAPTER 6

*Mummers,
Belly Dancers and
Morris Men*

SOMERSET

John Harris,
West Croft Farm, Brent Knoll, Somerset

Nestling under the great hill that is called Brent Knoll is the village itself, a long straggling line of old, well-proportioned red brick farmhouses. The Knoll is ancient and has been inhabited for thousands of years; it would have controlled the mouth of the Brue as well as the surrounding marshland. These are the real Somerset Levels, being just a few feet above sea level. Much of the land has been drained, but the fields are still laced with rhines (large ditches or canals, pronounced 'reen') and small ditches.

The village of Brent Knoll lies right under the lee of the hill, which protects it from the north-east winds. In the 1890s there were more than 20 small farms, all of which had strips that went up the hill, and it is on these slopes that the old orchards were planted. The whole hillside would have been covered in blossom in the springtime and each farm would have made its own cider. Much of the land was used as summer grazing and pasture for fattening cattle. The local pub is called the Red Cow, and this was linked to the Red Devon cattle that were brought here by sailing vessel to be fattened. Cattle were also brought across from Wales and even Ireland to be fattened here. At the far end of the village lies West Croft farm.

This is where John Harris has been making cider since 1993. His grandfather bought the farm

in 1918, just after the First World War, and ran it as a mixed farm. John has a south-west facing slope with two acres of old orchards and five acres on the flat just down the road over the railway line. He planted all of them.

Originally the family rented an orchard next door but two new houses were built on the land, so they then planted their own. As John says, 'This was the last orchard that came out of Showerings around 1987. They put together the mix of fruit for us.' Just after that John's father sold the dairy cows. It was the first farm in the village to stop milking and John reckons this was the best thing his family ever did.

John did not want to work on the farm without trying his hand at other things, so he took a foundation course in art and design at Bath and became a photographer. It was something he had always wanted to do and so he went to Cheltenham, where he worked as a photographer for seven or eight years. He did a lot of brochures for the campsites around Brent Knoll, Berrow and Burnham, as well as Cricket St Thomas and Bristol Zoo. 'I was good with people.'

Because John found himself working in Somerset, he came back to live at home and got slowly mixed up with the farm again. 'Dad used to say "Go and do this, go and do that". No such thing

as a free bed and breakfast.' And the orchard that John had planted before he left was starting to yield fruit: Yarlington Mill, Chisel Jersey, Brown Snout, Dabinett, some Morgan Sweet, Backwell Red and many more. But instead of picking up the fruit and selling it to the local cidermakers, John started to make cider for himself. He bought an old crusher and press from Draycott. Cidermaking was just something John had always wanted to try. After a while he phased out the photography and began concentrating on the cider.

He had one clear advantage, and that lay on the coast a mile or two away. If you fly over you see hundreds of caravans nestled in the dunes, and that means plenty of new customers on your doorstep every week. He couldn't go wrong. The beaches of Brean and Burnham draw people like a magnet and when they feel thirsty they move off inland in search of a drop or two of cider.

John makes around 10,000 gallons, grows about a third of what he needs and buys in the rest from Westhay and North Curry. Soils at Brent Knoll are heavy clay. It is good ground. The soil changes about

halfway up the hill, to a brown calciferous soil. As John says: 'The hill is very strange. There is a well halfway up the slope and if you go up the hill and dig a hole it will fill up with water straight away. There was an Iron Age settlement on top. Loads of springs on the hill, which is strange as it is above the village.' This must have been very useful indeed when grazing cattle and sheep in the summer, and also means that orchards on the side of the hill do not die in a drought.

John doesn't spray, and like many cider farmers is virtually organic; not registered, but his approach is as clean as a whistle. The fruit is hand-picked in sacks. October is the main month, but picking is, he agrees, getting slightly earlier. He makes a Morgan Sweet, which is very successful, and he says that with hindsight he should have planted 100 Morgans down the road. People love the new first cider in the same way they do a Beaujolais Nouveau, and it is often ready by December each year as the last of the late apples are being pressed, just in time for Christmas.

To make cider traditionally is simple, in his

Left. Pomace ready to be pressed out.
Right. Many old barns have low doors.

opinion. 'It is so easy. It is much more difficult when you start messing about with concentrate and chemicals, you need to be a chemist. You need to have a factory.' John also believes in orchard cider. Traditionally orchards were planted with the right mix of apple trees to provide the right balance of fruit. Why mess with nature? John is mildly amused that people have picked up on it as a marketing tool when it was there all the time.

Going completely organic wouldn't make much difference to John; it is quality cider he is after. And if the quality is there customers will keep coming back. 'I am only as good as the last pint of cider they have drunk.' It all comes down to having a good reputation. 'People come here, they can have a taster, they get served directly from the barrel.' John only does two ciders, dry and medium. Medium is the most popular by far. Even hardened cider drinkers like his medium, or they go for half and half.

John's ciders average out at about 7 per cent, which is half the strength of wine. It is a level that exists naturally. Why tinker with it? He has very few bitter-sharps. Fair Maid of Devon is a full sharp. 'High tannin is what we want.' And that is the secret to all great cidermaking in the South-west. It is simply allowing the natural qualities of the apple to come through in the cider.

John's cider is best drunk between six and nine months old. Some producers make cider from dessert apples and John is very scathing about those who use them. 'Dessert apples can't make cider, horrible things, horrible to press, the juice is pale and thin.' Some large-scale commercial cider-makers like to use dessert and culinary apples because they can get them cheaply as grade outs and mix them in, or even market them as single varieties. Coxes are good as eaters, but why mess with them as cider when there is such good-quality cider fruit available?

John also believes in natural yeasts and natural sugars. He is not a fan of sulphur. 'Natural yeasts are natural, it doesn't taint the final product, and it always works. That is my experience. I think the quantity is very important, and barrel size.' He racks off two or three times, extending the fermentation to keep 'a bit af fizz there. But you are better off

CHAPTER 7
Fair Maid of Devon
DEVON

Natasha Bradley,
Heron Valley, Loddiswell,
Kingsbridge, Devon

Kingsbridge lies inland from Salcombe. In this part of South Devon the land is riddled with small, steep valleys. All the rivers rise high up on Dartmoor and then find their own way down to the sea, twisting and turning through oak woods and quiet meadows. The valley of the herons is no exception. I drove down a long lane for over a mile and found a white farmhouse overlooking an idyllic scene. Natasha Bradley welcomed me with a cream tea. It was a wonderful afternoon as I sat down on the terrace and looked out over the fields. The farm has 80 acres, and some fine-looking South Devon cattle came nuzzling up to the fence. A calf had just been born. 'They just love the pomace at cidermaking time,' Natasha said as she poured me a cup of tea and chatted away. The clotted cream was thick and golden.

Talk about dynamos. Natasha is definitely the new face of cidermaking. Men watch out. She is very bright, well dressed and has a clear distinct voice – no chewing of straws here. If Natasha can market her business as well as she markets herself then there will be no stopping her. At the age of thirty-four she has bought out her parents and four sisters from the family business. She still employs her family, but the overall responsibility rests on her shoulders alone. She has kept Steve, her father, on to make the cider, as he is 'rather good at it', and he

also does the accounts. Two of her sisters, Kirsten and Britta, help in the 'bottling side of things, all the labelling and the distribution'.

And the herons? The farm is called Cranna-combe, which in Saxon means Heron Valley. There are rich pickings in the Avon river that runs through the valley, comes out at Aveton Gifford and runs on down through the estuary to Bigbury Bay. The small farm snuggles up into the side of the valley near Loddiswell.

Natasha read psychology at Plymouth University before pursuing a career in marketing. She worked on the family farm initially until she got a job promoting South Hams Food and Drink. Then she moved out of county and started selling surf-wear in Wareham, Dorset, and SatNav devices for boats: 'Wealthy marine clients including the MOD.' So if you are stuck on a sand bank Natasha might just be able to help you out, with cider of course.

Natasha is a real believer in her product and it is as if her soul is invested in the valley, the farm, the orchards, the cider and the apple juice. She is constantly going to tastings, getting feedback and adjusting the product to suit a wide range of people. Five years ago she would not have contemplated buying the other family members out, but now she exudes confidence and wants to take the

cider world by storm – 'Well, between Exeter and Plymouth will do for now.' And sure enough, the cider is reaching a wider audience.

Natasha took on the business in September 2006. 'I joined last April and there was a six-month hand-over. I've got four sisters. We are a big tribe of Amazons here. I am the middle one, so two older and two younger. Basically, it was very important that everything was done in a very fair way so I had to buy it as if I was a stranger. I bought everyone out so now it's my company, completely.'

Her reasoning was that she simply wanted to come back home and have a better quality of life with her children and her family. 'I have taken a risk and I've gone out on a limb, and the reason I've done it is not to have world domination or to make my millions; it is actually that I want to have a quality of life that allows me to serve a really fantastic product and have a family life and sit here with the birds singing around me. Actually, this table we are sitting at, with this view, is the works canteen and it is a soulful reason for doing it.'

Her analysis of where the cider market is at is spot on. 'Cider is our indigenous drink and for years and years it has been relegated. People had their first alcoholic experience on a really rough oxidised cider and lived to regret it. I find all my friends are now drinking cider. They are coming from the lager end, not from the wine end. My generation obviously knows the success of cider.'

What fascinates and excites Natasha are the future marketing possibilities now that cider is being drunk by people in their 20s and 30s. 'It is rather like the renaissance of wine drinking in this country 20 or 30 years ago, when people shifted from Liebfraumilch and Blue Nun and started to explore the whole range of wines. People's palates improved, their expectations improved, they then looked for other wines that they could drink with a meal. Then they were keen to experiment and to share their discoveries. It became a very sociable thing to do with a few friends round the kitchen table, rather than totally drowning your sorrows down the local pub with six pints of lager.'

As eating habits change, so do drinking habits. People want high quality and they want it bottled for convenience, and they have started searching out other varieties of cider. The nation is re-

Above. The Heron Valley works canteen: teatime.

training its palate as far as cider is concerned and that, combined with the real food movement, is a powerful force, and one that Natasha is keen to work to her advantage. People are now far more aware of cider and its provenance. Local food, farm shops and farmers' markets have helped enormously. *Terroir* was always here, but nobody bothered to market it.

For a long time, people were out of touch with the countryside. Cider has always been drunk by farmers or made in a small way, for personal use but not to sell. The tradition went downhill. 'Old scrumpy out the back. Is there a dead rat in there?' There was almost a bravery in drinking a pint of rough cider. For far too long cider was a poor man's drink and a rite of passage for teenagers vomiting in bus shelters. All it did was put people off cider for the rest of their lives. The secret is to let them try the real thing again and they often say, 'I never realised it could taste that good.'

Heron Valley sells a lot of cider to local pubs; some take three or four kegs a week. Natasha knows exactly where they are going, a lot of them for holidaymakers on the coast. The weather sells

cider, it's the perfect drink on a hot day: wine is too much. If cider is served really cold, in top condition, you can't get a better drink.

Heron Valley has been in existence for about 15 years. Natasha's father, however, has been making cider for about 25 years and learned the art at another farm that had an old press. He became a partner in a small, commercial, cider-making business and introduced farm-pressed organic juice to Devon, before going it alone at Heron Valley.

Natasha's parents met in London. Her mother was a West Country girl whose family lived in Plymouth, but spent most of their time in Cawsand. 'She went up to London and met my father, who was actually an actor. His father was a pig farmer from Wales so there was farming in the blood. They met and with a young family back in 1972 they moved down, bought a wreck of a house called Cumming Farm in the Dart valley between Totnes and Buckfastleigh. They had a house cow, chickens and it evolved. Mum made their own cream. Then we moved over here and they set up Heron Valley.'

Natasha's father is a director of Orchard Link, an organisation that helps connect orchard owners

Left. Britta Perkins with hydrometer.
Right. Liz Montague building a cheese.

and cidermakers and runs apple-related courses and events. Natasha buys apples from orchard owners in the South Hams. 'South Devon is very organised. We pay all their fees for the organic side, and then we guarantee them that we will buy their apples and while they are in conversion we will buy their apples for non-organic cider, so we have our own orchards and lots of local farmers,' says Natasha.

At Heron Valley she is planting a lot more trees, as well as looking at the soil conditions to see which will grow best: 'All the classic ones, like the Ten Commandments, Foxwhelp, Hangy Down Cluster, Pig's Snout, Sheep's Nose, Fair Maid of Devon.

'In the autumn, when the apples come in, we blend them as they go. Of course all the ciders end up being different and then we blend again and hopefully we eliminate those big swings in flavour. Yes at the moment we are going for bush, but we also buy from Lustleigh Community Orchard and

lots of small orchards. We have some lovely old farmers. We will probably have about 150 tons of apples this season, and that's a fair few. At pressing time it is an all-girl crew. We did 7,000 gallons last year, so we will probably press around 80 tons of apples this season to make around 11,000 gallons of cider. Quite a leap!'

Heron Valley sparkling cider is at 6 per cent, and very good it is too with a bit of bite, but Natasha feels there is also room for a slightly lighter cider at 4.5 per cent. It is just a question of being flexible.

Heron Valley also does a wide range of apple juices. 'At first it was the apple juice but now it is the cider which is the real challenge, because it can go so right and it can go so wrong. Apple juice is enormously labour intensive, but you have a pretty immediate idea of how things are going to taste, but cider is all about the waiting game.'

The qualities of taste that Natasha wants in cider are: 'Immediately you should get the appleyness, it is about understanding that this is made from an apple. For example, when you taste a great wine, you can smell the grapes, you can smell the oak, you can smell all those different fantastic contributing factors in the wine, if it's a great wine. With cider the first thing that should hit you is the appleyness and the right degree of tannin. I like very smooth ciders as well. I don't know if that's because we are women or if that's a difference in the palate. I think in many ways cider is very suited to women in terms of production, because one of the most important factors is cleanliness in cider production, the hygiene. You have to have very clean barrels, regularly checked. Yes we still use oak. We have different barrels. I actually like the rum ones. It's the tannins and the oak, you just get this sense of having more depth to it, the whole combination works very well.'

Being as natural as possible works with Natasha's general philosophy. 'We use the natural yeast on the skins; we don't add anything at all. No sulphur. It's completely natural, and thus far it's about the cleanliness being the important factor keeping it on the right track. And for the last 25 years my father has been making cider it's worked that way and I would hope to continue that.'

Natasha doesn't see the need for additives or preservatives or sulphites because her sister is allergic to sulphites in wines, and many other people have allergic reactions to them. 'The nearest we get to it is by making a slightly sparkling carbonated medium cider, which is basically our simple cider.'

Food and drink have always been among her passions and she loves cooking. 'I cook with cider. Mussels and shellfish are good with cider: pork obviously. We do a lot of mulled cider, vast quantities. At all our family parties we have mulled cider because the truth is, why cook with wine when you can buy infinitely superior cider for a fraction of the cost and less additives? It works really well, and with marinading.' Natasha has always had an allotment and grown her own vegetables. She thinks it is crazy that we are shipping most of our best fish and shellfish abroad. She sees cider as being a key part of the local food

and drink movement. 'We should be looking at what is around us, that is plentiful and produced in a really fantastic way, and actually we should be using it, and I think that will happen more and more with real cider.'

Natasha sees shopping habits changing with the local and Slow Food movements. She has seen a rise of better independent shops, such as Darts Farm near Topsham and Riverford near Dartington. She thinks we can learn a lot from our continental neighbours and hopes we become more European and less American in our cultural habits. She regards the fast food culture as very destructive. She also thinks we should have more exchanges with Normandy and Brittany and Spain. We have the ports – Dartmouth, Salcombe and Kingsbridge – why not use them?

Her optimism is very infectious. She believes in direct contact and direct sales. 'To be honest, we sell everything that we can produce at the moment, and I also enjoy the whole process of delivering. I have just dropped in six cases of cider and five of apple juice and I have chatted to the people and someone has bought a glass while I was there. That was just in Dittisham, they have our bottled cider there. And I just get an enormous soaring feeling of happiness that I actually know what has gone into it, I have actually been labelling it this morning and producing it and someone is enjoying drinking it

this afternoon, and that direct contact is incredibly valuable. Yes, that gives you a sort of sense of purpose and direction in life and soul really. Drink the view.'

Getting the label right is vital and Natasha may be making a few small changes. 'What I love about our labels, both in our apple juice and in our cider, is that there is a sense of soul there in the colour and the warmth of it.' For sweeter ciders Natasha is attracted to the challenge of keeving. 'I am quite excited about it. The Normandy method. Absolutely.'

When I talked about the future she was fascinated by the potential it holds. 'I think the future is really exciting. I think lots of new cidermakers will emerge from different backgrounds and bring different experiences, whether it's from other food and drink industries or from marketing backgrounds or from music. All these different fields. I think they will come with an energy, because I do feel that there is an energy now. My dad said this as well. He's noticed there's an interest and an enthusiasm, which is quite infectious really. At the Devon County Show, it's lovely there and people are hanging out and enjoying having a glass of something and having a chat about it, really interested. They are talking about their orchards, what varieties they've got, and can we come and have a look and see.'

Opposite. Natasha Bradley with her daughter, Jasmin.

CHAPTER 8
Whiteways' Phoenix
DEVON

Chris Coles,
Green Valley Cider, Darts Farm,
Clyst St George, Exeter, Devon

Most people in the cider world will have heard of the famous Whiteways cider works at Whimple in the Tale valley between Honiton and Exeter. It was founded in the 1890s by Henry Whiteway, who came from a long line of Devon farmers. For nearly a century the business flourished and in time became linked to Showerings of Shepton Mallet. Then in the spring of 1989 Whiteways was closed down with much sadness. It was such an old, established institution that many people were stunned: it had been a good and reliable employer. The factory site took up a third of the village. Many of the orchards can still be seen to this day, particularly from the train, and what a wonderful sight they are. Some are only just coming into their prime.

Not to be defeated, a small but enthusiastic group of former employees who could not bear the thought that cidermaking should grind to a halt in East Devon, decided to come to the rescue.

Chris Coles had worked as a biochemist in California and came to Whiteways in 1982 as technical manager; Nick Pring had worked at Whiteways for 20 years and was general manager. Their wives were involved as well. They bought some of Whiteways' oak vats, sought out a site, and by autumn 1989 they were making cider again 12 miles down the road, at Clyst St George. It was a brave move and a real gamble, but there was a lot

of good will and the farmers whose fruit had previously been taken by Whiteways were only too willing to sell them their apples. So they had the pick of the orchards.

The name 'Green Valley Cider' comes from the wonderful winding valley of the River Clyst, which joins the Exe at the port of Topsham. 'We were just trying to dream up a name, and we stood on the brow of the hill and looked down the Clyst and it was just a carpet of green.' Chris and Nick chose the site on what was then a bare patch of waste ground behind a small rough-and-ready farm shop with Pick Your Own. Now, of course, the wasteland has been rejuvenated and the shop is known as Darts Farm, one of the key outlets for local produce in East Devon. Some supermarkets have an in-store bakery, but none have an in-store cider works. In fact it is a unique arrangement that works very well indeed, and the shop has one of the best selections of ciders anywhere in the South-west selling more than 80 different ciders and more than 250 beers. It is a fantastic showcase for cider and perry. And just round the back you can see the three large wooden vats, each holding 5,000 gallons, that were dismantled at Whiteways and re-erected at Darts Farm. They are now more than 120 years old.

Chris admits he got into cider by accident. His

previous research in California involved working with mammalian heart enzymes, so a lot of his funding was from Heart Research Foundations. 'They compare mammalian cells and yeast cells, so we compared the enzymes in the two organisms.' Chris had a doctorate and was doing well-paid research over there, but he wanted to return. In short, he didn't want his children swearing allegiance to an American flag every morning in school, so he came back and got a short contract at the University of Exeter.

'I was looking around for professional jobs and one night the wife was reading the local paper, the *Express & Echo*, and she said, "There's a job here you could do. Whiteways are looking for a cider controller." So I thought, hmmm, sounds a bit strange. So I read it, and I'd got all the necessary technical background and I applied for the job, and for some reason they appointed me.'

This was making cider, quality control on the filling lines. The company had a canning operation and employed 250 people. Chris's department had about a dozen people. 'They had a laboratory with two or three people in it, then a cider crew who did all the fermentation and the filtering and the blending. They made about half a million gallons. At the peak, before the Second World War, Whiteways produced three million gallons a year, which with conventional hydraulic pack presses was a vast amount of work, but they were big, their beds were six foot wide. There was a row of about six presses along the side of the road. The trays were taken off by an overhead gantry and swung around to a different position. They used water hydraulics, but they had what's called an accumulator, which is a massive concrete block that was pumped up overnight, and was resting on a column of water, and it produced pressure whenever it was needed. The pipe went under the road and into the factory. It was very clever. I'm guessing they had 70 or 80 acres of orchard. Some of them were planted while I was there, in the mid-to-late 1980s, so they will be at their peak now. They're bush orchards so you've got stands of Dabinett and Harry Master's

Jersey and so long as the current farming family keep them pruned, they'll be good.'

Chris still regards the closure of Whiteways as a tragedy, which came as the result of various takeovers. There were certain agreements between companies owned by Allied Breweries, the worst of which was that Whiteways would stop selling bottled cider – its best-selling product – because that would have put Showerings and Whiteways in competition against each other. Instead Whiteways sold draught cider into the export market as well as Cidrax and Peardrax, which, interestingly, you can still buy in Trinidad and Tobago, because Showerings ship out the Whiteways formula to a factory there, where it is diluted and bottled.

Chris remembers the time he was made redundant. 'We were told in January 1989. It came as quite a shock. We thought they might take us up to Shepton Mallet, but they didn't, and the few people they did take up there were fired within two years.' Showerings continued to honour the Whiteways orchard contracts. Then Chris and Nick started the new business. They are the shareholders. As Nick was the general manager, he was virtually the last person left on the Whiteways site. Chris was keen to buy quite a lot of the equipment, so he and Nick walked round the factory and chose what they needed and bought it at advantageous rates. They also took on Larry Pope, another ex-Whiteways man, who had been winery foreman.

As to finding the site, a local farmer, Ivor Bragg, suggested to Chris that he talk to Paul Dart. 'Paul had this shed, just a conventional Yorkshire boarding shed, and he said, "Yeah, I'm looking for craft-type people to come on board." It was a very small farm shop in those days: this was 40 foot by 20, fruit and veg, and Doris made jam. That was it. I could see the site was ideal: it's between Exeter and Exmouth, it's close to the holiday areas, plenty of parking, good access. It had huge potential. We shook hands on it and I started paying rent from November I think.'

But it was far from plain sailing. All the machinery was lying in bits on the floor. They got

Opposite. The Vat-man cometh.

the press up and pressed that autumn. 'We got sacks full of Whimple apples, which were in the shed but were beginning to weep on the floor, quite juicy, and they smelt wonderful. To get the press built we had to hack a hole in the floor and build a pit to put the hydraulics in. The shed already had three-phase electrics and mains water and good drainage. At that stage we stored everything in about 20 black plastic tanks. We built the first oak vat that winter. We were on natural yeast.'

Getting the wooden vats down at Whimple before moving them to Darts Farm was a challenging experience, as Chris recalls: 'Not being a cooper, I thought, let's go about this carefully. We got a hammer and a drive chisel and knocked all the hoops up, and got left with the bottom one and we were just tapping around with this, and there was suddenly this BWOOMPH and the lid had dropped off inside. It wasn't catastrophic, it was on a cushion of air, and we realised we'd approached it the wrong way. No damage was done. The staves were two inches thick. Inside it was beeswaxed. You get carry-over of your yeast flora from one year to the next, which gives some character to the cider. We took advice from the vat company, who were just still there, and we put split water reed between the floor planks and the roof planks. Nothing at all goes between the staves, so you have a single pin half way up the stave and a notch in the bottom and a notch in the top, so you put the floor together and then start building the staves round the floor. When you get to halfway you have to put the roof in, otherwise you'd never get it in at all. Then you carry on all the way round. They were 5,000 gallons. So we had two of those, the other one was put up about two years later. We'd stored it dry in the interim. I wasn't over-optimistic about it after that much storage, but it worked out fine. They are still our main vats.'

As far as apples were concerned Chris and Nick were in an enviable position. Whimple was 12 miles up the road and they had the Whiteways supply books so they had a list of over 100 people who grew apples. But since then they have set up verbal contracts with people fairly close at hand.

'Luckily they have got quite a few old Devon

varieties, things like Fillbarrel, and Twos and Twos, Slack-Ma-Girdle, Brown's Apple, Court Royal, Killerton Sweet; there's a Tale Vale apple too. The only single-variety ciders that I've been able to conveniently make are Morgan Sweet and Dabinett. Morgan Sweet is always ready early and you know what you're getting, Dabinett because one of my orchards has a stand of Dabinett, so I know if I use all those it makes a good cider. We do a special cider from one orchard that has eight varieties of apples in it. That's got some Somerset apples in, it's got Tremlett's Bitter, Coat Jersey, Dabinett, Michelin, Fillbarrel, Twos and Twos, Fair Maid of Devon and Brown's Apple.'

Some of the old customers can remember the taste of Whiteways cider. 'A lady from Lancashire who'd found them on the internet and discovered we had a historical connection with Whiteways: "Do you do a sweet cider like the Whiteways sweet cider?" I said, "Well we think it's like the Whiteways sweet cider." She ordered two cases there and then and another two a week later.'

Green Valley Cider sells a lot of cider from the shop. The partners can't go wrong with the scale of Darts Farm as it is now. Each year they make about 10,000 gallons and their distribution area is about 40 to 50 miles, as far south as Plymouth, but North Devon is a little too far. It takes an hour and a half to get there.

As to soils, Chris reckons that soils do affect taste but the other thing that affects the taste is the season. 'So if you get a hot dry summer your tannin levels are going to go right up, and that's going to override any soil difference.' As to whether cider-making is a science or an art, Chris believes you cannot really separate the two, which coming from a scientist is remarkable. As he says: 'I think it's an art more than a science, but we use science to monitor what's going on. A lot of the art is choosing the right fruit.' Which means that it comes back to orchards, soils and varieties, weather and outlook: *terroir*, in other words.

To make an excellent cider Chris is looking for a good balance of sugars, tannins and acidity. 'You want to find a juice which has a gravity of 1055. You can vary the tannin level but I'd be looking for something of two to three milligrams per litre and the acidity about four grams per litre.'

As to that crucial question of taste, Chris reckons that his own cider is at the moment a little bit too traditional, still typically Devon, where the acidity is probably a bit high. As he says, people are getting a bit more discerning. Chris agrees that some manufacturers can make quite respectable ciders out of dessert fruit, but it is not a West Country tradition. 'You need the tannins and traditionally these would have helped to preserve the cider before such things as pasteurisation or chill filtering.' He doesn't use pasteurisation except for some of the sparkling ciders, which are in crown cap bottles, and those are bottled off site because you need a counter pressure filler.

Regarding carbonation, Chris finds that a lot of people are amazed that they sell still cider. '"This cider's flat," they say. It's not flat, it's still. We do a vintage cider, which is a high-quality still cider in a wine bottle, which comes as a surprise to a lot of people, to think of cider coming in that way. We've done that product for 18 years, but its profile has only just risen in the last few years.'

What is also interesting is the new wave of young cider drinkers who are switching from lager to cider. At Darts Farm they 'get a lot of Exeter University students in here and they're genuinely interested in it, mostly the bottled cider. The people who buy the five litres and the gallons are generally the tourists. They want something they can take back to the caravan, and later back home that they can have a good night with.'

So it's the younger ones who are taking it a bit more seriously?

'They're a bit more discerning. The students at Exeter University have never been short of money. It's very middle class. There are some quite wealthy ones there. A lot of pubs are seeing a decline as more people are buying bottles and drinking at home.

'We linked up with the farm shop in 1998 and up to then I'd sold half a dozen bottled beers, we were independent, and in 1998 I said, "We'll put a box display up on the wall there and we'll fill it up with beer." And so we did that, we had 40 beers, we thought, "This is amazing," and it worked. It's grown gradually since then, we got to 100, then 200 … Currently we have 80 ciders and over 240 beers. So that's an indication that people are changing their habits. The take-home trade has grown.'

Green Valley Cider produces a wide range of ciders. Devon Farm Cider, at 6.8 per cent, is a still cider, dry, medium and sweet. Then there are three sparkling ciders, two of them are 4.7 per cent, one is 8.3 per cent. There are also two still, quality ciders at 8.3 per cent. These are Stillwood Vintage and Clyst Orchard.

Chris has made perry, successfully twice and unsuccessfully twice. 'One of the successful occasions was when I got some pears from Bicton College, where they had some espaliers on a wall and they were sweet dessert pears and they produced a superb perry. They now sell the pears in the shop so we haven't got them any more. And the other occasion was there was a scattering of big pear trees in some of the cider orchards, and I had enough one year to do a perry, but they were biggish and they soften quickly and they're dreadful to press. If you can imagine filling up the cloths with butter and pressing that, that's about as difficult as it gets.'

And the future? Green Valley Cider is very stable and has good long-term prospects. 'It's growing 10 per cent, year on year, generally, it's going quite well. You never know what's going to happen, but at the moment it's stable. People love walking through the shop and going, "Oh look! What's going on down there? What's that mess?" And you say, "Come and have a look." And you ask them if they want to have a go, and they stand there with the rubber gloves on and the apron, and they hold this inner tube and out comes the apple. "Oh my goodness!" They love it. We have schools, we use this room for tutored tastings; we have stag dos and all the rest of it. In that sort of situation you can begin talking to them about the tannins in the ciders and showing them what the differences are.'

Opposite. Sampling is an essential part of the learning process.

I asked Chris, as a biochemist, why tannins are so important. 'I've always assumed that the tannins come through virtually unchanged, because if you taste the apple juice at the beginning and then the cider at the end that element, that tannin element, doesn't really change. If you taste Tremlett's Bitter cider over a period of months, it doesn't really change, does it? If you're drinking cider with food you don't want a cider that's too soulless. You want something with a bit of tannin in there to balance the meat or the cheese, or whatever it is. The balance there is quite important.'

Chris would like to see Devon cider keeping

its high tannins. 'Cider from this area should have tannins of two to three milligrams per litre.' He uses both natural and introduced yeasts. For the farm cider and the main vat cider he allows the natural yeasts to run the show. But for the vintage he sulphurs the juice and adds a wine yeast. It makes quite a difference.

There are major changes taking place in the pressing. 'In Devon you've got a huge range of machinery used to press apples, from horse-drawn mills; quite a lot of people use pack presses like ours, you get about 150 gallons to a ton, we press in nylon cloths. Not many press in straw, one or two do, but

now people who are investing in new machinery are putting in belt presses, because they're smaller, more convenient, don't require so much manpower, the only drawback is the cost. People quite like to see the old-fashioned pack press.'

Chris is now in his early 60s: he enjoys working and will carry on for as long as he can. 'One day somebody will buy the business ultimately, and what they do with it is very much up to them. I'm the older one, they'll farm me out I expect. They'll probably try and find someone a

bit younger to come on board. I've got a couple of daughters, but they both teach: they're not interested. I've got a grandson who absolutely adores the business. Whether he'll come on board or not, I don't know. He's nine.'

Henry Whiteway would no doubt be proud to know that the spirit of his venture is still going strong in East Devon, albeit a little bit further down stream. In 2007 Green Valley Cyder was awarded Bronze medal in the National CAMRA Cider Competition, and in 2008 a Gold medal.

Above left. Shelf life.
Above right. Dog tired.

CHAPTER 9

Cider Evangelists

DEVON

Ben and Ruth Gray,
Gray's Cider, Halstow Farm,
Tedburn St Mary, Devon

Halstow Farm is neatly tucked away in the rolling green hills to the west of Exeter on the narrow lanes between Tedburn St Mary and Dunsford, and it is well worth the journey. At 600 feet above sea level the farm is situated on the watershed between the Teign and the Exe with fine views of Dartmoor. Many of the fields are steep and drop down into small wooded valleys. The old set of farm buildings at Halstow are gathered round an enclosed farmyard that boasts a fine fig tree, which each year sags under the weight of its own fruit. The shade that the fig tree offers masks the doorway into the long cider barn, which is the cellar, a listed building, dark inside like a cave and lined with oak barrels tailing off into the distance. It takes a while to get used to the light. The walls are stone and cob, making it very cool. At one time every large farm had such a building and dotted around the farm are the various orchards that produce the cider apples. This is a rare example of a traditional Devon cider farm still in operation. This is, some might say, the very heart of Devon.

Halstow is mentioned as a Domesday manor and very little has apparently changed. The Gray family has been here since the 1660s. There is a feeling of antiquity and continuity, which is as solid as the granite in the barn. As Ben Gray proudly says: 'We have been supplying cider to Moreton-

hampstead and beyond since the Napoleonic Wars.' Ben and his wife Ruth and their three charming sons, John, David and Theo, are the present incumbents. The farm is an amalgamation of three farms, South Halstow, North Halstow and Duckshayes. Ben's antecedents were non-conforming yeoman farmers, the very backbone of Devon agriculture.

Ben is a busy man: he is a farmer at heart. When I met him he had just come back from taking some hogs to Exeter market. His time is taken up equally with sheep and cider and he is caught between the two. With 250 acres and 600 Suffolk cross mules, it does not leave very much spare time.

Ben can recall his father, Tom, pressing apples in the early 1960s with a hydraulic Beare press from Newton Abbot. His earliest memories of cider are of being allowed to go over to the barn with an eggcup. The men would stop for lunch at eleven o'clock with dinner at one o'clock, so they would sit over in the cellar and he was allowed to totter over with an eggcup and take a glass of cider with them – a small allowance. This is how it should be. Drinking under close supervision on a farm where there was always this duty of care and a feeling of imbibing something very special.

Cider has been commercial on this farm for at least five generations. As a boy Ben remembers taking nine-gallon barrels out with his father and

through the bad times when others were stripping the woodlands for hard cash. And also we have got a lot of granite from Blackingstone quarry five or six miles away with carts taking cider out and coming back with granite.'

But where do his customers come from? As with the apples, from a variety of sources. Some are entirely new and have not tried cider before. 'The real ale people are quite keen. A lot of regular wine drinkers would start by putting cider in their yellow fizzy category, then a little light bulb comes on … It is quite rewarding to think that the wine drinkers are now taking cider seriously. Nobody drank wine 30 years ago. A bottle of Blue Nun was a novelty. Now, even wine is too cheap. Worldwide there is a surplus.'

As a cider sales barometer Ben uses the Double Locks pub, which is down on the canal next to the River Exe. In 2006 the pub had the best cider summer they have ever had. But then again, even good cider has been too cheap for too long. It has not been valued for what it is, a purely natural drink. As with local food, you have to be prepared to pay more for the higher quality.

If Ben were to plant another orchard he would go back to standard trees: bush orchards take up too much time in management, at least for sheep farmers. He likes to see an orchard well grazed; the two systems in tandem have worked well for hundreds of years. But he would like the land to be flat enough for machine picking.

The soils and aspects of Ben's orchards vary greatly. One or two face south-west; the bush orchards face north, which means they are late flowering, but his favourite orchard faces due south and slopes at a 45-degree angle. Ben has the records for that orchard being planted in two stages, in 1790 and 1795. So it has yielded apples for longer than 210 years. The soils are shillet or impervious yellow clay.

At pressing time the apples are hand-picked and placed in the apple loft, then dropped down into the mill. Ben has just fitted a new hydraulic press, which gives 60 tons' pressure, far more than

the conventional wooden screw press. It also means that the juice gets pressed while the apples are in optimal condition. He uses natural yeasts from the apples and surrounding buildings. His old cider barn is perfect. The cider is dispensed from oak barrels, and as he says, 'You can't beat old buildings for insulation. We fill it up as much as we can. Most of those barrels I have bought in the last few years, the 110-gallon pipes and butts. I was always told that the cellar was built to take three rows of pipes, but when I was small they had rum barrels, ninety-eight gallons, four rows, aisles back to back but also two barrels high. So then there would have been a whole mass of cool liquid.'

Ben is concerned that some of the more commercial ciders on the open market are low in juice content, which is something that many of the traditional farmhouse cidermakers in this book have also mentioned. There ought perhaps to be minimum juice level for cider defined at higher than 90 per cent, because some ciders are apparently as low as 30 per cent. And shouldn't juice content be declared on the label? Perhaps there is not enough of a discerning market out there yet.

Above. The oldest listed cobb cider barn in Devon is at Halstow Farm.

But one day there will be and those taking short cuts will have to put their hands up. A level playing field would be appreciated by some of the more traditional makers.

As Ben says, it all comes down to marketing. 'We have the advantage over most farmers in that we have been dealing with the public since we could walk. And doing the shows, we quite enjoy dealing with the public.' Ruth often goes on the stand with him at the Devon County Show. 'This year, most of the people coming to the stand were coming with no pre-conceptions. People are coming to cider with a much more open mind; it has lost its rough farmyard image.'

Ruth originally came from Norfolk and slowly worked her way west. Prior to having her three children she read drama at Manchester University and worked as a postgraduate student at Guildford School of Acting and Dance. Following this, she did theatre work with school children and worked with special needs in Somerset around Wells and Glastonbury. She has also worked in prisons, before deciding to set up her own business in 1990 organising children's parties and catering.

But for Ben, cider was an historical and geographical accident. He was in a sense born to it. The sense of locality is very strong. Indeed Ben's grandfather said that he would only take apples from the three surrounding parishes, Tedburn St Mary, Dunsford and Cheriton Bishop, which are all on the same yellow clay, and there is a good reason for that decision. Ben feels that there is a lot more to the soils than they are given credit for. It is the compounds that come out of the soil that affect the flavour. The apples that grow well here do produce good cider.

Cidermaking is definitely an art at Halstow. And there is a very particular cider from this part. The farm is only four miles away from the red soil of Crediton and that would make a very different cider. One year Ben's father had several trailer loads of cider apples from Raymond Burroughs at Whimple and that cider tasted different again. 'In the cider world there is more unknown than known. There is so much there, we will never know what we have lost.'

CHAPTER 10
Blackdown Baler Twine
DEVON

Alex Hill,
Bollhayes Cider, Clayhidon & Vigo Ltd,
Dunkeswell, Devon

Hunkered down in the Blackdown hills on the Devon–Somerset border, Alex Hill is an unusual cidermaker. He is very charming and exudes an air of intelligent and jovial optimism, just like a country doctor. In fact, Alex might well have become a country doctor if he hadn't given up his studies as a medical student at Charing Cross Hospital. As an antidote to anatomy he started making wine and cider on a small scale. Little did he know where it would ultimately lead.

Over the years many cidermakers have phoned him up and asked his advice about an ailing hogshead or a terminally ill vat to find out if there were any chance of curing their cider, which has taken bad ways. Over the last 25 years he has become something of a local hero, providing employment and entertainment in this remote but beautiful backwater. He holds a wassail in his orchard every January, combined with a knees-up in the village hall, which goes on long into the night.

Homebrew wine and beer kits were all the rage in the 1970s and many an impecunious student started his drinking career on such small-scale ventures. Today, people may not realise that home brewing was technically outlawed until 1963, when the Chancellor of the Exchequer, Reggie Maudling, lifted the restrictions that had been in place since 1880 to protect the interests of the large breweries. Without Maudling there would be no CAMRA and few of the micro breweries would have got off the ground. There had been no restrictions on cidermaking until Dennis Healey introduced a cider duty in 1976. Exemptions on cider duty were made for small farmhouse cidermakers so long as they kept below the 1,500-gallon limit. This limit, arrived at somewhat arbitrarily, was taken, one assumes, to represent the annual consumption of an average farmer, his family and his workers in any given year – five people at 300 gallons each a year. This limit is unique to cider and allows many small producers to experiment and get on their feet before they become fully commercial. Alex Hill was no exception.

After medical school Alex did a series of odd jobs in London, including being a motorcycle messenger, which funded his travels in Europe and South America. He also financed himself at Sussex University, where he studied for a degree in International Relations. After university he worked for his brother-in-law shipping container goods around the world – Milwaukee one day, Japan the next. So he got a taste for buying and selling overseas goods. At Sussex Alex shared a flat with a Hungarian called Peter Davidhazi, who is now a learned Shakespearean scholar and academic. They struck up a strong friendship. In 1981 Alex cycled

from Tooting to Budapest and then for a few years visited Hungary every summer. In 1982 he saw a small but very beautiful fruit press in the window of a hardware shop in Budapest. He brought one back and showed it to his friends, and before too long everyone wanted one. These are the small, circular, green cast-iron presses with oak-slatted sides and a screw thread, which you tighten from above. The press combined simple aesthetics with function. The next year he imported twenty-four small presses, borrowed his sister's car and in two days' cold-calling at homebrew shops sold fourteen of them. The next delivery was a lorry full, unloaded by hand on to the pavements of Battersea.

Four years later Alex moved from Brixton to Clayhidon in Devon and the small-scale wine-making techniques of the Hungarian peasants were very quickly grafted into the cottage orchard economy of the south-west.

When Alex first set up in business supplying cider-making equipment, he started out from a prefab shed on Dunkeswell airfield, six miles up narrow lanes from Honiton. Then he became nomadic. For a year or two he was based in a neighbour's pigsty in Clayhidon, then back to a Nissen hut at Dunkeswell, followed by a unit in Hemyock at the back of the bus park. Eventually he found some upmarket sheds on Dunkeswell airfield where he is now. Today his business, Vigo Ltd, employs over twenty people.

Interestingly he still imports the small, green, oak Hungarian cider presses, Alex also imports state-of-the-art belt presses from Austria and has been known to supply huge quantities of oak chips to certain industrial cidermakers to give their cider the authentic oak taste and flavour. There can't be many cidermakers in the south-west who haven't consulted Alex from time to time to buy equipment from him. He is also in contact with many wine makers.

The cider Alex makes himself has won prizes

at the Devon County Show and Royal Bath & West Show. It is made at his home at Bollhayes Farm, Clayhidon, in the quiet and attractive Culm Valley. The cider orchard was planted the week his daughter was born, in November 1988. The trees were standards from Bulmers. By chance somebody had ordered an Austrian hydraulic press, but it arrived too late to be used at that farm that season. A friend of Alex's managed to get ten tons of late cider apples and so they made cider. Then he gathered up apples from other neighbours' orchards and pressed them. That was the real start to his cider-making career.

As Alex says, he came in just at the tail end of the farmhouse cider-making era and every farm sale he went to had a cider press. The old wooden presses had become obsolete and they were often dragged out of the barns, chopped up, cannibalised or even burnt. Many of the large beams were turned into lintels for fake inglenook fireplaces. There are still some orchards in the Blackdowns, but the really

old ones have just keeled over. County council grants have been very important in supporting replanting.

Alex presses about forty different varieties of cider apple. He goes round an orchard, tastes the apples and ties a bit of baler twine round the trees he wants and this tells the apple-pickers where to pick. This is done entirely by taste and instinct. He gets a feel for which apples work well in his cider. He admits that he does not know the names of many of the apples he uses, but believes that quality and flavour are more important than names. It is all a question of balance. Afterwards, he blends if necessary.

Alex's secret, apart from choosing his fruit in this way, is cleanliness and attention to detail with the equipment. He is a great believer in stainless steel. Scuffed plastic containers and old dirty wooden barrels are an absolute killer for good cider.

Alex only makes 1,500 gallons a year, so his cider is very select. He comments that he has the luxury of working free from any real commercial pressure and can make the cider that he likes. He supplies two pubs on the Blackdowns, The Merry Harriers in Clayhidon and the Culm Valley Inn in Culmstock. Both have restaurant menus and prepare fantastic food. This is where local cider really wins out. There is a venison farm just down the road. So you can eat local game with local cider. Alex's also makes a limited quantity of bottle-fermented cider and perry.

Talking with Alex about the finer points of cidermaking is always interesting. He regards the quality of the cider fruit as the single most important factor. 'It is extraordinary how many people think they can make good cider from lousy fruit.' One of the mistakes people regularly make, he feels, is using too much bitter-sweet fruit and not enough acid. 'You need to add some acidity, cider made from all bitter-sweets is insipid, and I think one of the reasons our cider does quite well in competitions is that it has a bit more bite and stands out from the crowd.'

His long-term association with wine-makers is also significant and the cider industry has much to learn from them about quality and finesse. 'Wine-makers know that you need acidity to carry the flavour and to give length, and it is an underrated element of cider. Too many bitter-sweets and not enough bitter-sharps. Not enough cidermakers understand the importance of acidity. It is the key to the whole thing.'

'In the West Country there is a definite shortage of bitter-sharp apples like Kingston Black, Lambrook Pippin, Porter's Perfection and Stembridge Clusters. Some cidermakers simply add Bramleys, which is cheaper than buying malic acid. If Bramleys add acidity then so be it. Many of the large cidermakers have been using Bramleys for years to sharpen up their cider.'

Alex believes that a pure bitter-sweet cider with an acidity of only 1.5 grams of acid per litre would be boring and prone to spoilage: an acid level of nearer 4 grams per litre would be better. The tannin and acid balance is important. Like many purists Alex is not terribly keen on sweet ciders, nor is he a great fan of single varieties: '… a

lot of them are insipid or one dimensional'. And he has a good point. Single variety cider is very good for learning about the individual characteristics of certain cider apples, but the cider that has depth and complexity only comes with a rich blend.

Like many traditional cidermakers, Alex is dismayed that there isn't a 'watertight' definition of cider. As far as definitions go I have a suspicion that the large makers wouldn't agree on anything above 40 per cent cider apple juice content and the small makers on anything below 90 per cent. Alex comments, 'If everybody could agree that cider should be made from 100 per cent apple juice it would help, and in the West Country it should be cider apples.' The general public is often not aware of the juice content in their cider, because the makers are not obliged to list it on the label.

Alex compares it to wine-making: 'If the rules for cider were as they are for wine, it would be far simpler. In France and England you can't add water and colouring to your wine. Saccharin in cider is "traditional" only because it has been used for over 100 years, therefore it is traditional …' As in the cheese world, the words 'traditional' and 'farmhouse' have many layers of meaning.

Curiously CAMRA, which has done so much for small producers of beer, and is normally squeaky clean about its rules, allows saccharin to be used in cider. Some purists feel that the only permitted sweetener should be the apple juice itself. Some use organic sugar; others keep the sweetness in by keeving and using the Normandy method.

Alex has his own views. 'cidermakers themselves should take cidermaking more seriously, otherwise people think they can get away with making cider from 25 per cent apple juice. The rest is often sugar out of a tanker, well water, pumped glucose syrup and orange colouring.'

There is clearly an impasse here, but the public has a right to know what sort of cider they are actually drinking. Part of the problem is that cider made from 100 per cent apple juice, too strong for some tastes and has 'too much flavour'. The trouble is that people who have been brought up on Coca Cola, lemonade and other soft drinks can't handle real flavour. But palates can be trained. 'People who visit from Norway, Belgium, Sweden, Hungary, France come and drink our cider and don't have any preconceptions and they enjoy it for what it is and refer to it as our wine. And they don't think anything unusual about it. English people will often say "Oh no. I only drink my Chardonnay".' If it is good-quality cider, it has probably had far less tinkering around than most wines.

Alex reckons that cidermaking is both an art and a science. 'If it were entirely science it would be soulless. And it would be less interesting. But you can't rely on art alone.' One of his many skills is in making bottle-fermented cider and perry. One year Alex had perry pears from a Long Ashton trial orchard and they made a fantastic drink, which sold in a flash. When I visited him he opened a very special bottle of perry. It was 14 years old – superb, smoky and apricoty, with just the right amount of small, lively bubbles. And drinking it in the sunshine outside the cider house beside the orchard, it was much better than most champagnes I have tasted.

When tasting cider Alex uses the same criteria as he does for wine. He wants the cider to look 'bright, but not necessarily crystal clear, to have a nice colour, to smell clean, not smell of sulphur or acetic acid or dirty barrels or farmyard. Interestingly, it shouldn't really taste of apples. Wine doesn't necessarily taste of grapes. It should have a full flavour, a natural alcohol of 6 to 7 per cent, which gives it body, then length of flavour and a clean aftertaste, which is where the acidity refreshes the mouth. We don't want over-pronounced tannins that leave the mouth all dried up, we don't want searing acidity to hit you as you take your first sip, but acidity that comes in gradually with a nice clean finish.'

Here in the Blackdowns, in the upper reaches of the Culm Valley, there is heavy clay and cidermakers have to make allowances for the altitude. They are at least 500 feet up. So they produce high-altitude cider in a frost-prone valley, sometimes with frosts as late as the beginning of June. To get round this Alex purposefully planted late varieties, because he knew his trees were in a frost hollow.

Alex doesn't pick them up till late November. The sugar level gives a specific gravity of 1055, which is adequate. In a good year Alex will grow about a third of the apples he uses and then he buys in from a multitude of small orchards on the Blackdowns.

Most people know Alex as the affable man at Vigo on the end of phone offering free advice and counselling about cider-making problems. What he has noticed over time is a shift in the psychology of cidermakers, and it is this shift that has kick-started the cider renaissance. Alex agrees that the decline of cider drinking since the end of the Second World War is simply because the older generation of cidermakers retired or died off. 'The ones who never changed their ways have just faded out because nobody wants to drink their cider apart from themselves. Often it was like vinegar, and this gave cider a very bad name.'

So, too, the cider drinkers. 'Cider was the traditional drink here even into 1960s. The landlady in the Half Moon at Clayhidon reckoned that 70 per cent of the drink served there then was draught cider. Once, when they ran out, somebody even came up from Wellington with a hogshead of cider in his linkbox on the back of his tractor. By the time she retired in the early 1980s it was less than 10 per cent, and then it was Blackthorn. The 1960s was the watershed. Tractors, lager and Babycham.'

The new wave of cidermakers can be divided between traditional cidermakers, who have revamped themselves and at the same time improved their manufacturing processes to make a consistently good but interesting product, and the completely new artisan makers who have come in

Above. Alex is a stainless steel man.

from the outside with the expressed intention of making a good cider. They are the purists who make cider from 100 per cent cider-apple juice, producing a perfectly natural product that does justice to the fruit.

Alex has seen a resurgence in cidermaking all over the country – not just in the South-west but in South Wales, Sussex, Norfolk and Yorkshire. He tells me that he has just notched up his first Scottish cidermaker north of the Tweed. 'It is all looking very positive. We have enough good-quality cider around but it is only now reaching a critical mass.'

He thinks this is because cidermaking fits in very well with the ethos of local food, Slow Food and environmental concerns. Cider also has a romantic image. 'cidermakers also have this immense advantage over most other food and drink producers in that deeply ingrained in our culture there is this romanticism surrounding cider. It is a fantastically romantic product. People love it for that, the ritual of the wassail, the orchard.'

Good cider is seen as very pure and healthy. 'Good for your arthritis and keeps you vigorous. It is a seasonal thing. There is the whole magic of blossom. The smell of ripe apples in the orchards, mounds of apples, just a very short period of pressing. They love it. A fresh glass of pure apple juice just off the press is magic.'

What also fascinates Alex is the social range of those who drink cider now. 'It can go from horse-drawn, New Age alternative hippies to Range Rovers and BMWs at weekends. Organic house-wives and bankers, beaten-up minis and genteel Bentleys: 18 to 85.'

Above. Bottle-fermented cider goes with a swing.

CHAPTER II
Tidal Cider
DEVON

Paul Gadd and Rebecca Jack,
RealDrink Ltd, Stoke Gabriel, Devon

Why is it that cidermakers always live in beautiful places? Stoke Gabriel in South Devon is one of the jewels on the River Dart. Upstream are Tuckenhay, Sharpham and Totnes; downstream are Dittisham, Agatha Christie and Dartmouth. The Dart, which I have known since childhood, slides by with unconcerned ease. In the 1950s there were cidermakers all over the South Hams. I can just remember cider being brought out to a threshing machine in the small fields on the cliff tops at Redlap near Stoke Fleming, and the way in which the stone jars would be hidden under the hedge or under a cart to keep them cool. This was cider's swansong.

Whenever I return to the River Dart I go to Stoke Gabriel. A good friend of mine once had a mooring here, the last in the line going down towards Pig Hole Point, and I would spend long weekends here when I should have been studying for exams in civil engineering. There is now a cheeky seal that has taken up residence on the bend near Gurrow Point, helping himself to migrating salmon. Succulent oysters are also grown in the clean tidal water.

So it is an enormous pleasure to have an excuse to visit Stoke Gabriel and meet Paul Gadd and Rebecca Jack, who have chosen to live just above the high tide mark on the River Dart. They left London to come down here and did so in unconventional style. For years they lived on a boat, an old 30-foot Westerly – a floating caravan in other words.

Tide and the river are important to Paul. For generations his family were lightermen on the Thames and he grew up with the sounds of Borough Market and Brixton Market ringing in his ears. Indeed, as a sound engineer his ears were a key part of his living. Rebecca, originally from Chester, was marketing for Polydor, a large record company. Together with their two daughters they chose to relocate to Devon and make cider, apple juice and elderflower cordial.

A hundred years ago Stoke Gabriel was thick with orchards and the mild maritime climate ensured that they cropped very well. The ebb and flow of the Dart meant that frosts were rare. As elsewhere, many of the orchards have since been torn down for housing, but there are still at least two orchards in the village; the one next to the church is a community orchard where they have their wassail. In 2008, 600 people turned up to celebrate twelfth night.

Paul and Rebecca invited me into their slightly ramshackle but delightful house, set in half an acre

Opposite. The Dart at Stoke Gabriel.

of field, and over a cup of coffee we chewed the cud and Paul told me how they got into cider-making. It all started up the road when they visited the two well-known local cider farms, Hunts and Churchwards that are side by side in Yalberton, another wonderful village not a stone's throw away from Torbay and Paignton – so plenty of thirsty customers after the attractions of the zoo and the beach have worn a bit thin. Here was a world of old tumbledown farmhouses and ancient barns.

When Yalberton Farm ceased making cider the house was sold and bought by some of Paul's friends. Unfortunately, the presses had already been sold, so they had the barns and the trees but no press. The solution was very simple. As a project between three families they built the presses from scratch and then embarked on communal cider-making. They found a screw in the field and built the rest of it themselves. This was in the late 1990s

and they must have been making nearly 5,000 litres, which is well within the limit on duty (1,500 gallons is roughly the same as 7,000 litres). And then Paul started a small company to sell the cider that they were making. Eventually they bought a second-hand hydraulic press and started making cider at a different location, Yarde Farm, in the middle of Stoke Gabriel.

Yarde Farm is currently in the process of being converted into holiday accommodation, the fate of so many barns these days. Paul now houses his equipment at a nearly nursery, where he has built a new shed for himself.

Paul and Rebecca pick apples up in at least a dozen local orchards. There are so many varieties in this region that Paul and Rebecca hardly know what they all are. There is no doubt room for a pomologist and a small research project here. The two of them believe in natural yeasts and allowing

cider to mature at its own pace. They believe very much in single orchard cider and apple juice. Each bottle has the name of the orchard printed on its label – ultimate traceability and *terroir*.

'Most of the orchards round here are totally underused. Compton Castle was the furthest we went last year, which is eight miles maximum.' Compton Castle is a magnificent fortified manor house castle and dates from the 1200s. They have a couple of orchards with around 150 standard cider apple and juicing trees. The occupants, Mr and Mrs Gilbert and the National Trust, are very pleased that the apples are being picked up and put to such good use. Paul sells his cider and apple juice at local National Trust properties, Coleton Fishacre and Greenway House at Galmpton, where Agatha Christie lived for so many years.

Another orchard that Paul and Rebecca have picked apples in is at Stoke Fleming, near where I

once lived. Paul uses the dessert and dual-purpose apples for apple juice and the rest goes into the cider. 'It's a hobby that gets bigger every year.' One of the problems he experiences is that no one wants to pick apples any more, which is a shame. The pub in the village is taking their cider, and the café down by the river takes the juice and the cider. The pair also do the cider as a bag-in-a-box. Paul has tried his hand at keeving to make *cidre bouchée* but you have to keep racking it a lot. With the Normandy method Paul admits that every year is an experiment. With keeving it is very important to get the middle section out, and he pumps it. 'I can't get it out gently.' Paul became interested in this while living on the boat in Normandy so they learned what they could off the locals. 'There's a nice man up in Cherbourg who helped us, and then we had a French student who came and worked for us last year. She was from near St Malo,

and she got us a lot of technical information.'

Paul doesn't use enzymes or chalk, but relies on getting the middle section out without disturbing the *chapeau brun*, the brown crust that forms on top. 'The secret is to keep racking it, and if you can slow it down enough, then bottle it.'

Paul makes two ciders. 'One I like and one I sell. I think a cider should be just like a red wine, rich, full-bodied and dry and quite thick. I'll drink that all day long, but what we end up making is what I call "grockle" cider, which has got to be as sweet as you can make it. I take the middle road. I won't do sweet cider, I can make a medium naturally and the dry I'll send out to discerning customers. I sip and savour cider, like I'd drink red wine. A complex taste is nice.

'We don't need to carbonate because if you put it in the bottle it'll do it on its own. I was thinking about pasteurising some of the bottles to get a more consistent product. I see the day when we may need to pasteurise it for some places.' Like many people Paul can't call his cider 'organic', although it is made in an organic way. All the orchards he picks are essentially organic. The trees aren't sprayed at all. 'We just say we're unsprayed. We can't technically call it organic because we can't be sure what the farmer might be feeding the sheep who graze the orchards.'

Paul has recently started having his cider distilled by Julian Temperley, so there will soon be Devon Cider Brandy. Paul is keen to add value to his product and will increasingly concentrate on the cider brandy and the sparkling cider. Paul's approach is more in keeping with the French

Above. Apple juice, honest!

124

tradition. 'We like their attitude of drinking cider in restaurants with families.'

Both Paul and Rebecca have spent many days and weeks working on their labelling. The customers like the packaging. And I can see why. The label is important. They used a friend of theirs, a graphic designer, and their brief was that they wanted it on craft paper, and didn't want a photograph of an apple or anything like that. And he came up with the apple potato print, which they thought was a stroke of genius – very earthy, very *pomme de terre*.

After an hour or two we gently sauntered on down to the quay at Stoke Gabriel with the couple's children and went out to Mill Point with a bottle of their Normandy-style cider and spent time watching the boats go by. When we came back the tide had come in and we had to wade for 100 yards or more but it was all good fun, the kids loved it.

CHAPTER 12

Coppy and
the Proclaimers

HEREFORDSHIRE

Tom Oliver,
Oliver's Cider and Perry, Moorhouse Farm,
Ocle Pychard, Herefordshire

Ocle Pychard lies about eight miles north-east of Hereford, and in the old, long, slightly rambling, red-brick hop kilns and drying sheds of Moorhouse Farm, Tom Oliver is quietly resurrecting the once noble art of perry making. With boundless enthusiasm Tom extols the virtues and idiosyncrasies of certain perry pears, and with panache imparts the mystique of this ancient tradition. He is a true ambassador for perry and has won many prizes, yet he only started making cider and perry in earnest in 1999. Like several others in his native Herefordshire, he is at the forefront of the perry revival, going back to basics, testing the boundaries, planting orchards, identifying old varieties and finding out what each perry is capable of. The sense of adventure is there for all to see.

Tom is a larger-than-life figure who is ruled not so much by his head as by his heart, in this case his passion for perry. And perry certainly needs dedicated enthusiasts, not just to make it but to promote it and drink it. As Tom freely admits: 'I have a history of allowing my passion to rule my head and then through brutal hard work I have to prove myself to be right.' His belief is founded not just on his own abilities as a cider and perry maker but on the quality of the raw material. As he says, 'I am a big believer in the bounty of the fruit and orchards.'

Not surprisingly, Tom's passion extends to the landscape where he was brought up and he waxes lyrical about the diversity of orchards, virtues that make the Three Counties look so fantastic. Tom could easily get a job with the local tourist board. Indeed, his farm once attracted a busload of perry makers from Austria and he baptised them with the 'real thing'. The Three Counties – Worcestershire, Herefordshire and Gloucestershire – are particularly good for growing perry pears and cider apples. These counties are drained by some of the country's finest rivers, the Wye, the Severn, the Teme and the Avon. Perry pears should, by tradition, be grown within sight of May Hill, which is near Newent, halfway between Gloucester and Ross-on-Wye.

As far as making the perry is concerned Tom uses wild yeasts and is a 'glutton for punishment'. By that he means he is at the mercy of organisms that can make his perry or cider taste fantastic or horrible. 'I let myself open to oxidisation but it is worthwhile. I get the ciders and perrys I believe in.' Tom is ever the optimist, always experimenting, always pushing boundaries.

But what is perry exactly? The word comes

Opposite. Ellis Bitter at Stoke Lacy.

from the Latin *pirum*, which simply means pear. Old English has it as *pirige* or *pirie* and Old French has it as *pere* or *perey*. Perry is defined as a beverage made from crushed and fermented perry pears.

Tom is no incomer. Moorhouse is a family farm. His great-grandfather moved here in 1873. In those days his family had extensive cider orchards and kept Hereford cattle. Like many farmers, they made cider and perry for their workers and when Bulmers started a factory in Hereford in the 1890s they grew cider apples commercially. But this all came to an end after the First World War. The price of cider apples suddenly dropped. Tom still has a letter from Bulmers that tells its own story. His grandfather was so impressed by Bulmers' latest price offer that he went and grubbed out 30 acres of orchards and put in hops instead, switching his allegiance from cider to beer. That was 1921. And it was a very good income for many years, relying as it did on gangs of casual workers from the Black Country and Welsh miners on their holidays to pick the hops. Tom's family stayed in hops till 1999

and the farm still has many reminders of the industry lying around: piles of twine, Salop trailers, slatted floors for drying and the rotating kilns.

Tom lives in a small cottage on the farm, which was once the estate cider house. In the garden he has the old circular stone mill, which his brother Matthew dug up and put back together again. Tom remembers as a youngster there being a single perry pear tree on the farm and it must have left a deep impression.

Like many other farmers' sons he went off to agricultural college in Devon, and graduated not so much from Seale Hayne but from 'Ye Olde Cider Bar, 99 East Street, Newton Abbot'. When he was 21 he told his family that he was going into the music business. Their reaction, as Tom remembers, was 'one of concern and bewilderment', not least because he had no visible means of income. The pop world was notoriously fickle. Tom thanked them for their 'patience and tolerance'. He had at least prised himself away from the cider bar and was now drinking Westons Centenary, a cider that he

Above. Old cider mill on Tom's farm.
Opposite left. Blakeney Red orchard near Bromyard.
Opposite right. Coppy blossom, Stoke Lacy.

particularly enjoyed. His local pub, The Three Crowns down in Ullingswick, used to get crates of it in purely for him to drink. He was, he recalls, 'a good customer: maybe too good a customer'.

Tom became a 'roadie', or, to put it more accurately, tour manager and sound engineer. One of his best friends was a home-grown Hereford musician called James Honeyman-Scott, known as Jimmy Scott who later became a lead guitar player in a classic post-punk rock band called The Pretenders. Twenty-five years later Tom is still on the road. Currently he is tour manger and sound engineer for The Proclaimers, the famous twins from Auchtermuchty, who play an amalgam of folk, country, pop, r'n'b and r'n'r.

The quiet seasonality of cider and perry makes a welcome antidote to the pounding music and constant one-night gigs. Touring is 'fairly thirsty work' but what really got Tom cidermaking in earnest was a realisation that the good cider and perry that he valued drinking as a youth were no longer around. He was dissatisfied with the large-scale commercial ciders, and like many others started making it for himself and his friends. He had always helped with the hop harvest and so after 1999 when the hops declined, cidermaking filled the vacuum

and he was able to take over the hop kilns at Moorhouse Farm. His timing was immaculate.

With Tom's return to Ocle Pychard such names as Winnal's Longdon, Blakeney Red, Thorn, Moorcroft and Coppy started to trip off his tongue. To anyone brought up in the cider tradition these names have a magic of their own. A whole new world suddenly opens up. As Tom quite rightly says 'perry has a mind of its own'.

Perry and cider logically sit side by side, as traditionally they share the same orchards, the same locality, and the same equipment, but after that, 'they go their own way, they have totally different traditions and they need to be quite separate now'.

'Cider is a hard master but perry is a beautiful but fickle mistress.' You never know what she is going to do next. She obeys no known laws. She can be brilliant one moment and awful the next or, as Tom likes to say, with some feeling, 'Perry is destined to pull quirky little stunts on you.' With perry you have a steep learning curve.

Although Tom is very keen on bottle-fermented perries, he has a sneaking suspicion that a good still perry is more than a match for many wines. As he says: 'The gentry two or three hundred years ago would have regarded perry as their wine.' They would have had great pride in serving top-class perry to a distinguished guest, a member of the clergy or more importantly their ladies, or 'hinds', as John Beale called them. There are hidden benefits, as Tom points out: 'A good dose of Blakeney Red cures all, keeps you regular.' And in those days with a very stodgy diet that was a distinct advantage.

The single perry tree that Tom grew up with has long since disappeared, but he has a small orchard behind his cottage and he has planted 60 different varieties. The bulk of his perry pears, however, come from other orchards.

Many of these trees were planted during the Restoration, when cider and perry were fashionable. But Tom is not just looking at the past, he has persuaded a local man called Farmer Parker of Stoke Lacy to plant a new 17-acre perry pear orchard with 420 standard trees. There are 18 varieties. This is a fantastic venture.

What concerns Tom, however, is that the skills of perry making have not been passed down from generation to generation. It doesn't take a JCB very long to do away with what nature has taken several hundred years to mature. Perry pear trees can grow to 60 feet in height and in blossom are magnificent giants. They have a more vigorous rooting system than apple trees, which is why they live so long. And the old standard orchards fit very well within a traditional mixed orchard, where you can graze sheep and Hereford cattle underneath their magnificent boughs.

'The hardest thing for people to grasp is that a perry pear does not always look like a pear. It can actually look like an apple, a cherry, a plum, any manner of traditional rural fruits. It can be incredibly hard, you can't bite into it; it can be like grape-shot or the softest thing in the world. One gentle squeeze and you have reduced it to a soft pulp. Those are the extremes and in terms of taste, the early ones are just incredibly sweet and not much else and very late ones, the very hard ones, are very astringent, not bitter but high in tannins. The acid levels vary quite a lot from year to year.'

One of Tom's favourite trees is Oldfield. He is happy to have 'as many Oldfields as anyone can pick and deliver here. Oldfield is a fantastic multi-purpose variety, it really is. It makes a good single variety, it has good characteristics, it is of interest, the taste, the aromas, the flavours; it is quite broad, it is not a narrow spectrum variety; it has a lot of character to it. It works very well on its own, and works very well blending.'

It is a bit like a Dabinett of the pear world. Tom is not even sure what some of the pears he is given are, and he gives them names to indicate where they have come from so he can recognise them another year.

'Blakeney Red is probably the most common perry pear, big trees, regular fruiters. If you pick, say, three or four times through the season from the same tree, you can really make use of the fruit. You ignore perry pears at your peril, they demand attention and you have to get it right. It is far more demanding than cider. The early season pears, when they are ripe, are off the tree and going mushy within 24 hours.'

Tom has gangs of hand pickers; some have been coming for ten years but no one is quite as enthusiastic as he is on his hands and knees.

He has his own ideas of why perry caught on in Herefordshire. For a start there was no point in growing dessert fruit in large quantities because of the long distance to any large cities. So it was eminently sensible to make perry, which could be bottled or put into a barrel and transported down

Above. Oldfield pears from Preston Wyne.

CHAPTER 13

Pip, Squeak and Wilfred

HEREFORDSHIRE

Tim Weston,
Westons, The Bounds, Much Marcle,
Herefordshire

The village of Much Marcle is well positioned, tucked in under the wooded Marcle ridge, and is therefore protected from the worst of the westerly weather. It has good soil, some of it marl, a mixture of clay and carbonate of lime, which is soft, loose and earthy, excellent for growing tall oaks, perry pear trees, cider orchards and bringing on young fruit trees. Much Marcle is also well positioned within the Three Counties. Gloucester is 14 miles, Hereford is 14 miles and Worcester, which is on the other side of Ledbury and the Malverns, is 20 miles. In many respects, Much Marcle is an archetypal village where the vicar might well be watching your every move: an unusual site, you might think, for a family business which has an annual turnover of £18 million and 30 different lines. But this is Herefordshire and family cider businesses are *de rigeur*.

Just up from the 1930s garage the tanks and vats of Westons ciderworks can be seen hovering above the village. I sometimes use that back road as a short cut to get to the Wye valley and Hereford via Sollers Hope and Woolhope, an area of wonderful hills and orchards. For the Westons, family history is as important as cidermaking itself, and to understand what makes the firm tick you have to understand the family history.

It all goes back to one man, Henry Weston, who was born around 1850 in Cheltenham. His parents, Thomas and Ann, lived at 413 High St, Cheltenham. Originally Thomas Weston came from Coleford in the Forest of Dean, and when he was in Cheltenham he was listed as a linen draper. This was an upmarket profession, which meant dealing with the public and with a quality product. Thomas's wife, Ann Webb, came from Upton Bishop in Herefordshire. By 1861 Henry, aged 11, is to be found living with his aunt and uncle, James and Mary Webb, at Crossington, a farm of 120 acres. So the young Henry had moved from fine linen and high street Cheltenham shops to Upton Bishop and livestock.

In 1871 Henry is listed as a farmer's assistant, but by 1878 he is a tenant farmer in his own right at The Bounds, Much Marcle, a farm of 165 acres, employing four men and a boy. The old farmhouse dates back to 1611. Henry had very little capital, and farming was not very profitable because of cheap imports of corn from America and Australia. So in 1880 he turned to cidermaking to supplement his income. Cider would, of course have been made here for hundreds of years, but this marked a conscious step to make cider in earnest, and Henry started to sell it not just locally but in the towns. This was no downmarket operation; he wanted to get the very best out of the apple. His original circular stone cider mill can still be seen in the garden today. It is a marvellous beast that would have been powered by a horse or two. Alongside it is the old cider press with a shingle roof, looking like a small Japanese shrine.

Henry was by this time married to Emily Bellamy, who was born at Westbury on Severn, another excellent area for perry pear trees. She was to bear him nine children. The 1881 census shows that Henry's eldest son, Hubert, was then aged eight months. Hubert later took on running the business with his brothers. By 1891 Henry is still just listed as a farmer, but now with eight children: three sons, Hubert, Stafford and Bernard, and five daughters, Edith, Lucy, Hilda, Dora and Jessie. Henry also acquired two more farms locally, Caerswall and Nuttal.

By this time Henry was really making his mark as a cidermaker. There is an in-depth interview with him in the *Hereford Times* of 1 December 1894, which reveals that Henry really knew what he was doing and applied modern equipment wherever he could. He used steam engines and granite rollers. There were power presses and slate tanks, wooden vats, cool, dark cellars hewn out of the rock, pumps and a filter called an Invicta, which could handle 100 gallons in 20 minutes. Young Hubert was in charge of this apparatus and he must have been all of 14 or 15 at the time. It removed all the bacteria, the acetic or lactic germs and thus made the cider clear and able to travel substantial distances quite safely. One cask was labelled to go to Devonshire. So even in 1894 export was on the horizon.

Henry Weston was fastidious about the quality of the fruit and all rotten apples were picked out. The article gives us many clues as to his high standards. 'Last year Mr Weston got first prize at the Hereford Agricultural Show for his draught perry and second for his bottled. The year before he got first for both cider and perry and he also had the privilege of supplying cider and perry at the House of Commons.' No doubt this was through the good services of Mr C. W. Radcliffe Cook, the MP for Hereford and 'Cider', who lived down the road at The Hellens, which has a fine avenue of perry pear trees, originally planted in 1710. What is really fascinating about this article is the impressive list of cider-apple varieties: Strawberry Norman, Skyrme, Redstreak, Foxwhelp, Royal Wilding, Yellow Styre, Cowarne Red, Kingstone Black, Cummy Norman; and the perry pears: Taynton Squash, Barland, Moorcroft, Oldfield, Butt, Pear, Longland, Huffcap, Red Pear, Old Dymock Red and Woodsell, being a local Much Marcle seedling.

Interestingly, the interview turned to the new Association of cidermakers. 'There is one thing it will do,' Mr Weston said, 'it will stimulate manufacturers to make a better article and consequently we shall get more attention paid to it. A vast number of people have not had the opportunity of tasting good cider – many indeed have not heard of cider at all – and the association will be a means of bringing to their knowledge the fact that there is a cheap and wholesome beverage.' These words are just as true today as they were in 1894, though ironically today it is more in relation to industrial mass production of cider than to the rough, acetic farmhouse scrumpy, which has thankfully almost died out.

Henry was a visionary, which is all the more remarkable when you consider that he was the son of a linen draper and brought up on a farm. Maybe the attention to detail was there and the desire to satisfy upmarket customers. He made quality his hallmark and this was applied to the whole process of cidermaking. He did not cut corners: in fact, he took every precaution to make sure the cider was made out of the best fruit and was stored so that it reached its destination in perfect condition. The fruit was only pressed when it was ready.

Henry apparently did not believe in advertising and instead preferred to let his cider speak for itself. By the 1901 census Henry is at last listed as a farmer, a cider manufacturer and a cider merchant. Another son, Leonard, has been born, now aged six.

When Henry died in 1917 his sons Hubert, Stafford and Leonard took over. The firm grew by

Opposite. Delivery in style.

leaps and bounds. Indeed, so popular was it in London that there was a famous 'Westons' cider house at 167 Wandsworth Road. There is a photograph, taken in the late 1930s of Nightingale's Cider House, which was a large, three-storey building, and outside there are four lorries each laden with ten barrels of Westons cider. Advertising had now caught on and the cider house itself had the name 'Westons Cider' on the frontage in large letters. The cider house was run by Mrs Nightingale, selling cider at 4d a pint. Westons would deliver 3,000 gallons every month.

In those days Westons made three brands of draught cider: 'Supreme', 'Bounds' and 'Farm'. The first two were available in sweet, medium and dry. 'Supreme' was very sound and full-bodied; 'Bounds' was for general use and the 'Farm' brand was for those having the 'acquired taste', which was in two classes, rough and medium rough. Added to this was the 'Marcle Blend' of perry, which was good for rheumatism and other kindred complaints.

Cider has always been seen to have beneficial health properties when drunk in moderate quantities and when I mentioned this to Maureen Weston, whose husband Norman ran the firm for many years, she produced an interesting press cutting taken from the *Hereford News and Chronicle* in July 1936. It included a photograph of Leonard Weston, in a cricket blazer, and his aunt, Miss Ann Bellamy, aged nearly 103, at a cricket match. She was Henry Weston's sister-in-law and a good ten years older than Henry's wife, Emily. Miss Bellamy's comments were most amusing: 'She thinks that the modern conditions are very much better than those in the old days; she is a great believer in a nightly glass of sparkling cider; she thinks young people are entitled to a good time and threatens that one of these days she is going for a trip in her nephew's aeroplane.' Certainly a nightly glass of sparkling cider seems to have kept her wit and faculties in fine trim.

Hubert Weston, Henry's eldest son, sadly had already died of blood poisoning in 1929, aged just 48. He had been a very well-respected farmer and had helped to keep some of the old Hereford cattle

blood lines going. He had two sons, Norman and Dennis. Norman was only 12 when his father died and so the business continued to be run by his uncles Leonard and Stafford Weston, neither of whom had children.

It was only while talking to Maureen, Norman's wife, that I realised how difficult it had been at certain times. She has been at Westons for 55 years. Dennis enlisted as a Sergeant-Observer in the RAF, and was killed in action coming back from Germany during the Second World War. As Maureen remembers: 'He was the only one killed on that plane. Wasn't it a misfortune? He was only 26, I think. Stafford never had any children; Uncle Leonard never had children. So that left just us, really. We managed to keep it going, we had to work jolly hard, it wasn't easy.'

Westons never compromised on the integrity of the cider or the business. When Leonard and Stafford died in the 1970s, Norman ran the business on his own. These days the company is ably run by Helen Thomas, Norman and Maureen's eldest daughter, who took over the role of managing director in 1996. Her brothers, Tim and Henry, are also active company directors. Maureen is proud that they have never had to advertise on television.

These days there are so many different types of

cider made in Much Marcle that it is difficult to know where to start, so I had a chat to Tim Weston and Heather Mead from the PR Department. Annual production on-site is around 28 million pints, or nearly half a pint for everyone in the UK. Tim is still a gallon man, I was pleased to hear, and this equates to 3.5 million gallons. Tim told me that Bulmers, the other famous cider family in Herefordshire, started out in 1888, which means that Westons was just that little bit earlier in 1880. Unlike Bulmers, Westons is still run by the family. Tim also remembers that all the wooden barrels had 'Westons of Dymock' stamped on them, because that was the nearest railway station, which Westons used to transport their cider to customers around the country, and the railway men knew exactly where to return the returning empty barrels. It must have been a lovely rural station, a bit like Adlestrop, which was on the Oxford line.

Edward Thomas, the poet, was a great frequenter of Dymock, as were Robert Frost, Lascelles Abercrombie, Rupert Brooke, Edward Thomas, Wilfrid Wilson Gibson and John Drinkwater. They are still known as the Dymock poets to this day, and no doubt they drank cider and let it colour their rural contemplations.

Dymock is also the home of a great promoter

of cheese, cider and perry, Charles Martell. I once helped to make a BBC Landlines programme for Radio 4 on his farm and what a pleasure that was. Charles makes Stinking Bishop, the well-known smelly cheese, which is washed with perry. The name comes from one of the perry pear trees that grows in Charles's orchard. Its other name is Moorcroft, or the Choke Pear. Charles is not just a cheesemaker, he is a keeper of Gloucester cattle. At present he is compiling a vast compendium of Gloucestershire perry pears and cider apples.

Tim explained that this was a good area for mixed farming and that Westons was going back into Hereford cattle, the wonderful red and white beef animals that are slow to mature but have such presence. They now have 30 of them. The cattle were once housed where the Westons offices are. Farming and cider go well together and nowhere is this better illustrated than in a standard orchard with cattle or sheep grazing underneath. During cidermaking, the pomace can be fed to the stock and in the past the finished product would be given to the farm hands to keep them working.

Westons gets 10–15 per cent of its apples off its own land and the rest is from the three counties, covering a radius of about 30 miles, with a few producers 50 miles away. As Tim tells me, 'We've got about 50 acres of organic standard orchards on our own farm, we are getting up to 100 acres of bush orchards, and 10 acres are perry pear.' They have all been given names such as Nardene, Ox Park, Rough Meadow, Pool Meadow, Well Field, Nuttal Orchard, Nuttal Shirehill, Point, Marcle Meadow, Slag Meadow, Hazerdine, Shirehill, Caerswall Orchard, Sheep Wash, Joiners, Horse Moors, Top Orchard, Fish Ponds, Applegarth, Clock Meadow, Venning Orchard, Long Meadow, Big Walta and Pear Orchard.

In terms of perry, a few years ago Westons planted a 17-acre bush orchard which has a wide range of perry pear trees: Brandy, Green Horse, Hellens Early, Hendre Huffcap, Taynton Squash, Thorn, Winnal's Longdon and Yellow Huffcap.

But Westons, as Tim mentioned, is about to embark on a large-scale planting programme with local farmers that will see another 1,200 acres planted up under contract. Some of these will be organic. Westons can sell as much organic cider as

Above left. Maureen Weston, next to an old perry tree.
Above right. Apples showered and ready for pressing.

it makes. Organic cider began about ten years ago and this was initially led by Sainsbury's, but 'now we can't get enough organic apples'. The cider world can be unpredictable. Five years ago people were ripping their orchards out.

Tim remembers growing up on the cider farm and it was obviously tremendous fun. 'When it was snowing we used to go on the press floor and chuck snowballs at the workmen, who used to retaliate, and they would come out and chuck snowballs at us as well. His sister Helen, who now runs the firm, used to work on the bottling line. They had three wet presses and one dry press. They would always press twice to get the last bit of juice out. These were all the old hydraulic presses, but they have been replaced by three massive Bucher presses, which work around the clock in the autumn. They can press 20 tonnes an hour, which means more than 300 tonnes of fruit a day. In the past the apples would have been piled high on a vast concrete apron at the back of the mill and then washed down via channels within the concrete to the pressing floor inside the mill. Now they are tipped from large lorries directly into deep pits like vast swimming pools from where they are washed down into the mill, where they feed the presses continually. Westons presses around 12,000 tons of cider fruit each year. Today the chief cidermaker is Jonathan Blair, who curiously enough used to work for Bulmers in Hereford.

For storage of the traditional cider Westons has 59 large wooden vats, and some of these are enormous. They are over 200 years old, and they have names such as Darby and Joan, Pip, Squeak and Wilfred, Faith, Hope and Charity, Hereford, Worcester and Gloucester, and Wembley. Wembley is just behind Hereford because it's the closest that Hereford United will ever get to Wembley! Some of these vats are 24 feet high and are made from oak staves. Squeak holds just over 42,000 gallons, which is fairly large. Pip, Squeak and Wilfred were cartoon characters that appeared after the First World War in the *Daily Mirror*. The naming of the characters in the strip was due to the artist's wartime batman, whose nickname was 'Pip-Squeak'. Pip was a dog, Squeak, a penguin, and Wilfred a rabbit. Westons has

invested in 24 new 200,000-litre tanks to increase storage capacity, each one holding about the same as Squeak, but these vats have not yet got names. All 24 will hold around one million gallons, which will allow for a modest expansion.

All of the waste water from Westons cider-making is treated in a natural wetlands area where reed beds clean and oxygenate the water. It takes nine months for the water to go through, then it is pumped back up to irrigate the bush orchards in the summer when it is dry, particularly the young perry orchard. Trees need a lot of water when starting out. Conversely, too much water is bad for them as well and the roots can rot.

Every company needs to keep experimenting with new ideas, and some old ones as well. As Tim says, 'We are forever looking at ways in which the market might go and we recently brought out an "in bottle" conditioned or bottle-fermented cider. We try to deliver full taste.' It is a fine line to tread sometimes. When you dance with the super-markets you are not quite sure who is playing the tune or when the band will stop. Though it must be said the supermarkets have been making good progress in showcasing premium cider, especially organic cider and perry. Some supermarkets have their own brand ciders made by large companies, some even with fruit from their own farms, as in the case of Waitrose and the Co-Op.

Tim told me a nice little story. He is visiting his local pub and sitting there minding his own business and in walks a lady and asks for pint of a certain well-known commercial brand, and she is told by the publican that they 'only have Westons'. She says, 'Oh no. That tastes of apples.' Tim had a little chuckle and thought, 'Oh well that's fine, carry on then.' This highlights quite nicely the public's perception of cider. Some don't even realise that it is made from apples.

My guide to the various different ciders Westons produce was Heather Mead. The range includes Bounds brand, a still cider; Old Rosie, a cloudy scrumpy named after the company's 1921 Aveling and Porter steamroller; draught scrumpy; organic premium cider; vintage; perry; an oak-conditioned cider; Stowford Press; a premium

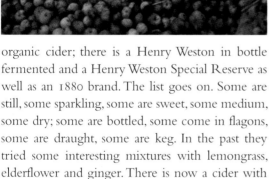

organic cider; there is a Henry Weston in bottle fermented and a Henry Weston Special Reserve as well as an 1880 brand. The list goes on. Some are still, some sparkling, some are sweet, some medium, some dry; some are bottled, some come in flagons, some are draught, some are keg. In the past they tried some interesting mixtures with lemongrass, elderflower and ginger. There is now a cider with raspberry.

Here Heather told me an amusing story. Originally their raspberry cider was called 'Kiss'. But this had to be abandoned as the Westons workers felt a little uneasy about going up to a butch barman in a pub and asking for a Kiss. Or come to that saying, 'Three pints of beer and the wife wants a Kiss'. So now it is called Cider with Raspberry, as opposed to Cider with Rosie.

Westons is one of the largest traditional cider-makers in the UK, and that is because it has concentrated on a niche market. The company also exports to about to 20 different countries.

So Henry Weston would, I think, be very proud of his great-grandchildren running the company. Not only are they selling cider with his name and his photograph on the bottles, they are employing many more people. He started with four men and a boy, and Westons now employs around 120 people, producing nearly 30,000 gallons per employee per year and most of the employees live within 5 miles of Much Marcle. Westons is a good example of a family business and factory operating discreetly in the countryside. I wonder if Henry Weston ever dreamed that his small enterprise would grow into such a giant.

CHAPTER 14

Blakeney and Butt, the Birthday Pear

HEREFORDSHIRE

James Marsden and Helen Woodman,
Gregg's Pit Cider and Perry, Much Marcle, Herefordshire

Much Marcle is not just the home of Westons; there are two other craft cidermakers, Gregg's Pit and Lyne Down. The name Gregg's Pit refers to a local variety of perry pear tree, to the smallholding itself, and even to a marl pit, which can still be seen in an adjacent orchard, often full of water and providing a home for newts, ducks and damselflies. We don't know who Gregg was, but the marl from the pit he dug in the eighteenth century is said to have been used to make the lime mortar for St Bartholomew's Church in the village. The Gregg's Pit pear is much valued for its ability to make a single-variety perry and, while past their prime, the trees are still to be found there 250 years after they were planted.

The present-day owners of Gregg's Pit, James Marsden and Helen Woodman, are heirs to an ancient and important tradition. James and Helen are very well organised and plan the cider-making season like a military operation. They'll put a calendar together around weekends from late September to mid-November, see which friends and family members are available to help, and blitz it. James says, 'We still pick up all the fruit by hand, us and our co-workers, into sacks, and then it comes back here in the back of a trailer. We try not

to wash the fruit. We wash if we think it really needs it but on the whole I like to pick up clean, because I want the wild yeasts on the fruit. That's why I want livestock out at the right time so there's no risk of cross-contamination. Six weeks before fruit fall, ideally. And when the cattle leave, I like to have the grass at about an inch and a half or two inches.'

The length of grass is important. Just enough so that the pears and apples bounce a little and are protected from bruising, but not so long that you lose them. James is very lucky because he is able to borrow some traditional Hereford cross heifers from Great Moorcourt Farm next door to graze the orchard over the summer months each year. On the other side of the property is a large old organic orchard belonging to Awnell's Farm and he has the use of the Blakeney Red pears from there, which make a good single variety in the Normandy style. They also provide the volume for blending with several different varieties.

For single-variety perry, James, of course, favours Gregg's Pit. 'It's fabulous, but I've only been able to make it once because I simply haven't had the volume, and then again it's a difficult pear to get, it's one of the early ones, but instead of coming

Opposite. Pedigree Hereford cattle at Awnell's farm, the next-door neighbours.

145

all at once, it comes in bits and bobs over a couple of weeks, and they don't keep very well. Thirty-six hours and you've lost them. It's very difficult to get enough volume unless you've got a very heavy crop. To make a single variety of that is quite unusual.'

The favourite blend for James is Gregg's Pit, Aylton Red and Blakeney. 'That combination is really good and I've made it year on year since I started. I just happened to discover that they were ready at the same time and found, following nature's course more or less, a combination of 30 per cent Gregg's Pit, 50 per cent Blakeney and 20 per cent Aylton Red makes a rounded, rich, complex and quite spicy perry. The other combination that I'm very fond of for a late-harvest perry is Blakeney and Butt. Butt is a late-season pear and I call it the birthday pear, because it's never ready for pressing before my birthday on the 30th October, and people often make the mistake of picking it far too young. This pear needs to be yellow and waxy before it's used. It's no good at all if it's still green and hasn't got that sticky, waxy feeling. But when it's fully ripe and blended with some late-harvest Blakeney, you've got a lot of natural fruit sugar to work with and high tannin and acidity from the Butt. The Butt has to be macerated for eight hours or overnight to lose some of that tannin, but a combination of about 70 per cent Butt, 30 per cent Blakeney works consistently well. I have occasionally made a single-variety Butt, but it works better with some Blakeney and in recent years I have been adding a few bags of Oldfield, another good late-season perry pear variety, to this blend.'

James really does know what he is doing and makes some of the best perry I have ever tasted, on a par with Tom Oliver and Kevin Minchew. And here the small producers win out. They are only making a small quantity, but what they do make can be exceptional.

James mills the perry pears straight from the orchard, macerates them in half barrels overnight and then first thing the following morning he'll press them. Like all small producers, he is very keen to experiment and he has learned by trial and error

what works and what does not. Thorn is quite variable, it can be very sharp, which has the advantage that in the right year, if you've got the right balance of acidity, tannin and residual sugar levels after the first fermentation, you can then make bottle-fermented (*méthode champenoise*) from that variety very successfully.

One of the godfathers of perry pears was Ray Williams from Long Ashton, and until Ray came to visit, James didn't know that he had an indigenous variety of perry pear. 'Ray came and he looked at the trees in the home orchard and he looked at the trees over there, and he was quite clear that this was the Gregg's Pit pear, which was obviously thrilling, and I then propagated loads of it because I wanted to have more trees of the home variety.

'The pear is named after the property. The cottage we're sitting in now, where the stair went, that would have been a ladder, just a hatch through into what was really just a loft bedroom. It wouldn't have been full height at all, and what is now the kitchen was the cowshed, a lean-to against the north wall, a two up, two down, and this frame here is 1785 or earlier. Probably earlier, because I've got a deed of 1785 with the house on it. The pear was obviously around then, because on the map, on that 1785 map, it shows both the name of the property and the orchard with the marl pit in it. So all of that tells us something about the history, and the pear follows the name of the property and the pit.'

The story gets better, because when James took the graft wood to propagate the new trees in 1996, he took it along to Mac-the-Knife, a well-known grafter, at Bulmers Field Farm. They hadn't got a mother tree of Gregg's Pit, so it was a new variety to them, and then they grew on the new trees for him. This sort of story about recovering old varieties is extremely important, because they are so easily lost.

But it is not just the perry pear that James has rescued, it is the whole property. He bought Gregg's Pit in 1992 and it was unfit for human habitation. 'The property was condemned, and the orchard – you couldn't see that it was an orchard – looked like a wood. Scrub, ivy up the trees, bramble, you name it. It was as derelict as the house really. So I spent all that autumn and winter clearing the orchard and there was no harvest in '92 at all.'

Then it was a matter of getting some stock in to graze the orchard and get the pasture back. In 1993 he was able to harvest two tons of pears and took them down the road to Westons, load by load in the back of his car. He made ten or twelve trips to get the volume there, but these beautifully nurtured, hand-picked pears were just going into the tump (the long mound of pears) with all the others and down the chute. James thought, 'Damn it, I've got to do something better with these.' So he talked to Jean Nowell at Lyne Down round the corner and she said, 'Why don't you bring them here?' So in 1994, James took his harvest to Jean, and did a deal where she taught him the tricks of the trade. He came away with his first barrel of perry and hasn't looked back.

Jean Nowell was well known for the quality of her perry and James could not have learnt from a better tutor. She had been making perry for at least ten years. In 1995 James made three or four barrels at Lyne Down and then in 1996 Jean suggested that, because what he was producing was reasonably drinkable, he should enter it for a few competitions. James entered his blend of Blakeney and Butt for the Big Apple, the annual event that is centred on Much Marcle, and the Hereford Cider Museum competitions that year, and it won both, which was remarkable for a novice. He has since won the Big Apple Champion Perry trophy eight times, most recently in 2007.

The next step was bottling, and in those days you could go to Three Choirs Vineyard and they would process a barrel or two at reasonable cost. And that's how James's hobby evolved into a commercial enterprise, in true Cobbett style – William Cobbet wrote a famous book called *Cottage Economy* in 1821, which extolled the virtues of being frugal and inventive, as every true cottager has to be. James's business has grown tenfold since then, and now he is making about 5,500 litres, which is just over 1,000 gallons. The increase in volume has enabled James to invest in shiny new stainless steel vats and a wonderful green oak-

147

CHAPTER 15
Adam and Eve
HEREFORDSHIRE

Ivor and Susie Dunkerton,
Dunkertons, Pembridge, Leominster, Herefordshire

As I approached Pembridge on the main road from Leominster I was held up behind a Welsh haulage lorry going west carrying big square bales of straw for bedding and fodder to Rhayder and beyond. It meant I could have a good long view of the fertile rolling farmland. Pembridge still looks medieval, and is very pleasing on the eye in that understated half-timbered, black-and-white Herefordshire way. Take a left turn at the New Inn and follow your nose till you reach Hays Head, a farm that proclaims itself as Dunkertons Cider and Perry. You have reached the holy of holies in this area. When I last visited, there was a young man who had come all the way from Seattle just to test the cider.

Ivor Dunkerton was charming, as always. We chatted a while and then he took me out into the orchard and introduced me to Claes Mark, the Swedish pruner and orchard keeper who was hard at work in the Foxwhelps. Claes is quite a character and is zealous about pruning. This part of Herefordshire feels untouched by such things as computers and satellite dishes, but you can sometimes hear Polish being spoken down the lanes as PhD students pick strawberries for Tesco. 'Every little helps.' Just down the road is Luntley Court and its 1673 dovecote, an exquisite little building beside Tippet's Brook. Vernacular architecture in Herefordshire means oak. Things are deeply rooted in the soil here.

When Ivor and Susie moved to Hays Head there was no cider orchard, only Bramleys and eating apples – the previous owners had been teetotal. 'So we came here with 18 acres and started to try and make a living. That was about 1979.' They have been planting orchards ever since, even an avenue of perry pears, including Thorn and Moorcroft. But as Ivor says, 'Perry pears are very difficult. Moorcroft, for example, are very difficult to grow, but Thorn are very easy. Moorcroft are reckoned to make the best perry, but Thorn makes a good perry too.' Planting avenues of perry pear trees is a peculiarly Herefordshire thing. Many large houses had them and one or two still do. The avenue of The Hellens in Much Marcle was planted in 1710 and one or two of the original trees are still there. In blossom they are magnificent.

Ivor is very keen on his perry. Over the road they have just planted another 150 standard perry pear trees, with about a dozen different varieties, which are growing extremely well. 'They've only been in two years, but they were loaded with pears.' Last year he had to go around with a pair of scissors 'chopping off thousands of pears, otherwise they would have snapped. Simple as that. It's rather a shame. A hundred and fifty trees is an awful lot of pears.'

Ivor and Susie have been making cider for 26 years. Before that Ivor was in London working as a senior television producer for the BBC with Fyfe Robertson on the much-admired *Tonight* programme, a forerunner of *Newsnight* with Jeremy Paxman. Current affairs were served up by such illustrious names as Cliff Mitchelmore, Macdonald Hastings and Alan Whicker. Ivor was earning good money but he was spending a lot of time abroad. 'My wife and I wanted to be together more so we sold up in London, bought 18 acres and wanted to live off the land.' They chose a part of Herefordshire they had discovered on their honeymoon. Ivor remembers people saying that 'I was an absolute idiot to leave the BBC. Nick Ross particularly said I was a fool. I saw him again about a year ago and he decided that perhaps I wasn't so stupid after all.'

'Our eighteen acres was the size of the park that we lived next to in London; it seemed vast to us.' The soil is fairly heavy clay but not much stone. In the spirit of John Seymour and the self-sufficiency movement, the couple got into cider-making just for survival. They multiple-suckled

cows with lots of calves and they were very successful. They had auctioneers ringing them up and saying 'Have you got any more?' They have bought more land since, but farming and cider production were interlinked.

Dunkertons is one of the few commercial organic perry producers. Last year it supplied Waitrose, and the perry was so successful that it ran out, which is always one of the problems with small high-quality producers.

I asked Ivor if he was related to the Somerset Dunkertons, who come from the Glastonbury area and even have the ultimate accolade of having a cider apple named after them, the Dunkertons Late. Robust and fairly disease resistant, it was raised in the 1940s and is sometimes known as the Dunkertons Sweet. Ivor received a letter from Bill Dunkerton, whose father had raised the apple, but there was no direct link, although Ivor's family did originally come from the West Country.

In those early days Ivor freely admits that he was slowly sliding towards becoming a peasant and quite liked it. 'My wife Susie noticed that there

Right. Claes Mark pruning Foxwhelp.

were cider apples lying about underneath trees and Bulmers hadn't been buying that year, so off we go, thanks to a really lovely guy, Geoff Williams. He's the guy who started most small cidermakers off. Originally from Long Ashton, then he went over to Bulmers and started tins of Scrumpy Jack. When Bulmers finally got hold of him, because he was working for Greenall Whitney I think, he had it written in his contract that he mustn't help any small cidermakers. This was absolute nonsense because he came over here, sat over there with the first cans of Scrumpy Jack. To my horror it was quite good, but he knew what he was doing. So that started us off, and we started with black plastic vats. We bought a press for £100, we bought a mill for £100, we built a barn out there which could, if necessary, be converted to cattle.'

So Ivor and Susie started from scratch but they had expert advice. When Ivor's mother died she left him £20,000, and they bought the field next door and planted a few thousand trees. Because they decided to be organic, they had problems with some varieties. Why go organic? Ivor says it was a gut reaction. 'We watched what was going on around here and being outsiders you see things perhaps more sharply, and we noticed that hares were disappearing, the curlew were no longer crying out there in the spring, and so we decided right from the word go that we would use only unsprayed apples. That was the beginning. Then we moved over to being totally organic. We were the first cidermakers in Herefordshire to become organic. So we started making cider. We made very curious cider, I would say, then it slowly went on and we now sell all we make, which is quite good.'

Ivor and Susie started bottling in 1981 and they showed me their original label 'May 1982' with all the apple varieties listed on it. 'Sherington Norman, Old Foxwhelp, Hope, Medaille d'Or, Yarlington Mill. We designed the label with a local artist, Peter Horrocks. Though I have to tell you it was an Indian friend who I was chatting to here, and I said we were trying to find a logo, and he said, "You've got one hanging in your bathroom", and that was Adam and Eve.'

The label is superb, with a muscley Adam and

a voluptuous Eve stepping out of a Herefordshire Garden of Eden. Other cider varieties are Sheep's Nose, Brown Snout, improved Kingston Black, Balls Bitter Sweet.

The first labelled cider was dry, in other words fermented out. Other cidermakers feel exactly the same – what they want to do is sell dry cider because that is where the full flavour is, not masked by sweetness.

Ivor and Susie then started making single-variety ciders. They started with Court Royal, which is a Somerset apple, sometimes known as Pound Apple. It is a large green apple with an orange flush. Ivor also tried Breakwell's Seedling, which is a Monmouth apple. They still ferment their apples as single varieties and then blend them afterwards, so Ivor can always know exactly where they are. Ivor is helped by Rob West, who has been making cider with him for 20 years. And because Ivor has planted his orchards in specific rows, picking single varieties is easy. He pays a good premium for excellent hand-picked fruit. 'We pay £130 a tonne you see. That keeps all the organic

growers happy.' The going rate is anything between £60 and £90 for non-organic fruit delivered in.

What was Ivor's first taste of cider? 'Those first glasses of cider in childhood were just stunning. It was certainly still and I think quite sweet. It was appley and lovely, which we can achieve here sometimes. I got one the other day that we bottled, and I thought, it's exactly like the cider when I was a child.' Ivor is keen to keep his cider naturally sweet if he can and won't buy in bitter-sharp apples such as Bulmer's Norman, which is actually a French apple; and he won't use Tremlett's Bitter and the Jersey apples.

Ivor started out with the aim of making the best bottled cider in Europe and he might just have got there. They started out with a wine bottle with a cork. Even in the early 1980s they were trying to push cider upmarket, which was no mean task in those days. Since then they send their cider to Fortnum & Mason. 'Harrods couldn't take it because the bottles were too big. We went to smaller bottles simply because we found that old ladies, who were quite keen on the cider because it

Above right. Ivor Dunkerton testing the latest batch before bottling with Rob West, the cidermaker.

brought back happy memories, couldn't carry them around because they were too heavy, and it was too much cider. So we went to 75s [cl], and 33s [cl], and 66os [ml]. Our 500 ml bottles are a bit different to everyone else's.'

Not all of the trees survived under organic conditions. Kingston Black suffered badly from canker. Ivor lost about 1,000 trees, which had to be cut down. 'There were two things we were going to do here: one was to make cheese, we thought, and then cider. We thought we'd make cider at one point. And then when old Bill Dunkerton wrote the letter, he said, "Dunkertons have been making cider and cheese for centuries". So we thought, oh well, there you go. This must be in our genes. Although you wouldn't know it.'

Talking of genes, one of Ivor's sons runs a well-known clothing firm called Cult in Cheltenham. Ivor hopes he might buy a field or two for his old dad so that he can keep up with the planting schedule.

One of the things Ivor loves is pouring the sparkling cider. 'We experimented with French cider and I found it quite fun, but it's just not as interesting as English cider. If you get English cider right there's a lot of background and depth. It's quite exciting.'

What does he look for in his cider? 'I suppose the truth is I would be looking for a small amount of sweetness, and I would be looking for complexity of flavours. That's really what it's about. Some of them are quite extraordinary. Some sweetness, but that's because I had it when I was aged fifteen and cycling in Devon. My first impression was how lovely this was. This was at a pub I'd stop at at lunchtime and I hadn't any money. I remember cycling up Porlock Hill. When I was very small my parents would buy me Cidrax. But I remember going to Brixham in Devon during the war, and the interesting thing there was eating a crab sandwich and having a half pint of cider. That's a memory which I cherish.'

But to go back can sometimes be disappointing. 'Susie and I went back there a few years later and every pub on that harbour sold Bulmers. I mean, what's happened to all the people in Devon?'

Above. Cider, perry and upmarket chocolate.

Ivor also does specialist bottlings for weddings and special events. 'Sparkling perry is particularly popular and is best drunk before the meal. It is so subtle that it can often be overshadowed by such things as mutton. They need a good chunky cider to go with them.'

It was Susie who suggested that they ought to be bottling perry. To begin with they just sold it as draught. But visitors to the cider house were slightly confused. 'They'd say, "Perry? Do you mean water? Perrier water?"'

Ivor says that most people think perry is just cider made from perry pears. 'It's very different. I would say perry is perry and I wish they'd leave it alone. It's on its own in my view, it's nothing like wine. I think it should be an aperitif, and I don't think it should be there on the table. Most food will knock the flavour out.'

I asked Ivor what varieties of perry pears he uses. 'Merrylegs is one, Red Horse. It's reliable but it doesn't make very good perry. What we would tend to do is get bulk off the Red Horse and then hopefully get others to mix in, but good perry is not easy to make. We've got some out there which is absolutely stunning, one of the best we've made, very subtle, very fragrant. We do a still perry, which is the best one, and we do a sparkling perry.

'We reckon that the people we sell to are the middle classes. Fortnum & Mason, Waitrose. Our cider's quite strong. The stronger it is the more it keeps its flavour. If you don't have it at 6.5 per cent, it'll go off. We've got Foxwhelp, for example, which is one of the greatest cider apples; there's about 2,000 gallons out there. Dabinett are on the trees for much longer, we've actually had it to nine and a half degrees.

'Black Fox. That's a blend. We don't filter very heavily, so we don't have very bright cider. We use only the cider apples. My feeling is that the complexity that we're talking about is there with cider apples but it's not there in cooking apples, certainly not Bramleys. If you go into eating apples, I remember Geoff Williams at Long Ashton going through eating apples, and it's pretty awful cider. If you take an apple like Foxwhelp, the nose on Foxwhelp is just stunning. You just open the tank and you're knocked out. You don't get that with eating apples. Cider apples are cider apples.' The Foxwhelps are quite early, a bitter-sharp grown widely in Herefordshire and Gloucestershire and dating from around 1600.

The year's crop is often dependent on the weather at blossom time and the effect it has on the bees. Lots of rain will actually stop the bees from flying. Ivor feeds the bees in the orchard at certain times and his hives are flourishing. 'It was autumn so I fed them.' It is all part of the interdependence of cidermakers and nature.

Ivor's gamble has paid off. He and Susie now have 38 acres of orchard and are possibly the only ones with organic bush orchards. They make around 50,000 gallons of cider and perry. As far as keeping cider is concerned, Ivor reckons wood is a waste of time: he has top-grade stainless steel vats. 'The apple we put into this is the apple we get out. If you put it in wood, it can sometimes be more unpredictable.'

Ivor is very much a man of the moment. Sensibly, he will drink what's good at that particular time, whether it is beer, cider or perry. 'I drink Black Fox cider, and I drink the medium still cider.'

At one stage they thought of putting a distillery in their Cider House Restaurant, but distilleries require enormous capital and a bonded warehouse and dealing with too many regulations, and besides, real peasants don't like paperwork. Susie is now using the kitchens in partnership with Lorraine Williams for making upmarket chocolates, some of which contain King Offa Cider Brandy.

As I drove back into Hereford I got stuck agian, this time behind a small flatbed truck, and in the back I could see great bundles of mistletoe with white berries gently bouncing as the vehicle proceeded towards Hereford at a sedate 30 miles an hour, no doubt destined for a farmer's market or one of the mistletoe auctions held in Tenbury Wells. Adam and Eve?

Opposite. The 1673 dovecot half a mile down the road at Luntley Court.

CHAPTER 16

Winnal's Longdon and the Cider Horn

HEREFORDSHIRE

Paul Stephens,
Newton Court Cider, Newton,
Leominster, Herefordshire

Newton Court is a very pleasant farmyard just tucked away off the main road three or four miles south of Leominster near the large Cadbury's chocolate factory at Marlbrook. Like many of the up and coming cider and perry makers, Paul Stephens is relatively young and only started making cider commercially in 2000. Paul took a course on cidermaking with Peter Mitchell at Hindlip College in Worcestershire and this gave him the confidence to get started. He need not have worried for, as he says, his 'grandparents were heavily involved in cider and perry'. One grandfather was at Ivington Farm, near the River Arrow and his other grandmother was at Bartestree, on the Ledbury road out of Hereford, which is famous for its perry pear, the Bartestree Squash.

As with many Herefordshire families, their business was hops and cider. Peter's grandfather, Jack Stephens, worked in a hop yard in his younger days and then went on to work for Bertram Bulmer. 'He was in orcharding, all sorts of jobs. I think one of his main jobs was looking after horses. This would have been in the 1920s. This was my father's father, the one with the cider horn. It would have been fascinating to see what it was tasting like then.'

By cider horn, Paul means a small horn cup, which farm workers used to have about their person just in case a flagon of cider happened to appear in the fields. Horn cups are very light and practical and, unlike glass or china, rarely break when dropped. They are made from cow horns, no doubt from Hereford cattle. Often they are only two or three inches long. Paul found this particular horn in the cider barn when he was tidying up and he uses it for testing his cider and perry.

Paul knew his grandfather well. He was still alive in 1991 when they all came to Newton Court from Ivington, where his grandfather had a small cider orchard. Paul's uncle, Doug Stephens, being the elder brother, carried on making the cider just for the family. He died at quite an early age: 'He was only about fifty-one, fifty-two; it was quite a shock, but he had two or three barrels made each year up until then.'

Paul has his own ideas as to why farmhouse cidermaking stopped suddenly. Tractors. He could well be right. 'Talking to people who made farmhouse cider, what really came to the crunch was when tractors started coming on to farms and people lost their horse and you didn't have anything to mill fruit with, and I think that was one of the reasons why you lost a lot of the farmhouse cider. Every farm in Herefordshire had a cider mill and a horse up till that point.'

When the family arrived, Newton Court was

set up for hops and had its own hop kiln as well as a cider mill, cider press and cellar. It was one of the biggest working cider mills Paul has seen to date and had facilities for making large quantities of cider. A loft in the barn above where they made the cider must have been able to store many tons of cider fruit, which would then drop down into the mill. That old building was converted to a dwelling, but the orchards were replanted in 1950. Paul has 15 acres of cider apple orchards, and a lot of it is on a lime soil. There are lime kilns down the road in the banks. 'It doesn't seem to affect the trees but the fields do change quite drastically in their soil structure, and you do notice it does make a different drink. It's chalk underneath.'

Paul's father also worked in a hop yard and he used to help make cider when he was a lot younger, with his father and brother. But as Paul remembers, 'what really got us into making cider was when a chap came to stay with us from New Zealand, Brian Shanks. We were taking fruit into Bulmers, and it was when Bulmers were struggling to make ends meet in the late 1990s, and he had a few tons of cider fruit. Bulmers have a small facility for doing small trials of cider and he had some of our cider fruit and made a few hundred bottles of cider for us and the rest is history really.'

Paul had been to Hereford Tech to do a course in agricultural engineering and so by trade he is an agricultural engineer, which is mighty useful if you are keen on welding and playing around with cider machinery. He made his own cider press, which sits up in the barn in the corner of the orchard. Paul had also been on various training courses in Austria and he could see that there were a lot of perry pears out there. Then one day, by chance, a group of Austrian perry makers visited him in Newton Court: 'They brought some of their perry over, which I tried. It was very nice. They bottle it very young, it's very clean, very well-balanced perry; it was carbonated, it was a very distinct perry.' Paul had tried perry in France and had found it insipid with not much body. What intrigued him about Austria was that they planted their perry pears, not in orchards, but in avenues in the fields, instead of hedges. 'I would love to go back over there in the autumn.'

Paul buys in a certain amount of fruit and, like many producers, says it is very difficult to get people to pick perry pears. 'It's fiddly getting them off the tree, it's fiddly picking them up, and it's fiddly to make it.' He has access to some old orchards but with perry, 'you have a few perry pear trees, which have remained amongst the standard cider fruit, and they're growing about twice the size of the rest of the orchard so we have to try and go into the orchard without damaging the rest of the fruit that's fallen on the ground. I hand pick but

I've got a little picker, and if I can, get hold of them before they've been on the floor for too long. You've only got a very narrow window in which to go in and pick the fruit, and it has to be pressed almost immediately.'

He puts them into sacks or straight on to a small trailer, so they're not handled too much. 'We've got plenty of room and it's washed off and stored ready for pressing.' The press he made is hydraulic and if he has three or four helping he can press more than 1,400 gallons in a day, and that is a lot of fruit. How much juice you get per ton depends on the quality of the fruit and the juice content. Paul reckons to get between 600 and 700 litres, which is about 120 gallons per ton.

His favourite pear is Winnal's Longdon and he has access to a lot of them. 'For me, that is the best perry pear for making a good drink; they're a pretty good all-round pear. This is a young orchard; it's not too far away from here. I'm very lucky; I look after the person who owns it. They say they are biannual but we've found that they're very productive orchards actually. It's a standard or even semi-standard orchard.' Winnal's Longdon, according to Dr Robert Hogg, technical editor of *Herefordshire Pomona*, published by the Woolhope Naturalists' Field Club, was raised by Mr Winnall of Woodfield in the parish of Weston-under-Penyard, near Ross, in about 1790. It tends to ripen in the first two

weeks of October and gives a medium-to-high acid, low tannin perry of good quality.

Because of his job, Paul meets a lot of farmers and has noticed that they are planting more bush orchards. Even the Austrians are putting in a lot of bush orchards of perry pears. Paul knows of one farmer who has a contract with Westons, but 'if you're going to start doing that you need to know what varieties you can mechanically pick. There's no use planting Thorn or something that's going to be ready in the second week in September and is going to go to mush straight away'.

As Paul says: 'Jim Franklin, who's retired from cidermaking, he reckons that every seventh year you'd have a vintage year, but I'm very interested in the Normandy method of preserving cider. I found the best way for me was to bottle it in the late part of the winter and to have it naturally cloudy, the sediment in the bottom, but a sparkling drink the following year. Today's customer needs a sweetness in their drink, so you've got a naturally sweet, naturally fizzy fantastic drink. I will continue to do that.'

He has been winning prizes, and got first prize in the Hereford Museum of Cider competition for his sparkling perry in 2006. His secret is to keep everything clean. 'Hygiene. I do take a lot of time, it's a lot of work to keep your cloths clean, but they have to be pristine. Your fermenting vessels have to be spotlessly clean. Good ripe fruit, I wash my fruit

before I press. If I'm doing a draught product we will use a yeast, but if it's for my bottle fermented, I let it ferment naturally.'

Paul makes roughly 8,000 gallons every year, so that is quite a commitment at harvest time. And almost half of that is perry. So he is making 4,000 gallons of perry: some is sold draught and some bottled. He is going to start some contract bottled and carbonated for various shops. Unfortunately draught perry doesn't travel well, and the only way he can supply that is through his own shop. 'We sell our products in the Hop Pocket [Hop Pocket Wine Company]; they take a considerable amount – Orchard, Hive and Vine – they market that on the internet. Local village stores, Canon Pyon and CAMRA are probably our biggest customers.'

He has about 15 acres of cider fruit, but buys in certain varieties such as Yarlington Mill, Dabinett, Stoke Red, and Kingston Black if he can get his hands on it. 'It's not a very productive tree so there are limited supplies.'

Like many cidermakers, Paul doesn't make a living out of it, so during the week he is working as an agricultural engineer and at weekends he makes the cider and perry. During the week his parents run the farm shop. Customers are mostly local and passing trade and Paul is getting a good following. But he feels it could be better. What frustrates him are the tied pubs. 'I cannot get into our local pubs. There's still a stigma attached to draught cider; there's still some ropey cider being made.'

The future? At the moment Paul is very optimistic because there seems to be a huge demand for cider, and providing people still want it, he'll continue to make it. 'People are hugely aware of what they're eating and drinking now, and I think cider definitely fits into this new food culture. Cider goes so well with food, we've always enjoyed cider with the Sunday roast, we've always had cider or perry.'

His parents are equally positive. 'They have been taken aback by how popular it is, and the awards give you confidence. I've taken overall champion at the Big Apple cider trials at Putley in 2003; I've had a couple of awards from CAMRA; and definitely had first prize at the Cider Museum last year; and I've picked up various prizes for the bottle fermented.'

It pays to be patient. 'A lot of my perry seems

to take a long time to ferment out, and I've been led to believe that the longer it ferments the better. One of the problems with the cider trials is they have them too early; they could do with being six weeks later. I've seen corks popping out of demijohns on trestle tables in village halls.'

Cider and perry making is for Paul both an art and a science. He puts a yeast in for his draught products just to make sure that it ferments all the way out, because you can get stuck in fermentation and this runs the risk of it going off. Ciders he blends, but once his perries are finished they are not touched at all. 'It does not like being thrown in with other perries once it's finished fermenting. You can blend cider but you can't blend perry'.

The qualities he is looking for in a good perry: 'it's got to be well balanced, it's got to have quite a powerful taste when you bite into it, an almost harsh taste, some of them have a higher juice content than others. We use Winnal's Longdon, Blakeney Red and the Gin trees that I have access to are not very productive for some reason, but they make fantastic perry.'

Orchard work is always important. 'We're always replanting trees. We have an old orchard which always suffers when we have a gale. We've lost up to 15, 20 trees this year, so it's an ongoing process. The rest of the farm is organic.' It is registered with the Soil Association and runs to 155 acres of mixed arable, beef and sheep. The cider is organic but is not marketed as organic. 'We can only say it's made from organically grown fruit. We can't put organic on the bottle. The only time I will do that is if we're competing on a supermarket shelf, and the organic bit on the label will give us the edge.'

As an agricultural engineer, Paul works on combines and tractors. His work takes him all over the local countryside so he sees a lot of orchards. 'It's fair to say I've got a good idea of the location of perry orchards, not only in Herefordshire but also in Gloucestershire.'

Paul has also noticed a change in the perception of cider over the last five years. 'There's still a stigma attached to it, but it's shaking that off. I think we're going to see an explosion in the interest in perry. I think people like ourselves have to make sure that if the interest is there, it's followed up. If you've taken the time to pick that fruit and make it, you're going to make sure that it's reasonable to drink. It's fair to say that it's half as much work again as cider. It would be nice if the price reflected that!'

He does pasteurise sometimes. 'If it's going to be carbonated and sweetened, it'll be pasteurised, but again, this is why we've gone back to the bottle fermented. Some of the French ones are still very sweet, with an alcohol content of only around 3 to 3.5 per cent. So if you think your average cider is 7 to 8 per cent, half of the sugar that went into making that apple is still in the bottle, so you've still got all that sweetness there, and if the fermentation isn't controlled properly it's going to want to become dry, to ferment out. So the trick is to make sure that when the cider is put into that bottle it goes on to ferment a little bit to give you the effervescence, but not so much as it's going to go completely dry. The yeast then dies off and you're left with a nice carbonated drink.

'I do keeve, we press it, I add salt and calcium and keeve, and within about ten days of pressing it you're left with a brown cap and a little sediment in the bottom. So the trick is then to retrieve what's in between the two and then let that ferment out to whatever sweetness you want, so your cider is then a sweet cider.'

Half the trick is to get your friends to drink your cider and perry, as they are your best ambassadors. What is reassuring is that Paul feels he is part of a continuous tradition passed on from his father and grandfather. 'For me it's always been in the family, so this is a natural progression, and to be able to make a living from it as well is fantastic. We're expanding slowly, and to comply with the local legislation is proving to be costly, but once you've done that then you're away. The future's fairly rosy. There's no reason at all why it shouldn't be.'

Paul is a very good example of a go-ahead young man who has made it his mission to make the best perry and cider he can, and all this in his spare time. No doubt his grandfather would like to have another nip out of his horn cup.

CHAPTER 17

Faith, Hope and Charity

HEREFORDSHIRE

Mike Johnson,
*Ross-on-Wye Cider and Perry Company, Broome Farm,
Peterstow, Ross-on-Wye, Herefordshire*

Ross-on-Wye, at the southern end of the county, is a marvellous town. The Wye here is quite wide and slightly lugubrious as it winds its way down to Monmouth before gaining momentum on its famous run to Tintern and Chepstow, before it meets its big sister, the Severn. Mike Johnson's farm is tucked away at Peterstow. The Wye is only a mile away and so his small, sheltered valley is part of the benign weather system that is often associated with large rivers. The red sandstone soils around Ross are reckoned to be some of the best in the country; they can grow anything, and drain very quickly. Orchards, soft fruit, poly tunnels and asparagus beds abound. The market in Ross is always bursting with fresh produce.

Mike has been making his own cider and perry for more than 20 years and before that his father made it at different intervals: even his grandfather made it in the early years. Mike's family came here in 1930 from near Leominster in north Herefordshire. His grandparents had cattle and sheep and they wanted to move to a bigger place; his grandmother also ran the farm as a guesthouse. At the end of the 1940s their farm was only about 20 acres, but the next farm came up for sale, which was another 40 acres, and Mike's father wisely acquired it.

In the 1950s they actually stopped making

cider and his father sold all the equipment to a neighbour, which left the shed free to rear calves in.

But as Mike says: 'We're now 65 acres. We'd always grown apples, of course. Herefordshire is probably the best climate because we have a lot of sun and probably a bit less rainfall than Somerset, so you're guaranteed much better quality apples, generally. All the fruit trees were on the original farm and around the buildings here. From my memory when I was a kid, there were about half-a-dozen different perry pears down the bottom here, but very old trees and eventually they all disappeared.'

So they kept the orchards on and sold the apples every year to Bulmers. And that might very well have been it if certain key decisions hadn't been made in Hereford. As Mike comments, 'We didn't really make cider seriously until about 1984 or '85. Bulmers were buying all our fruit until that year and then suddenly they decided they didn't want it all because I think they were buying cheap concentrate from France, so we had about ten tons that year and they said they would only take four tons. So we thought, what shall we do with the rest? So we turned it into cider, and from that time on we've made cider for selling.'

So in a sense Bulmers did him a great favour.

As for Mike, it changed his life and now he has

replanted the whole area. About 25 years ago he bought a collection of perry pear trees from Bulmers. 'They were the nursery trees and they'd got a bit out of shape, and they were clearing them out and redoing them, so we got a job lot of about 27 varieties and there were 84 trees, and we put all those in then and now they're producing quite a lot of perry. They straightened up when they were allowed to grow. We lost one or two from a bit of disease, but apart from that, they're producing quite a lot of perry now.'

Broome Farm was a dairy farm until the late 1970s, and then Mike went travelling. 'I went to Europe, lived in Germany for a couple of years and Australia for a year, and other parts of Britain for a couple of years. The Wye Valley is a funny place. Most of my school friends moved away when they were young but most of them have come back because there's something about it; you just love being here. I feel I'm really lucky in my lifestyle. I'm not well off in the cash sense, but it's still a fantastic place to live. My sister and brother-in-law now run the guesthouse. They've got a small restaurant here, but my sister was saying the other day, she's so tired, but she's completely booked up for the month. We don't actually advertise, it's just regulars and word of mouth.'

Word of mouth makes a big difference. Mike is very proactive and runs his own small music festivals. He does the wassail in January and has musical events in the summer, about once a month. 'We're going to have Blues in July, Folk in August and then the festival in September, which has a whole mix of people.' He usually gets about eight other cidermakers to come. Last year they were Harechurch Cider from Gloucester, Seidr Dai from Wales, Barbourne Cider from Worcester, and Dennis Gwatkin, Rob Uren and James Marsden from local Herefordshire. 'One of the rules is that you should be there selling it yourself so people can come in and talk to you about it. We don't advertise it very much; we don't want more than 300 people or so because of fitting them in. We hold it in the big barn so it's under cover. We've been doing it for five years now. It's always the first weekend of September. We chose then because it's close

enough for people to go out in the orchard and see the apples, and before we start getting really busy.'

'These sorts of events are magnificent because they get people on to the farm and they can see the fruit and they can talk to the cidermakers and drink their cider and perry, listen to the band and then hopefully find their way back to the tent in the early hours. Any profits go to a named charity, usually in Africa or a third world country.'

It sounds brilliant, like a mini Glastonbury festival, but much more mellow. But one word of warning: certain perry pears can get their own back. One of the oldest pear trees on Mike's farm is called Holmer, well known for its diuretic qualities, which is graphically reflected in its local name of Startlecock.

Mike starts making cider in the middle of September. 'We've got an early pear called Paske No. 1. It came with the collection from Bulmers. It comes in the middle of September and then there's usually a few windfalls as well that we put in with it. Applewise, what we tend to do is pick up quite a few of the windfalls in the early part, try to resist

shaking any because they're just not ready if you shake them. We do a bit of apple juice for the festival, which is our first pressing, which is usually Discovery or Worcesters.' These he buys in from his neighbour. He has varieties that would suit apple juice, but they are October varieties.

He makes a single-variety cider, Foxwhelp. 'It's a really good blending cider. It adds a lot of attitude, it's got plenty of acidity, it always smells of apples. I would say it's a really high-quality apple. I don't have a lot of Kingston Black. I wish I did. I have planted an orchard of them, which is about three or four years old, but it's a standard orchard, so it's going to be years before it comes into its own.'

Kingston Black makes a single variety but is also very useful for blending as well. 'Most single varieties are unbalanced: sometimes they work – a bitter-sweet cider, for example – you've got to have the taste for it. A lot of people don't like bitter-sweet ciders because they don't give you anything when you first put them in your mouth, it's all in the swallow, but I actually prefer them.' Mike also has some customers who love what he calls 'the

Above. Picking up apples in the autumn with a Pattenden Grouse self-propelled harvester.

sharp stuff'. Most of his ciders tend to be a blend of about 20 to 30 per cent of a bitter-sharp or a sharp, and the rest is bitter sweet. He continues making cider right into December. Butt perry pears are usually the last things that he presses. 'Some years I've gone on pressing into January, when it's really cold, and you get a much better cider if you leave them longer.'

Mike does not just drink his own cider; he is a connoisseur and all his regulars bring him ciders from all over the country whenever they go away, which he likes to compare. 'The thing that strikes me most often is that people have pressed under-ripe fruit. They're quite hard ciders, even the tannins are hard when you swallow, and it lacks that mellow quality that you get from ripe fruit. I think we did a lot in the early days. It's a temptation to press early because the apples look great and you can get on with it, but if you want a soft cider ...'

So it pays to be patient, and this is where the small-to-medium-sized producers win out: sheer quality if they really know what they are doing. In the old days, from the photographs Mike has seen, they used to let the apples mature in the yard before pressing them. But it doesn't work with all of them. 'You wouldn't do it with the Foxwhelps because they don't have the keeping quality, but when you get to know the fruit you know how well they keep. A lot of the perry pears can be left, but you have to watch them carefully because they can change every day.' This is real hands-on stuff. No computers, just human judgement, intuition and local knowledge.

Mike initially learned cidermaking from his father, and he's perfected it over 20 or so years. 'I'm a great believer that you must drink it regularly and develop your palate. You have to keep sizing up the cider just to check whether it is taking bad ways. Basic hygiene is important and in a farm situation when you rack from one barrel to another obviously the new barrel has got to be clean.' He uses all natural yeasts, 'But you must put that 50 to 100 parts of sulphite in just to stop off the flavours. I always put cling film around my bungs because what you tend to do is put the bungs down on all sorts of dirty places, and then you put them back in

the top without thinking about it.' Small things like that really matter.

His father really enjoys the cider. 'I think he's quite pleased with the way the cider's going. We started it because on 65 acres nothing's really viable.' And there is another Bulmers twist to the story. A few years after Mike started making cider, the price of apple concentrate went through the roof. 'So Bulmers turned round and offered us new contracts for 30 years from date of planting, and I then decided I'd plant every field that I could that was machine harvestable. So we've now got 40 acres that we harvest for Bulmers. Until five years ago we made 1,500 gallons, just below the limit, then when Bulmers had a financial crisis again five years ago, they said, "We're sorry to say, but when the contracts run out we won't be renewing them because we're oversupplied."' Mike had one year left on one contract, so he thought, 'What am I going to do with 30 tons of apples? The only thing I can do is start straight away and make more cider, and see if I can sell it.' Luckily it coincided with the new cider boom, so he has gone from 1,500 gallons to 8,000 gallons in about 5 years. Bulmers has since decided that it will now renew contracts.

What also appeals to me is the diversity of other interests that cidermakers have and how they bolster their income from other sources. In Mike's case it is not just the small festivals, which are very popular, but also the bed and breakfast that his sister runs. 'Lots of people want to come and stay down here because of the cider. Also, naturally enough, they buy cider for themselves or as presents.' Mike's busiest time serving customers is July, August and September, but what he's found is that people who really like his cider become regulars, 'maybe only three or four times a year, but they call in when they're passing'. And these visitors become your ambassadors and your cider goes countrywide and even abroad.

Mike helps other cidermakers who are just starting. 'My philosophy is if anyone's interested in starting making, I encourage them. I help them if I can, because it seems to me, the more of us there are, the more people will be introduced to it.' And that is one of the reasons he started the festival, 'to

give everyone a chance, and it's quite nice because you get to know all the other cidermakers.' His approach is broad and generous. 'I think you should never worry about competition, because if you make a good product, people will come to you. There's no point in being secretive; surely you want everyone to make good cider so people will enjoy it. It's terrible for people who aren't into cider and perry if you get together, because there's nothing else talked about. Some of the commercial cidermakers are good at what they do, millions of people enjoy them, but there seems to be something wrong about the descriptions and the image and the marketing.'

He has put his finger right on the crux of the matter. It is about marketing and perception. The problem is that the small producers cannot compete with the price being charged by the large companies and at the same time they cannot get their products into tied houses. So cidermakers sometimes reach a ceiling beyond which it is difficult to go, even though they feel that their product is superior.

Mike's hydraulic press runs off the back of a tractor but it is still quite hard work, time consuming and labour intensive. Several cidermakers I know have been given grants to buy belt presses, which has greatly speeded up their operations. But there is still some debate about how much juice you get out at the other end.

As to perry pears, Mike's favourite is Butt, because it has more tannin. A well-known saying

Above. The sharp end: cidermaking in full swing.

with Butt is, 'Gather your Butts one year, mill them the next and then drink them the year after.' And this is pretty good advice. This is a high-tannin perry and will therefore keep better than some of the others. It will, however, precipitate out tannin during storage. Mike likes Gin, which is from the Newent area, because it has 'that elderflowery flavour' that is so light and characteristic of good perries. Mike has also experimented with Aylton Red in a rum barrel. 'It came out really nice. That recently won at the CAMRA festival in Sussex.' In 2006 Mike got the CAMRA Silver Perry award, the Gold went to Welsh perry makers Seidr Dai from Cardiff.

He also likes Thorn, Moorcroft and Hendre Huffcap as perry pear trees, but cropping can be a bit sporadic. Interestingly, only about a mile to the west is a small hamlet called Hendre, which is still surrounded by orchards.

The local soils are all red from the sandstone, which gives Ross that rich colour when the fields are ploughed, just like parts of Devon. 'It's pretty good soil, you can have torrential rain but within a day or so you can drive back on it with a tractor. No problems with harvesting. The disadvantage is that it dries out very quickly in the summer.'

Mike likes Foxwhelp to blend but drinking, wise he prefers Dabinett and Brown Snout. 'Chisel Jersey is a really, really good apple, but not on its own. Blended I think it's fantastic. I've got a nice medium-sharp apple called Reinette Obry, which is really good to add to Dabinett or something to give it some acidity and a real appley flavour. Ashton Bitter, although it's a new variety, as long as you let it ripen it produces a fantastic cider. It's a little bit astringent for some people.'

He likes to make single-variety ciders from the apples when they're pressing, 'but if they don't come out right you can always blend two barrels together. You often come across a cider which has been well made and tastes OK, but it's just unbalanced and if the two barrels are mixed they can make a fantastic one. But the danger is that you make too many ciders that you like, and that's not necessarily what everyone else likes. I try to be aware of that.

'It is not just that the customer is always right, it is more that if the customer has bothered to come on to your farm and find you, they are more open to suggestions and learning a bit more about the cider apples and perry pears and the key factors in choosing fruit and making cider.'

At small farms like Mike's, the producers get to talk to their customers direct. No telephone surveys or multiple-choice questions here, just the real thing in a glass poured straight out of a wooden barrel, and in the dark cool of Mike's cider cellar it is difficult to leave when the conversation is flowing. 'At the end of the day you have these apples and you have to make the best of what you've got. I think they all have a quality and you just have to find where each cider's place is.'

Mike's sons, Jack, Albert and Martin, and nephews, Toby, Kenelm, James and Tom, help him quite a lot. 'Their palates are developed even though they're quite young.' So hopefully the tradition will continue. One or two others who help him out are already making their own ciders. Mike is full of praise for the Big Apple Trials at Putley, which have really helped him. The event is a good platform for new cidermakers to try out their products on the cider cognoscenti. The cider is judged democratically by the cidermakers themselves, so it is a level playing field, not just down to one or two judges' preferences.

Mike also reckons that a lot more women are drinking cider and perry. Women, in his experience, 'tend to prefer perry and the lighter or sharper ciders rather than the bitter-sweet ones. They don't go for the heavy tannins, although if they do like the tannins they really like them, if that makes sense. My girlfriend Sophia likes more or less the same cider as me. She doesn't like them quite as heavy as me.'

What he finds is that people expect to have a cider that is sweet and fizzy, whereas farmhouse cider is often flat and full of tannins. 'Many people come in here and they want something much sweeter than I produce, and although I won the sweet prize at Putley this year, I just happened to have a barrel of Knotted Kernal single variety, which is a sweet. It obviously had residual sugars

and it was like an apple juice cider, and it just stood out. I didn't have to add anything to it, it was 1016 [specific gravity] and it had finished fermenting. It was a fantastic cider.'

Mike is also very aware of his surroundings. 'We are so lucky to live here, I remember a few years ago sitting in the orchard with Dave Matthews, of Seidr Dai, and we were saying how lucky we were, and that it didn't seem fair that other parts of the world had such terrible struggles, and that's what made me start doing the charities. We choose a charity every year, and we have social nights, and when we do these events, after the expenses then the money can go to whatever charity we're supporting. We have a social night here on the first Friday of every month. Everybody drinks for free because I'm not allowed to sell it, but they put donations in the box later. We were supporting a trust this year that was building schools in a small area in Zambia.' Such social conscience is not uncommon and it is a great way to raise money for Africa.

Mike is helped on the farm by Sophia, Phil, Cindy, John and Henry. As a business they don't want to grow too big or too quickly and are quite happy where they are. 'The whole idea of the cider company was not to borrow money.' Mike's cider can be found in three local pubs: The White Lion in Wilton, The New Harp at Hoarwithy and The King's Head in Ross-on-Wye. The great thing, Mike says, is that 'they've sent people here. There's also a couple of shops in Ross and the delicatessen.' Another pub Mike supplies further afield is the Valley Bar in Scarborough, which won CAMRA Cider Pub of the Year in 2007, as well the National Collection at Middle Farm, Firle in Sussex.

As to prizes, it is sometimes difficult to get cidermakers to own up to them. Mike has been champion cidermaker at Putley three out of five years. 'The other nice thing is that one or two of my friends here who make cider have also won at Putley.'

So Mike has had faith in the cider apple and perry pear; hope that quality will out; and an inner drive to put on musical events to give charity where it is needed most.

CHAPTER 18

History in a Bottle

GLOUCESTERSHIRE

Kevin Minchew,
*Minchew's Real Cyder and Perry, Aston Cross,
Tewkesbury, Gloucestershire*

Kevin lives in a small, picturesque cottage in a smallholding next to a vast army camp. Rose Cottage, this is where Kevin was born. Not the most obvious place for a cidermaker but he has consistently turned out unusual and interesting ciders and perries, going commercial in 1993. He is always keen to experiment and loves a challenge. Even as I sit down on the bench outside his cottage he is extolling the virtues of his trees as he points to one in front of us. 'This is a nice eating apple from a seedling, this tree here, and I've a bitter-sweet up the top which I've got ten grafts off. I might call it Harry Minchew after my father. It's immortality almost. People say, "What's this cider apple like?" or, "What's that cider apple like?" And I say, "Get a demijohn, make one gallon and see if it has any characteristics, and if it has and you like it, go ahead with it." You'll get an idea from one fermentation.' Kevin is always keen to give an apple a chance and will not rest until he has drawn out its most interesting attributes. He is very definitely a 'back to basics' man.

Kevin made his first cask in 1984, but prior to that his father Harry always had a barrel of cider or perry at home. So he was brought up with the rich flavours of Gloucestershire. 'It used to be half a crown for a little demijohn of cider from the shed opposite the youth club with the chickens running

about. When I was a lad, I was told, "If you can't see your fingers round the back of the glass, don't drink it."'

Kevin's father was in the Royal Navy more than 20 years and a Royal Marine commando, and when demobbed he went off to work at the army camp, moving various prisoners of war around. 'This house here was the village stores, run by my grandmother and I think there's still a jar of pickled onions in there from 1940, so this was the heart of the community.' Even as a boy Kevin took a great interest in the soils. 'The soils change here: you move into the vales and you've got much sandier soils, gravel deposits from glacial terminal moraine, it's very good for growing crops. This side we've got heavier soils. And the dialect changes. You go to the other side of Bredon Hill and they've definitely got the Midland twang. I don't think enough research has been done into how a particular variety of fruit changes in character depending on the soil conditions.'

At Tewkesbury the River Severn meets the Avon, which winds down from Stratford, and these rivers affect the microclimate beneficially and help to make this area so good for fruit growing. Upstream are Evesham and Pershore. 'At Aston it can often be dry and belting it down in Tewkesbury. It's too windy on the top, it's cold up there, but there are some people growing cider and perry trees in sheltered valleys. But on the top of the Cotswolds is stony ground and full of wheat. It's these small things that make all the difference.'

His father did not have his own press but 'there were two presses down at Northway, a couple in the village and a cider factory in the parish of Ashchurch, called the Tewkesbury Cider Company. I've got a ceramic mug and some cork bottles with the labels on with the address at Fiddington. In the late 1960s Bulmers acquired the business and as a result of the loss of the local production, a lot of orchards were seen as having no value. Particularly the pear orchards.' Kevin can remember them being sawn down, the roots grubbed up and dragged into ponds, and the wood was then taken to the toy factories in Gloucester. 'Shepton Mallet did take the perry pears, but you load ten tons here in Gloucestershire but down in Shepton Mallet you might only have five tons when you arrive.'

Gloucestershire is famous for its perry pear trees but the fruit has to be processed locally. To Kevin perry is as different from cider as wine is. 'Fermentations are generally a lot slower, and this is using the same wild yeasts, but a fast fermentation tends to blow all the flavours out in the gas stream. I can generally predict what a cask is going to taste like from experience. Condition of the fruit prior to milling is vital because if you mill something that's underripe, not only are you going to get less alcohol, you won't have the full depth of character.' Kevin has spoken to a lot of old men, he has read a lot, and he has arrived at a method of production that works for him. 'I've been awarded many prizes for doing things the same way, which I regard as the correct way, then I'm going to stick to it. If it ain't bust, don't fix it.'

Just around the corner from where Kevin was growing up there were three cider houses. 'One was the Yew Tree at Conderton, on the foot slopes of Bredon Hill, another was the Monkey House at Defford, and the third was The Plough at Elmley Castle. They all made their own cider and we'd go on our motorbikes and have half a pint at each pub, start chatting to the other lads. It was wonderful listening to these old boys. You'd go there and trade

things, asparagus and bacon, and people would meet in pubs. The Mop Fair in Tewkesbury would be the place to recruit labour in early October. Everyone would want to work for the farmers and growers who made the best cider, so he'd have the pick of the workforce. There was this kudos and a real reason why people strove to produce a good cider. The role of the cider house was vital.'

When Kevin left school at 15 he got a job in a nursery growing tomatoes. Kevin learned a lot of plant husbandry skills such as grafting and control of bacteria, which were very useful later when it came to cidermaking. After eighteen months he got an apprenticeship on the army camp and did five years as an electrical and mechanical engineer with the REME. He then went into precision engineering – that was when he had a mortgage – after that he baled out and went to New Zealand, spent three months hitchhiking around, which was a great experience. Then he was self-employed and ran a motorcycle spares and repairs place in Worcester. He did auto jumbles at the same time and raced British motorcycles, but cider was still the culture. 'What else have I done? I'm a qualified bricklayer, I use the level on the press; intercontinental truck driving, I've had a go at that, and cidermaking; although you're doing it for what seems to be nothing, it gives me a great sense of pride.'

In his spare time he had already started cidermaking. He found references to some perry his father was making in the 1950s. The local formula was ten bags of cider apples to two bags of perry pears, then matured in rum or whisky barrels. 'You'd have an enormously powerful drink. Cider was currency: you'd get invited to parties, other guys would have barrels in their shed, and you'd go round to their place for a drink.' But Kevin wanted to make a better quality cider.

The real skill of cidermaking is knowing what is going right and what is going wrong and how to correct it. 'You can't just go "Ooh arr", chew on a bit of straw and think it'll be all right, it won't be all right.' Some may be all right when the cask is opened but it won't keep. Kevin is a perfectionist and his product has integrity.

He is also a very keen naturalist. 'I've got a

great sense of conservation. I can name nearly every native plant in the UK, every orchid, every butterfly. You lift a stone up and I can tell you out of 16 species of ladybird, which one it is. The latest thing is, I've got a snowdrop, unique, that nobody else has got. I found it by chance and I've had it bi-stemmed, as they call it, chopped up into pieces, and now this one bulb is starting to flower. They're white with a green chevron on the outside, so I've met all the galanthophiles by accident. Also I won't open a new cask until I hear the first cuckoo. That's culture, that's what I grew up with.'

One day Kevin was at The Plough at Elmley Castle and he got talking to a man called Dave the Cheese, who was a MAFF farm inspector, who said there was a cider course running at Hindlip College. So Kevin went along and learned about cidermaking from the expert Peter Mitchell, taking notes and watching practical demonstrations. 'I think we even made some cider, we took home a demijohn and fermented it, but I was learning to make cider here to the best of my ability.'

Kevin had another friend who was interested in cidermaking, a dry-stone waller in the Cotswolds. 'We picked a bag of fruit, different varieties of cider apples, took them over to some exhibition to be identified, and the guy wanted £1 per apple. We had a sack full, so we thought, "What are we going to do?" So we shot over to the cider museum at Hereford, where we knew there was a display of cider apples. At about four or five in the afternoon, just before it closed, we went into the cellar and picked up a Major. Eat into it. Crunch. Make a few notes. Hide it. Then we picked up a Dabinett. We had to physically taste the fruit. Somebody should have helped me a long time ago by saying, "tannin is red wine, acid is white wine", and just a simple analogy like that and then of course hand in hand with biting these things and having these new flavours, because bitter-sweets are scarce here. I had to knock on doors and ask if I could taste their apples. At one point I was scrumping. Well you start picking and you wait for someone with a shotgun to turn up and you say, "Oh hello, pleased to meet you. Is it yours? Can I buy it?" And sometimes they say, "Yes," and sometimes they say, "Get off my

land!'" Kevin was flying by the seat of his pants and learning orchard skills fast.

'I never did science at school, but we were looking at titration, litmus paper, basic chemistry. So I do acquiesce to some of the scientific principles like cut your apple open and paint it with iodine, that sort of thing [to test the starch content: too much starch, the apple isn't ripe]. Some of the Bulmer's Norman apples – eurgh! And some of the perry pears – eurgh! But the magic is, once they're milled, something that's inedible becomes really magical. It struck me as being magic, something that changes so quickly from being in one state to being in another. It's like a painting: the more you look at it the more something reveals itself. I've had a few casks that I haven't liked; I never throw it away. We'll go back several times to pick if they're not ripe.

'My job is to keep a representation of the original fruit. I made a batch of Foxwhelp. I read in a book that it would keep 40 to 60 years in a bottle, and this was written in 1880, and I thought, that's interesting. I've still got some 1990 Foxwhelp now, and I have groups round to try it, the malolactic fermentation has occurred and now it's carbonated after 14 years in the bottle.' And very excellent it is too. Kevin took me into his shed and we tried some. His press is in a low building with open sides and he has wonderful pieces of stained glass with an apple tree fruiting.

Kevin has his preferences when it comes to the fruit. 'People rave about Kingston Black, but I think it has the reputation because it has the highest specific gravity I've ever measured in anything. Foxwhelp again, it's got gravity in the 1070s, but Kingston can be 1080. I've learnt to like bitter-sweet ciders, soft ones; Dabinett, lovely; Harry Masters, superb; Sheep's Snout, very soft, subtle, it's like it's got honey overtones. Reine des Hatives, it's got a citrus nose to it, it's not in the profile of the drink. Foxwhelp is a distinct apple, you bite it, smell it, process it, bottle it, and when you taste it, it's still Foxwhelp. Even when you piss it out afterwards, it's still Foxwhelp. Dabinett, lovely. Each of these fruits has individual characteristics.'

As to local favourites, Kevin likes Corse Hill,

and has made cider from that, but it is sharp. 'Most of the Gloucestershire apples used for cidermaking are sharps, but all over Gloucestershire it was perry that people made in profusion. You can still see remnants of that today. The public are aware that these things are disappearing now. Perry pear trees are usually of a grand stature, 40-, 50-, 60-foot trees. In the spring, to see an orchard in white, they're like a bride and bridesmaids at a wedding, they're just gorgeous, it's stunning. And what also fascinates me is that you've got a complete range of profiles of perry pears, from sharp acidic perries to soft drinks with great character and depth.

'I like Blakeney Red, it's a regular cropper, a trouble-free tree, easy to shake, not too tall, large-size fruit and a very nice perry. A favourite is always going to be Moorcroft or Malvern Hills because my dad made that; another one is Hendre Huffcap/Yellow Huffcap. Huffcap pears have got character and merit. There's one round here called Jenkin's Red, which is the only red-flushed Huffcap. I had Ray Williams' book, and I'm looking at perry pear trees, and I'm like, "Ah, that's a Butt tree", because some of them are conspicuous. And I went to an orchard at the next village over at Oxenton and said, "Do you mind if I try and identify your perry pears?" He said, "Go on, son", and so I wandered about looking at the book, making a few

notes, disappeared and a few weeks later I went back to the orchard, and they said that two guys had arrived and asked if they could look at the orchard the day after I'd been there, and they'd said that a young man had been the day before, and they said, "Who is he? What was he doing here?" Long Ashton and I were looking at the same thing. It was meant to happen, and then I realised that we had to start finding these rare varieties.'

To make the cider Kevin uses a rebuilt scratter mill, and a stone. 'It's a Forest of Dean sedimentary sandstone, same as all the stones around here. It's got a greenish tinge to it. You can't break it. The press came from Forthampton, which is a tiny little village just on the other side of the river from Tewkesbury, and the guy I bought it off was 84. He said, "What do you want it for?" and I said, "I want to make some cider", and he laughed. His sons weren't interested, so I brought it up here, recondi-tioned it, rebuilt the scratter, and away we went. We had an 1880 handbook, an 1880 press, we had varieties that were around then, and I thought, I'm going to adopt what was happening around then and try it now.'

Then Kevin would go back across the Severn and take the old man a couple of bottles. 'There was a candle going and the old radio, which was there in 1939 and crackled out the news of the

Opposite. Kevin's old cider press in full working order.
Above. Old volumetric measuring stick used by gaugers.

outbreak of the Second World War. Warm up a poker in the fire, then stick it in the cider [to create mulled cider], "whooph", and then smell it. There is definitely some change, and there are bouquets, smells, odours, nuances, tastes when you plunge the poker in, white hot, you get a bit of slag that falls off in the vessel, but you get a little layer of smokey gases staying on the surface of the drink. Sniff that and taste that, it makes it something else.

'But that was part of the learning curve. I saw that historically people were paying different amounts for different types of perry. A Huffcap perry was twice a Gin perry. A lot of perry pears from this area were shipped off to Bristol or London to stretch out the imported wines. Five hundred years ago perry would have been on the top table in the manor house and I've always thought that it deserved to be there. Why support another country's wine economy when we've got this here? The time is coming when people will appreciate us, but at the moment it's still a bit quirky. I'd like a pound for every time someone asks me, "What's perry?"'

So who is drinking the perry? Kevin says, 'I'd certainly go along with perry's a lady's drink, even today. I don't know why. It was helped along by Queen Elizabeth I visiting Elmley. I've seen a copy of the menu that she was served; on that were ales, cider and perry, and there are still pear trees in Elmley now. She sent a runner back from London to insist that they put three pears in the Worcestershire coat of arms, and I think that ties in with the experience she had in this area.'

But it is also the physicality of it all that interests Kevin. 'The scratter makes different noises with different pears. I'm serious. The texture of the pulp's different. This maceration business, in the past we made a cask of perry just as quickly as you make a cask of cider. I avoided the maceration and I found that the resulting product furs your tongue. It's a thoroughly nasty experience to drink it. The key is to adopt what the older boys will tell you, which is that certain varieties need a period of maceration to allow these tannin levels to fall to an acceptable level. I don't keeve. We disintegrate the fruit, leave it overnight, covered over, and you find that a lot of juice is released, and then we'll press that the next day. It should be worth more than cider because it takes longer to make. We considered using hairs, but cleaning them out is too difficult, so we use nylon cloths. We keep them in a tub of SO_2, and you shake them dry, so a small amount of sulphite does get into the product. Temperature's very important. You can press something into the cask and that afternoon it'll start fermenting. Then it goes straight in a cask via a filter, which most people call a kitchen sieve, and that's just really to catch the wasps or pips or any fibrous material that gets through the press, then into the cask. I would say that cellars are crucial.'

As to the making, Kevin has his own chronology. 'I start with Moorcroft/Malvern Hills in September and try and make as much of that as possible because I like it and it sells well. That one doesn't need maceration. Wait for the gentler fermentation to ensue, then in with the top-up juice, and then I use a cork with an airlock, vaseline around that to stop the flying boring beetles, and then just wait. And through the winter it'll stop because it's sub-zero, but as long as you walk past and hear a little "bloop", you know that's safe. Some people rack their juice off into another cask, but I don't do it, I just leave it in there, *sur lees*, and it's all cobblers because people who've racked it have won prizes, people who haven't racked it have won prizes.'

For his cider and perry Kevin has a very distinctive label. 'That was a wedding present. A friend worked in the graphics department of the National Health. She asked what I wanted, and I said I wanted something triangular, so we've got air, earth and water, something Celtic, because my mother's Irish and I believe the Celts were drinking this stuff 1,000 years ago – and the tree had been done to death [see p.221]. And she came back with several designs and she said, "What about that one?" and I said, "That's got to be it." It jumped out at me.'

What Kevin is looking for in good perry is:

Opposite. The natural sparkle.

'First of all bouquet, nice and interesting nose to lure you into it. The colour is really irrelevant to me, whether it's still or sparkling, that doesn't really matter, and then the taste, and the first thing I'm looking for is a fault, something that shouldn't be there. Next thing is a balance, under the tongue, under the teeth, all around. Let it warm up in the mouth, warm up in the glass, and then swallow. And then I like a long finish that stays the same and doesn't change.'

It may come as no surprise that Kevin has won the prestigious Pomona award from CAMRA for longstanding achievements in the cider and perry world, and it is richly deserved.

Kevin's perry has also been featured on the Great British Menu with Mark Hix. 'He said, "This is great. Can we have this in our restaurant?" I said, "Yeah." He said, "We've got several restaurants", The Ivy, which I've heard of, Caprice, which I've heard of, Scotts and something else. I said, "Of course you can have it, I'll just get some postal rates." Presumably they want it to make this dessert, which may become popular. It was a circular mould with perry, a bit of gelatine and then Dorset blueberries, wild strawberries and raspberries set within this mould, in the middle went a scoop of ice-cream, flavoured with elderflower cordial, and on the top of it he had deep fried chervil, but he made the batter out of perry, which was a double whammy.' The full recipe is available at http://www.bbc.co.uk/food/recipes/database/perryjellyandsummerf_86328.shtm

Once Kevin made thousands of gallons a year, now he doesn't even make enough profit to pay income tax. 'But I don't expect a lot out of it, just happiness. And that's what we've got in the bottle. History in a bottle. This is a lot of hard work for three months: you work so hard you don't feel any aches and pains. But it keeps you young at heart. I still think I'm 25.'

So in his lifetime the cider house culture has almost died out but what has replaced it are these small pockets of highly skilled makers like Kevin who have gone back to basics and really understood what is going on. His dream is to find the Herefordshire Redstreak. Wassail!

CHAPTER 19

Wordsworth and Emma Hamilton

GLOUCESTERSHIRE

Keith Orchard,
Orchard's Cider and Perry Co., Yew Green Farm, Brockweir, Gloucestershire

Nobody has a more apt name for cidermaking than Keith Orchard, and he has chosen to make his home in a small farm with two orchards overlooking the beautiful Wye valley. The River Wye is both frontier and trade route, and a mile or two above Tintern Abbey lies the village of Brockweir. The name has nothing to do with badgers, but dates from around AD 620. Before that it was thought to have been called Pwll Brochuail from the Welsh *pwll* for pool, and Brochuail or Brockmael, which was the name of a sixth-century prince of Gwent. No doubt salmon had something to do with it and a fish weir could well have been used to help catch migrating fish at certain times of the year.

Certainly from ancient times Brockweir was an important crossing place and there was a ferry here until the iron bridge was built in 1906. The girders were brought upriver from the foundry in Chepstow. Brockweir's reputation is colourful and its benign tranquility on an autumn day belies its turbulent past. For hundreds of years there was no church and no vicar, and it had a reputation as the most lawless place in Gloucestershire. It was the haunt of boatbuilders and quarrymen, salmon poachers and charcoal burners, stevedores and hobblers who had to haul the boats upriver in gangs. It was a place of refuge for rough diamonds

and was described as a den of iniquity by the Moravian missionaries who came here in the nineteenth century at the behest of the Duke of Beaufort to bring some law and order. Emma Hamilton apparently stayed here in the Royal Arms in 1802 when visiting her lover, Admiral Nelson, in Monmouth. No doubt the village turned a blind eye. Nelson was visiting Monmouth because Emma's husband, William, had estates nearby and he used it as an opportunity to assess the oaks for shipbuilding.

Four years earlier a young William Wordsworth stayed at Brockweir and wrote his famous poem 'Tintern Abbey' (1798). If you look carefully at the title of the poem it says, 'Lines Composed a Few Miles above Tintern Abbey, on revisiting the banks of the Wye during a tour. July 13th 1798'. In the poem he mentions 'tufted orchards' in line 11 and the various cottage gardens: these 'pastoral farms' and 'wreaths of smoke sent up in silence from among the trees'.

It was on just such a day that I visited Keith Orchard at Yewgreen Farm, at the end of a long track. Keith was brought up in Somerset and comes from a village called Backwell near Nailsea. Backwell is famous for giving its name to a cider apple, the Backwell Red, a mid-season bitter-sharp. Nailsea is itself famous for Coates, which was the

largest cidermaker in North Somerset until it was bought out by Showerings. 'They had a good cider house there, The New Inn at Nailsea, and then there was the Black Horse at Clapton in Gordano, where Adge Cutler and the Wurzels used to play.' Acker Bilk was a local boy from Pensford, and Coates even named a large wooden vat after him (as well as one after Adge Cutler), both of which Rich's Cider now own (see Spitfire, Acker Bilk and Adge Cutler). Long Ashton was four miles down the road. 'The other cidermakers were Richards between Yatton and Congresbury and of course Thatchers of Sandford, who have gone very modern.'

Keith's introduction to cider was being taken to the well-known Backwell cider farm run by a family called Williams. 'It was always a treat when I was young, and I mean nine or ten, when my brother and father used to take us down to the farm, especially in the summer, to buy some medium cider in flagons, the old traditional flagons, and have it with our food. This was in the late 1960s. The family sold up about 15 years ago. A big shame really.' Keith has even planted half-a-dozen Backwell Reds just to remind him of home.

His father was on the road in the early days selling furniture and he ended up having a furniture business based in Portishead, which then expanded to Nailsea. Keith's brother now runs the business. There were wheelwrights in the family, and cart makers, which must have been useful, but no coopers.

As a young man Keith worked in transport for 'an international haulier based in Avonmouth, transporting ship's stores and general haulage, working across Europe as far as Poland and Greece. They had quite a big independent fleet at the time'. Keith next moved to Chippenham and then Reading, both office furniture suppliers, and then on to a furniture manufacturer, project managing large installations. After that he was instrumental in creating an installation company based between Swindon and Manchester. Eight years ago the partners bought Keith out and with the lump sum he was able to refurbish the buildings at Yewgreen Farm. Keith had always wanted to make cider and when the farm came on the market his sister-in-law, who lived in the area, tipped him off.

Keith told me about the shipbuilding at Brockweir, which was an old tidal river port, one of the highest on the Wye. You can just see the old slip down by the river. He has elvering rights but no salmon fishing rights. A lot of villagers still go elvering, but it requires having to stay up all night. The Wye is tidal to Bigs Weir, just below the bridge. The *Belle Marie*, built in Gloucester in 1860, was Brockweir's 'market boat' and carried local produce

Above. The old boat-building slip on the River Wye at Brockweir.

to Bristol every week. In 1914 she became the last boat to sail to Brockweir.

The Wye Valley was at one time alive with ironworks and glassworks and small shipbuilding yards. In 1827 a sea-going schooner of 180 tons was built in Brockweir. The largest ship was the *Constantine*, 509 tons and 121 feet long, in 1847. Just upriver on the Welsh bank is the village of Llandogo, which gave its name to the Llandogo trow and a famous pub in Bristol near Welsh Back, where Daniel Defoe met Alexander Selkirk, whose real-life marooning inspired *Robinson Crusoe*. The last trows (a River Severn and Bristol Channel sailing barge) were built here in about 1925. Vessels would often have to be pulled upstream and the goods transferred on to smaller barges and vice versa. This was seriously hard manual work. There were also coal miners and charcoal burners in the Forest of Dean. These were all thirsty occupations: so plenty of custom for cidermakers.

In those days there were no fewer than seven public houses, which, for a population of only two hundred, was a little excessive. 'The New Inn, that's the oldest in the village; that's now the Brockweir Inn; then the Royal Arms, where Emma stayed; The Carpenters Arms or Tumpkin Hayles; The Severn Trow, almost joining the New Inn, was a cider house; The Old Boat Inn, that was close to the river; Live and Let Live, a cider house in Hudnall Wood frequently used by charcoal burners and stone millers from the woods; then The Spout, a beer house.'

Keith was full of stories: 'At one time there was no drinking on a Sunday in Wales so the village would get crammed, especially on Sunday nights. One of the old boys in the village was telling me he saw Shirley Bassey in one of the pubs; she came over to sing.'

Keith has a book about the railways and at one time Brockweir had its own station. 'It must have been a scenic route and there would be unofficial stops when the guards used to go and test the local ciders because they knew where the best ones were.'

'At one time every farm around here must have made its own cider. We come under the Royal Forest of Dean, and the first recorded family lived here in Brockweir in the 1500s. They were farmers and in my porch we have two sitting stones and we believe they came from Tintern Abbey.'

Like many in the area, Keith believes that the first experiments into bottle-fermented cider were conducted here in the Forest. The glass makers here were some of the first to use coal, and the combination of higher temperatures and the essential impurities of iron and manganese meant that they discovered bottle glass accidentally. And once they

Above. Beehives in the orchard.

185

had a strong glass they could control the fermentation in small batches.

When Keith took over this farm it had been derelict for at least ten years. The previous owners had goats, cows, pigs, hens, a milk round and made cheese. When I visited he had the builders in and the place was upside down. In one of the sheds he found an old 45-gallon drum of cider, which must have been there since the 1960s. The drum was lined with plastic and Keith tried some. Apart from being a bit citrusy, it was fine but didn't last long once the air got to it. But what really impressed me was the base stone that Keith had rescued from the house next door. It was round and made from Forest of Dean stone and must have been at least 300 years old. Between Brockweir and Bigsweir Bridge there is a quarry where they used to cut the pressing or milling stones. Many would have been taken downriver on barges, and they were much sought after. 'There are the round ones with the lip. You can see where they are half cut out of the rock now and they have half fallen down, and they got rolled down the hill to the river and loaded on to the boats. Someone said if you go to Newnham there's a lot in the water where a boat tipped over.'

Keith's task at Yewgreen Farm has been jungle warfare, particularly with brambles in the old orchard. He has found old perry trees, old cider trees, old cherry trees, plums, vines, grapes and a 200-year-old box hedge. Keith sent some samples to Brogdale, Home of the National Fruit Collection. 'One variety was a Blakeney; the others, they weren't too sure about. The Forest of Dean was famous for the Welsh Druid, which was actually an English apple. It was a south Forest fruit. You break it off and put it in the ground and it self-roots. There was one in the village but it's gone now. Another apple that is extinct is the Forest Styre apple but that's long gone, about 20 years ago'.

Living as he does on the Welsh border he has to be diplomatic when selling his cider. But he is quick to applaud the renaissance of Welsh cidermaking. The Welsh cidermakers are very enthusiastic and there are some large-scale plantings just across the border, Springfield Cider the other side of Trellech and then there is Seidr Dai in Cardiff.

For Keith, hacking through the undergrowth, planting his own orchard and then cidermaking, has been a voyage of discovery. I asked Keith about William Wordsworth and he had some very interesting information. Apparently in the adjacent field is an old ruin of a cottage and that was the place where Wordsworth used to stay when he was in the area. 'So from where we are sat, it's about 400 yards.'

But Keith was more interested in cider than poetry. When he found the old cider and perry trees he knew they had made cider and he vowed to do it himself, so he planted ten trees straight away. 'The first were Sweet Coppin, Harry Masters Jersey, Dabinett, Kingston Black and Browns, then a couple of rows of Monmouth Fredericks and Breakwell Seedlings, then some Severn Bank, some Chats Hill and then of course some Backwell Reds.'

What Keith is trying to do is to get back to the taste of Gloucestershire cider and he is now much more interested in local varieties. He also co-owns a 300-year-old orchard in Little Dean, which has about 14 varieties of perry pear trees, 'which is where I get the perry pears from'. It has a Dean Stone in it, which shows the boundaries of what would have been Henry VIII's hunting grounds. Keith also gets some apples from Thornbury, which is over the Severn Bridge but still in Gloucestershire.

To learn cidermaking Keith went on one of Peter Mitchell's courses and then combined the new knowledge with his own techniques. He doesn't want his cider to be the same year in year out because that defeats the object of what he is trying to do. He is after something special and of that particular year, a vintage in other words. And this is more like 'wine speak'. You have good years and bad years and middling years and that's what makes it really interesting. Although he hasn't been making cider for very long Keith has won a number of prizes, which just shows that the enthusiastic amateur can come up trumps.

Keith sells some of his Wye Cider and Farmhouse Cider at the Slow Food market in Bristol. North Somerset is a stronghold for dry ciders, they like their tannins. Keith has also obtained a PGI for Gloucestershire cider. 'I think I was one of the first in Gloucestershire to get it. It's Protected Geographical Indication, so all my fruit comes from Gloucestershire or the Three Counties.'

One thing that concerns him is that when you sweeten something the flavour gets lost. He wants the flavour to fight through. One year he made a Hagloe Crab with fruit he acquired from Charles Martell, a very old Gloucestershire apple from near Awre on the River Severn that used to be swapped, barrel for barrel, with whisky in years gone by. It was deemed the cider of the time. William Marshall in 1796 mentions the Hagloe Crab being produced in around 1730 by Bellamy's [a local farming family] nursery at Hagloe near Blakeney.

And Keith has experimented with perry. 'I normally make a Blakeney Red and a Cannock, which is unique to the orchard on the other side of the Forest, and generally create a blend. Last year I just did the one; it got first prize at the Three Counties.' He has not been short on prizes: First prize in 2006 for his dry cider at the Bath & West Show and in 2004 Orchard Mist, his bottle-fermented cider, became the Supreme Champion at the Hereford Museum International Cider competition. Keith is keen on his bottle fermented but it was a lot of work so he has only made it once, as the high duty is a deterrent to making more.

Saving Wye Valley and Monmouth trees is very important to Keith and he has helped Charles Martell to re-find Pig's Snout and Old Josie. He also thinks Jim Chapman is doing an excellent job near Newent. 'It requires real enthusiasts like them who have time and energy to preserve what we have got.'

Keith supplies some of the local pubs: The Boat at Penalt, The Wye Valley Hotel at Tintern, The Brockweir Inn at Brockweir, The Wyndham Arms at Clearwell, The Miners Arms at WhiteCroft and Newhall Farm Shop. The Brockweir Community Shop, which is owned and run by the village, is his main outlet. This highlights the need for cidermakers to be proactive in their local communities as well as going to shows and festivals. They need to get their cider known to as wide a market as possible. Keith even takes cider across the Severn Bridge to the Nailsea and Backwell Rugby Club when they have their annual cider and beer festival.

CHAPTER 20

St Cuby and Lord of the Isles

Andy Atkinson,
Cornish Orchards, Westnorth Manor Farm, Duloe, Liskeard, Cornwall

Cornwall is not well known for its cider but it certainly should be. Once you cross the Tamar you effectively leave England behind and enter the land of St Piran and tin mines, saffron, surf and pasties. Cornwall has a rich history of cider apples and cidermaking but it never went industrial or commercial like Devon, Somerset or Herefordshire. In that sense it has more in common with Dorset, where the traditions have been kept alive by a few dedicated families.

The county has its own apples varieties, such as Captain Broad and Manaccan Primrose, Breadfruit and Cornish Gilliflower, Cornish Mother, Queenies, Ben's Red, Tommy Knight and Tregonna King. There are more than 75 Cornish apple varieties and they are hard to find, often multi-purpose and steeped in local tradition.

One cidermaker who is dedicated to using these Cornish apples is Andy Atkinson, from Cornish Orchards at Westnorth Manor Farm, a Duchy of Cornwall farm in the manor of Duloe in south-east Cornwall. In 1992 he had the foresight to plant an orchard of 200 trees in front of his house in an attempt to preserve rare varieties and find out which ones were really useful. Seven years later, Andy, a committed dairy farmer of twenty-seven years decided to press Cornish apples to make excellent juice and sell it in bottles. His timing was perfect.

What started out as a small experiment soon became a core business. He sold his dairy herd and switched from milking cows to pressing cider apples. From the start he wanted to get the very best from his apples and soon realised that he had an excellent product and local people relished the fact that the apple juice was made with Cornish apples. In 2002 he started making cider and that was also very successful. Demand soon outstripped supply. The same year Andy planted another 1,300 trees, which included Improved Keswick and Lord of the Isles.

Cornish cider apples can be used as cookers and eaters as well. They are not as high in tannin as some of the Somerset cider apples such as Yarlington Mill and Dabinett, but tannins are essential for good cider. With his recent orchard planting Andy hopes that in ten years' time he will be able to make his cider entirely from organic Cornish cider apples, because currently he has to buy in some of his apples from across the Tamar.

Some of his earliest outlets were the Eden Project and the Lost Gardens of Heligan. Andy was so short of apples that he advertised in a local newspaper, the *Western Morning News*, and many traditional orchard owners contacted him. But Andy was very selective; he wanted the right balance of fruitiness, sharpness and tannins.

One person who encouraged Andy's cider venture was his mother. In the 1930s, as a young girl, she lived opposite a cidermaker called Abbots in Lee Moor, near Ivybridge in South Devon. Her bedroom window overlooked the cider press and in the autumn she used to wake up in the mornings to the heady scent of ripe apples and pomace. And of course she drank the cider; she was a Devon girl.

Andy's father was from Yorkshire and he was born there but the family moved back to Devon when Andy was ten years old. His father was a tailor, then a carpenter, as well as being a keen poacher. He told Andy many stories about catching hares and pheasants. For Andy, school was Teign-mouth and he remembers a very poignant moment when the headmaster turned to him and said, 'What do you intend doing in life?' Andy hadn't really thought it through. His father's comment was: 'He wants to go to Seale Hayne.' Andy's comment was: 'What is Seale Hayne? What is it?' He did go to Seale Hayne Agricultural College and became a farmer. 'I drank quite often in the cider bar at Newton Abbot, as did Tom Oliver, and opposite was the striptease artist who performed in the pub over the road. A good education. Newton Abbot has got a lot to answer for.'

Andy was first introduced to real cidermaking by John Mortimer, a farmer who lived up the lane from where his parents lived in Ideford. 'I had bought a Series One Land Rover and was looking for somewhere to do it up, as you do at college. John generously offered the use of an old granite-pillared cart shed. And I remember one vivid moment when I was under this Land Rover with my feet sticking out and John came along and said, "Andy fancy a drink?" And it was a really hot day in the middle of summer and he took me into his cider barn. I can just smell it now as I walked in there, this dark, dank building and there are these 110-gallon cider vats, and the proverbial happened. "Try this one. Try this one." Eventually we got to one that I liked and could drink and it was fantastic. I still have it in my memory. It was very, very dry and very clear, verging on the wine, like 8 per cent plus, and the barrels had been used a number of years, so no oak or great spirit in there. Clean fermentation, no acetification. John could see a young strapping lad like me was useful to him for haymaking, so when I finished he used to have me there helping in his haymaking gang and I am proud to say I have ridden on the back of laden hay trailer with a flagon on my shoulder, drinking cider: the sort of thing that could never ever happen now. So that is where the cider kicked in …'

His first ever memory of cider? 'My dear dad,

and I can't have been more than five. Every year we came down to Cornwall on holiday to Hayle, caravanning. I have this wonderful memory of my dad walking towards the green Ford Anglia; we wound down the window, my brother and I in the back, and Dad came walking over silhouetted, with a tray, and he passed in these two small glasses of golden liquor. And that was when I took my first tipple, it was in a Ford Anglia outside a pub.'

In the 1970s and 1980s dairy farming took Andy from Winterbourne Steepleton in Dorset to a farm in North Devon near Holsworthy, and then to another Devon County Council holding at Down St Mary where he saw the Down St Mary vineyard being planted. Then in 1992 the tenancy came up at Westnorth Manor Farm where he is today.

But Andy felt there was more to life than producing lakes of milk, and in reaction to the greater intensification of the dairy industry Andy found himself being drawn towards more sensitive farming. In 1992 the Farming and Wildlife Advisory Group (FWAG) influenced him to plant an orchard in front of the farm. Cornwall County Council, helped by Mary Martin and James Evans from the Tamar valley (who have been saving threatened varieties for the last 25 years), came up with a scheme to propagate 3,000 apple trees. Andy

applied for 200 of these trees and got them: traditional varieties on M25 rootstock. 'We planted 18 varieties of apple trees: Tregonna King, Tommy Knight, Hockings Green, Colloggett Pippin, Queenies, Ben's Red, Cornish Longstem, Breadfruit, Snell's Apple, Cornish Gillifower, loads of different varieties.'

In 1997 Andy's daughter was getting married and as a wedding gift a college friend from Cheshire brought down a box of apple juice and a 25-litre barrel of cider. Andy was astounded by the juice's flavour. Almost 20 years previously Andy's farm manager in Dorset had given him some very useful advice: 'To be successful find something that someone else isn't doing; something that someone wants to buy.' Andy's mind was suddenly focused. 'I thought, you don't see this apple juice around. Maybe we could make some from our apples and diversify the farm business.' It was as simple as that.

The first apple juice was produced in 1999 and sold in 2000 and Andy hasn't looked back since. The cider followed in 2002. 'We now have two more orchards making 15½ acres.' The varieties that Andy has stuck with are: 'Improved Keswick, Collogget Pippin because it is a beautiful apple, Hockings Green and Lord of the Isles. Rita and Colin Vincent are still traditional cidermakers at Lerryn in the Fowey Valley: this apple came from them, looking

almost like a Bramley, big and green, but definitely a cider apple. Originally it came from the Isles of Scilly. Ben's Red and Queenie, because they look nice. I then had a nursery man from Somerset come down and take some bud wood away. He phoned me up 18 months later and told me, "your apple trees are ready". So lo and behold we had another 1,300 trees. Those were planted in 2002.'

But with Andy impatience had kicked in and around 2000 he ordered another 300 to 400 cider-apple trees from Bulmers: Yarlington Mill, Dabinett, Brown's, and a couple of rows of dessert apples, Falstaff and Crispin, which were hopeless. 'They have not got the natural resistance to Cornish wet weather.' The third orchard was planted where the original orchard was in the 1800s, again a bush orchard of old Cornish varieties. They are very early fruiting; most things in Cornwall are early. Andy's farm is only three miles from the sea and the fishing port of Looe.

To make cider well Andy has devised his own methods. He feels that in the industry, making cider is a bit of a free for all. 'It is important that some of us try to marry the heritage of cider and the quality of cider production so that the image matches the reality.' A bold ethos, and through hard work Andy has just about succeeded. His secrets are hygiene and a few simple laws. 'To make a good-quality traditional cider you don't need any added preservatives at all; a good natural apple juice will produce a 7 to 7.5 per cent cider, loads of alcohol.' Storage is in stainless steel vats and oak barrels, and he believes in cider production that relies on natural yeasts without using sodium meta-bisulphite.

Andy met Dr George Kington, a chemist who had been very well known in the MOD. When he retired, George came down to Cornwall and planted grape vines in Veryan on the Roseland Peninsula. George soon realised they did not produce particularly good wine so he replaced the vines with cider-apple trees and made cider by the same method that he would have used for wine. This produced a very dry, very strong cider, which won a national cider award in the late 1990s. Andy bought George's business in 2000, and with that came George's method of making cider. What Andy got from George was an insight into his scientific mind and all his wealth of knowledge. So Andy became, in his own way, a farm microbiologist.

Andy has also grasped the challenge of keeping his products within the bounds of honesty and integrity. 'What you see on the label is what you get. The public generally like a medium cider, they want it fruity.' So Andy uses apple juice to sweeten his cider, which infuses back the fruitiness. He also has new flash pasteurisation equipment, allowing him to sell naturally sweetened draught cider and apple juice with good keeping quality.

He still makes Veryan-style cider, the closest he can get to a traditional dry cider, but in practice he sells a lot of cider to the Cornwall visitors, which has to be less challenging. 'The public has lost its palate for traditional dry cider.' Andy has adapted by producing a whole range of ciders from 7.4 per cent bone-dry cider to a draught 5.2 per cent, a medium tannin cider for social drinking, and the Black and Gold range, the national colours for Cornwall.

The business is only a few years old, but with five million people visiting Cornwall each year, Andy's dream is to supply them with local cider and apple juice entirely from Cornish orchards. In the next ten years Andy wants to bring Cornwall back onto the map as a cider producer. He is encouraging others to plant orchards for this to happen.

But Andy is no spring chicken and it is a large-scale, hands-on business to be starting in your mid-50s, bearing in mind he still has to pay the rent to keep his landlord happy. But as always Andy comes back to cider philosophy and the methods of production. He is organic. 'It is very, very important that Cornish Orchards stays true to what is very obviously becoming its key area of ethical focus.' And that is becoming clearer and clearer to Andy as time goes on. 'My products should reflect that; the philosophy and *terroir* must come through in the integrity of the cider. So that is where it must be.' The National Trust takes his products at its shops in Cornwall. He has more than 600 outlets, including restaurants, hotel and cafes. 'We supply many of the famous chefs – Rick Stein and Richard McGeowan.' The only supermarkets he supplies are Waitrose and Booths.

Andy is very much a 'pure juice' man and thinks that it is high time there were some water-tight definitions of cider. The industry is, he feels, addicted to using apple concentrate, artificial sweeteners, glucose and carbonation. 'Why can't they make cider the way it is supposed to be made, as nature intended? Cider is what it is, apples pressed, fermented with wild yeasts, drunk at harvest time, that is what it is.' He thinks there is a need for cider to be defined by the percentage of juice it contains and for this to be displayed on the label.

He has not made perry, but he is keenly aware that at one time there were pear trees in Cornwall. One of the gardeners at Trelissick Garden near Truro came across about 140 stamped name tags of pear trees that were once grown in the valley. None are there now.

One of Andy's newfound passions is bottle-fermented cider and his is named St Cuby, after the son of a Cornish king who became a priest and then a bishop before being anointed a saint. On his father's death he declined the throne, instead wandering round the countryside preaching. In his lifetime he built four churches, one at Duloe, the others at Tregony, Cubert and Landulph.

Andy went to France to learn how to make bottle fermented. And after about three years he reckons he cracked it. 'It has a lot to do with the nutrients and the complexities of fermentation. So it is one of those things that you do at your own peril.' He ferments this cider in the vat for four to six weeks then ferments it in the bottle for three months. He makes about 5,000 bottles a year.

For Andy cidermaking has been a second career that has brought great rewards. He has also planted orchards with local Cornish cider apples and learned the microbiology of fermentation. Perhaps, more importantly, he has understood that you need to have a real ethos and integrity to succeed. For him there are no short cuts. He is making his mark in Cornwall and at the same time raising standards and keeping things local.

Opposite. Andy outside Westnorth Manor with a 5-litre bag-in-the-box.

CHAPTER 21

Called to the Bar –
Upstream from
River Cottage

DORSET

Simon and Amanda Mehigan,
Netherbury Cider, Netherbury, Dorset

Netherbury is a large West Dorset village just a mile or two downstream from the market town of Beaminster. The River Brit flows through the picturesque village and then winds its way down to Bridport via the film location of Hugh Fearnley-Whittingstall's infamous River Cottage. Until the 1950s the whole valley erupted in blossom every spring and orchards abounded on either side. There is still a commercial orchard at Elwell and several people have just planted vineyards locally. At one time Netherbury boasted two commercial cidermakers, the Warrens and the Olivers, both of whom learned their cidermaking at Long Ashton in the 1920s. Olivers went on until the 1960s but Hubert Warren only died recently. Simon Mehigan is following in their footsteps.

However, Simon is not your average cidermaker. In fact there is no such thing these days. He bought a cottage in 1988 in West Milton next to the well-known cidermaker and organiser of the ever-popular Powerstock Cider Festival, Nick Poole. Then Simon moved to the Old Rectory, Netherbury, in 1994. Originally he came from East Anglia on the Suffolk/Essex border. He became a lawyer, was called to the bar, but always wanted to be in farming. So by day Simon is a barrister and by night, or rather at weekends, he is a cidermaker in partnership with his wife, Amanda. It is Amanda

and her friend Lisa who actually press the cider. And soon it won't just be cider, because Simon has taken the very brave step of planting more than 1,000 perry pear trees – Blakeney Red, Hellen's Early, Hendre Huffcap, Judge Amphlett, Thorn and Winnal's Longdon – on special root stock.

People usually associate perry pears with the Three Counties, but the old name for perry pear is *pirig* or *pere*. Parnham is a large Elizabethan house just up the road, which used to belong to John Makepeace, the designer and furniture maker. Earlier versions of its name are Perham in 1228 or Perhamme in 1413 and Parnham in 1431, which can mean 'pear in the corner of the river or low-lying land'. And Perhay is down the road. So there are early indications that the valley was suitable for pears. Other 'pear' names that I know are Parham's farm in Melbury Abbas near Shaftesbury, Puriton near Bridgwater, Perry Street near Chard, Purton near Swindon, Pershore in Worcestershire and Paulespury and Pury End near Towcester in Northamptonshire. Pear trees were often used for boundaries and as markers where paths diverged and on roundabouts. Intriguingly, the crest for the Parnham family is a chevron azure between three pears gules.

Simon only started out with cider in 2004. Since a young lad he had liked the taste of it. 'If you

went to a smart party in your late teens, the trendy drink was Bulmers Pomagne. As a boy my favourite drink was Cidrax, absolutely lovely drink. Apparently now it's only seen in Jamaica. I loved Cidrax. It had a hint of cider to it. It had a wonderful flavour, I thought.'

When Simon came to Netherbury he was looking for some land to plant cider-apple trees, and fortuitously the babysitter's former husband was selling some cider orchards. Instead of having to buy the land and plant the trees, he was able to buy some ready-planted orchards at Pineapple Lane. And then there was another orchard in Melplash. 'So we took over those orchards and they had contracts with Matthew Clark, which were continued. One was about fifteen acres and the other was about six acres. Bob Chaplin [the chief cidermaker at Matthew Clark] was very helpful to me, because before I bought the orchards I had Bob and Martin Ridler [the main orchard manager at Matthew Clark] down to talk to me about them, and the contract, which was at that time pretty non-existent on both. And Bob said, "Don't buy

these orchards, they're a complete disaster, they haven't been looked after for years." And they hadn't been. "We only pay a contract price for orchards that are in a tiptop condition. I haven't inspected these orchards for years, and if I had done, he wouldn't have been supplying us for as long as he was".'

The long and the short of it was that Bob agreed to give Simon a ten-year contract on each of them, so long as he improved the orchards. This was in 2002. So Simon had 20 acres of orchard to maintain.

The first year the apples were picked up entirely by hand by Polish students. 'Fifty tons, which is hardly worth sending. It's four lorry loads. Bob Chaplin told me it wasn't worth picking the apples up the first year, but we did. The first lot we picked up were in October 2002. We then pruned heavily that winter and the next year instead of 50 tons, we had something like 240 tons. That was the best year we ever had. All destined for Shepton Mallet.

'They had some "dreaded" early French

Above. Bringing on gribbles.

varieties and Michelin, but we had some interesting varieties, ones that I think are excellent for making cider, Harry Master's Jersey, Yarlington Mill, Brown's Apple, which has the most extraordinary honey scent to the juice when you're pressing, but huge trees, heavily biennial. You couldn't rely on that alone because one year you'd have no cider and the next year you'd have a lot. Probably the most interesting variety that we had was Porter's Perfection. This had been planted by Taunton Cider in the 1970s and my predecessor, at one stage, was getting £133 a ton for them, which was very good money then. You are lucky if you get just over half that now. It was £133 less £2 haulage; now it is £85 a ton with £10 haulage. In the late 1970s, early '80s, people were making real money, and what's interesting is that nearly all the people around Melplash here who planted cider trees were ex-army or ex-navy, and they obviously saw some sort of reward there.'

'In fact, in this particular parish, Netherbury, the Ordnance Survey map from 1906, the whole of this area was covered in apple trees. For example, the Edwardian house behind this house is called Orchard Hill. Before that was built it was just an orchard, and that's why it's called Orchard Hill. Phenomenal amount of orchards around here, mostly apples, but some perry was made around here. But going back to the varieties, Porter's Perfection is a fantastic apple, it's a bitter-sharp, but it's related to Kingston Black. It's a full brother, and like Kingston Black, it's very difficult. The apples are tiny, they're well known for producing what are known as dollies, often about five apples squashed into one. The other problem that it has is it's such a late cropper; they don't want to come off the trees until late November. Sometimes they're still on the trees at Christmas and sometimes they're still on the trees in March. And nowadays the commercial cider mills don't stay open long enough. A lot of them open in September because so many people have earlies, their main month is October, they do go into November, but they're not too keen to go too far into November, certainly not the last week. So Porter's Perfection is absolutely hopeless from a commercial point of view, and in fact, every cider orchard that was planted around here with them in Beaminster and Melplash, they pulled them out. So we had sixty-four trees, we had one row only.'

Simon is very keen on the different characteristics of his apples and as always is trying to get an interesting and unusual cider. 'The only people around here now who produce, and they do make a very nice single-variety cider out of Porter's Perfection, are Hecks at Street, but they only have something like 24 trees. We also have Dabinett, and we have Sweet Coppin: there are two rows of Sweet Coppin, although it's a funny thing, isn't it, having a sweet apple, because as you have to ferment to complete dryness, it's pretty irrelevant what you start off with in many ways. We've used it in our own blends, but we've had to ferment it virtually to dryness for stability purposes. Brown's Apple was dual purpose, you can eat it and it doesn't have that horrible cotton wool interior. We also had some Tremlett's Bitter, some Taylor's – you do need those two together for pollination – and they were quite successful. We didn't have the Majors that people go for now. In some orchards apparently, they've finished by the end of September. We also had Nehou, which is a disastrous apple. It's horrible. It is quite early, tends to almost rot on the tree, and when it falls on the ground it certainly does rot. Matthew Clark do have some of that in their orchards, so they're quite understanding if you send a load of Nehou off. It would look disgusting but they wouldn't complain. I think they like Michelin, it's very dependable, but the juice is very bland, it's good for bulking.'

The intricacies of orcharding and cider fruit are forever unravelling and one farmer's experience may well be the opposite of another's, depending on the location, soil and seasonal variations.

As far as pressing is concerned Simon and Amanda started with a single screw press. 'It came from Exmoor, but by the time I got it, it was basically a whole load of railway sleepers. It had been used by a chap on Exmoor, his father had used it, he said even his grandfather had used it. I knew him when he was about 75/80. We started making our own cider, the next year. After that we made more, we only made 2,000 to 3,000 litres, but we started selling it in plastic bottles at the local farm shop, Washingpool, near Bridport. It was quite successful and then they started to bottle it in glass.'

They now use a modern hydraulic press, not a belt press. Amanda and Lisa do all the pressing and they build cheeses with style. 'They do a lot of the work, they've become very expert at pruning, and the big thing about pruning is the time is taken in deciding which branch you're going to take off, and they just look and do it, they don't really need to think.'

Out of the blue Simon was offered an orchard in 2006 in his own village of Netherbury, which had belonged to Hubert Warren. 'They had been very successful. Richard Warren, who helps me in the orchard, is one of Harry Warren's grandsons and Richard remembers, as a boy, going around in a van to all the big houses between here and Dorchester every week delivering cases of cider. We were offered this orchard, which was a Dabinett-only orchard, 30 years old, right next to the River Brit, never ever sprayed, not for ecological reasons but entirely for reasons of saving money: not pruned very much; we've now pruned it once. Very closely planted, so no question of mowing between the trees, you have to keep the grass down with sheep. So that's slightly under two acres, but the great thing is it's very productive and it gives us enough to make all the cider at the moment.'

Following this, Simon decided to sell the other orchard at Pineapple Lane; in effect he has downsized and is concentrating on making high-quality cider rather than sending his apples to Shepton Mallet. The 'new' orchard is called Hatchlands Lane Orchard.

To make his cider Simon uses a champagne yeast and he's just done an experiment with a German yeast that gives 'a huge amount of fruitiness, and we haven't racked that off yet. We ferment in stainless steel and we store in stainless steel.' He is keen on stainless steel; he wants to keep the purity of the apple. 'I don't want my cider to taste of wood, I want my cider to taste of apples,

and unfortunately with oak barrels you can leech an awful lot of oak into the cider, and I'm not interested in that. They look nice but they're not useful from a flavour point of view. Cleanliness, they're a problem.'

Cleaning barrels was always tricky but in the old days they would be deconstructed. 'They had a massive press on the Crutchley estate in Nettlecombe, but in the 1960s they would have at least one chap on the farm who would cooper the barrel. You'd take the end off and you'd scrape the inside of the barrel with a piece of glass, you'd clean it out with caustic soda and you'd put it back together again, but very few people can do that now, so the difficulty would be cleaning a barrel, and then the third problem you have is keeping air out of the barrel. All of those things aren't a problem with stainless steel. The disadvantage is it's very expensive. Luckily I managed to buy all our kit second hand. We can keep it in stainless steel for years. This year [2007] we're still bottling our 2005, and we haven't even gone on to 2006.'

What Simon is looking for in a good cider is that 'first of all you've got the aroma, you really want it to smell of apples in the glass. I think the texture and the viscosity of the juice is very important. I don't like seeing a thin watery juice. There needs to be an oiliness there which is quite important for the body, and that really is part and parcel of the experience, and then it's the taste. I like a dryish cider but not too dry. You want the dryness and some fruitiness. You want them both there. And a nice, long, thirst-quenching, haymaker's drink. The problem with so many ciders is that they're either commercial, fizzy and bland and sweet, or they are so astringent. There are some farmhouse ciders that I've tasted around here which are just beyond belief. Also you've got to have it at the right temperature. I think it's got to be quite cool. You don't want it at room temperature.'

It is interesting to note that apples can be exported as well as imported. 'There's even a Spanish company that's buying apples. They get pressed in Spain. And what's interesting is that in the old days Harry Warren used to buy apples in from Normandy, and they'd come in to West Bay and then be brought up here to be pressed. I think the Spanish are buying because the climate is getting too hot now. I did try a very good Spanish cider which I think had a good deal of perry in it.'

Simon is very keen on perry. 'Perry should be such a premium product that you wouldn't want to waste your perry. I think really nice perry is fantastic and I don't know why it isn't more expensive.'

Simon quite rightly has an upmarket view of cider. 'I think good-quality cider should be viewed as a wine equivalent, I think mass-produced cider should be viewed as a lager equivalent, that's the way I would look at it. Carbonation can mask an awful lot of sins. Ours is just still. We drink our cider when we're eating a lot of the time. We also drink cider like you would drink beer, to quench your thirst.

'I think most roast meats go very well, I've never had it with fish, but traditional things like pork and chicken go very well with cider. It goes well with cheese, I think it's versatile, it's an alternative to wine, it's an alternative to beer. I don't think any of the Indian restaurants have taken it on yet but who knows?'

Simon has a few outlets: one or two restaurants, the Bridge House in Beaminster, the Broad Street Restaurant in Lyme Regis, the Washingpool Farm Shop and Framptons in Beaminster and Majestic in Dorchester. 'The future? I'm hoping that we'll do some perrymaking, and I'm hoping that we'll expand our market sufficiently so that people will recognise the product and the quality of the product.'

Simon is a bit of a dark horse, he is also an expert on betting and gambling law and an expert on the law regarding licensed premises, and he has just spent a significant amount of time updating the bible of regulations, Patersons Licensing Act published by Butterworths. The world of real cider and perry is, however, I suspect, a law unto itself.

I look forward to Simon and Amanda's Netherbury perry when it comes on stream.

CHAPTER 22
Cider with Rosie
DORSET

Rose Grant,
Cider by Rosie, Winterborne Houghton, Dorset

Tucked away in the middle of Dorset up a lovely narrow valley lies the village of Winterborne Houghton. The name Winterborne means simply a river that only runs in the winter. Rose Grant has made cider her third career. No one else in this central part of Dorset makes cider commercially and so she is almost single-handedly pioneering the art in this county. True, I once made cider down the road in Durweston with my brother in the early 1980s, and there were cidermakers in Okeford Fitzpaine and Shillingstone but they have ceased production. A thatcher called Andy Banwell took over making cider in Durweston, so the thread was not entirely lost. There also used to be a cidermaker in West Knoyle called Coombs. Very good cider and perry are made in Stour Row near Shaftesbury by Bo Rutter and again the art has been resumed at the Mill House Cider Museum at Owermoigne. The cider clubs of West Dorset are now legendary. This is where informal groups of friends or farm workers gather together to pick the apples and make the cider on a communal basis and then have the pleasure of drinking it together. One of the clubs at Monkton Wyld is led by Maureen Westons nephew, Winston Chapman. Liz Copas, who was a pomologist at Long Ashton, is also now trying to identify many of Dorset's lesser-known apples, one of which is called Buttery Door. So even though

the cider tradition is alive and kicking in Dorset, they seem to drink it all themselves!

Rose Grant was brought up in a thatched cottage in Huntingdonshire. She moved to Somerset in her teenage years and used to drink cider at the Churchill Arms in Churchill, which is next to Sandford. (This is John Thatcher country, and Thatchers the cidermakers was then just a farmyard operation, but now it has got a little bit larger …) Rose went into the Royal Air Force as an avionics specialist. She served in various bases in East Anglia and the West Country, becoming a Flight Lieutenant before returning to civilian life. She became an engineer in a small electronics firm in Dorchester, making optical-electronic sensing equipment. In her lunchtimes she would go down to Captain Thimbleby's cider den at Wolfeton House, a well-known haunt that was feudal to say the least, the barrels being kept in the stables, as if the Normans had only just arrived. It reminds me of a man I know in Meavy on the edge of Dartmoor who still refers to the Norman Conquest as 'that French Invasion'.

Rose was experimenting with making cider in the early 1990s. The idea of going commercial happened by accident. She just got rather good at it, learning from such illustrious cidermakers as Jean Nowell at Lyne Down in Herefordshire and

Andrew Lea in Oxfordshire. No chemicals or sugar for Rose: just a few sulphur candles to sweeten the barrel, a technique used for centuries. Her apples initially came from a two-acre orchard 200 yards up the hill from her cottage; she planted these in 1990. This was not very good soil, the drainage was good but there was no loam. This is a real problem for Dorset, which is mostly chalk upland. It is only the narrow bottoms of the valleys that are any good for loam, unless of course you prefer clay in the Marshwood Vale or Blackmore Vale. Kingston Black did quite well on the chalk. Other apples she planted were Dabinett, Stoke Red and Ashmead's Kernel. She managed to acquire a few other orchards to see her over and from this her 'empire' began.

She also gets apples from Sparkford in Somerset. These are traditional orchards, which are harvested with a mechanical harvester and a tree shaker. At Bloxworth in Dorset they let Rose have the apples as long as she picks them up, something she really enjoys. 'Lovely job. I just love going down there. People just don't know what to do with them. I just take her a few bottles of cider. I can always find enough. There is another farmer has an orchard in Waytown; they grow tremendously well. Never seen such beautiful cider fruit. Dabinetts like grade one Cox's. Twice the normal size.' Must be the microclimate and the ideal soil.

Rose likes Kingston Black, Dabinett, Yarlington Mill, Porter's Perfection. Tremlett's Bitter, Redstreaks; some of the early sharps to give it the balance, Cider Ladies Finger and Brown's apple. 'I am very much a Dabinett and Yarlington Mill person. I like the richness and flavour you get from those apples. Cider Ladies Finger is quite an ugly little apple and yet as far as cider is concerned it is just as useful as Tom Putt, having similar acidity and tannin.' Rose is enthusiastic and even has an article on the ukcider website (ukcider.co.uk), which is very useful for beginners or for people who want to appreciate the joys of pressing their own.

She affectionately calls her press St Em as it comes from St Emidiceau near Paris. She bought it from Vernon Bland in Gloucestershire, who was retiring from cidermaking: he had brought it across the Channel. It is an old French water hydraulic press that develops 60 tons of pressure. It works from the bottom up and dates from around 1930. The firm also made 100-ton presses. There was an artisan version that was operated by a lever, but Rose was glad she had an electric motor. At least she had a manual to go with it, which was, of course, in French. However, she has to stop it when it gets to pressure. She had a new oak tray made for it in a furniture workshop, Lou's Place.

Rose is a firm believer in natural yeasts. 'Natural yeasts, absolutely. I read that old Warcollier book [*The Principles and Practices of cidermaking*, 1928, by Professor G. Warcollier from Caen with the translation in conjunction with Dr Vernon Charley].' This is a rare book. Rose found it very interesting indeed. 'A passage in there talked about developing yeasts from cider fruit, and the fact that the yeasts did seem to impart the characteristics of the tree from which they came. And I thought about that, Kingston Black comes too late but I do have eating apples, and so I do a starter bottle of Discovery juice that I use to kickstart the cider all the way through. That is the dominant yeast that I transfer from vat to vat.'

Being a modern electronics engineer Rose is a 'great believer in stainless steel, particularly having seen James Marsden's lovely little cider works. I thought "that is the role model". Throw out the oak barrels. I had oak for quite a while, but I didn't like the flavour, they were whisky barrels. I don't like whisky; don't mind rum. I used to use the sulphur candles. The cider was perfectly good but it wasn't tainted with rogue yeasts, it was tainted with whisky and I didn't like that; other people do. I like to make a cider that tastes entirely of apples.'

So Rose slowly progressed from barrels to stainless steel vats, a sputnik or two as she calls her oddly shaped steel vats. Her knowledge of scientific matters came in very handy as she used the infallible principle of trial and error to perfect her

Opposite. Rose in action with her French cider press, Ste Em.

methods. The basic law, as always, is the best fruit in the best condition and pressed out at the right time, using natural yeasts and meticulous hygiene. She still uses a little sodium metabisulphite at the beginning to make sure the fermentation goes the right way, and then leaves nature to do the rest. The results are superb: she won a first prize at the Putley Trials in Herefordshire in 2007, which is a rare achievement for a Dorset cidermaker.

Rose likes a good blend of bitter sweets and bitter sharps. She blends everything together, in all about 6,000 litres (around 1,300 gallons) of draught. She monitors the acidity as she goes and obviously if she needs a bit more acid she looks for a sharp apple to add to it or the other way round. 'I might put in more Dabinett. I am looking for fruit with character and flavour. I think blending extends over the whole pressing season as you are watching what you are building up in the tanks. And it gets a bit crucial towards the end. I keep checking all the way through, I may be looking for a more acid apple towards the end.'

Her scientific training has not been wasted. 'The secret is to keep tasting all the time. Even when it is still fermenting, taste it. Your taste buds are the best instrument you've got.'

Rose is very meticulous with racking. She knows what she wants from her cider – stillness, depth and complexity. As she says, 'I am particularly averse to carbonated cider. I feel that the gas in it masks the flavour; you could be drinking pop, or anything. Even good commercial ciders like Stowford Press are spoilt with carbonation. I am looking for a fairly still cider. I don't mind a little bit of natural carbonation; that is nice. I don't like anything that is at all tainted with the mouse; it has to be totally mouse-free. And any other off flavours, a rich balanced flavour.' Rose likes her tannins. There is quite a bit of tannin in Tremlett's Bitter.

Rose supplies 15 pubs in Dorset, including the Square and Compass at Worth Matravers, The Greyhound at Corfe Castle and the Vine Inn at Pamphill. Interestingly, it is the whole age range that drinks her cider. She has investigated it by asking the landlords. Of course it varies from pub to pub. 'A lot of the old fellows like it, they say it

reminds them of the old days, it reminds them of what cider used to taste like. At The Anchor at Shapwick, a lot of the old fellows go in there, they love drinking it. I am keeping the old men of Dorset happy. The local thatcher got very interested in it; he drinks it down at the Bakers Arms at Child Okeford and the Plough at Manston. So he is quite fan.'

Rose also does keeved cider, the Normandy method. 'This is a way of making naturally sweet cider by adding an enzyme to the naturally fermenting juice, and the enzyme then precipitates out a lot of the pectin components in the cider and this then rises to the surface and produces a thick brown crust on the cider known in France as the *chapeau brun*. And the thing then is to get rid of it, or to siphon the cider from underneath, and the result is that you can get a beautifully clear cider, which is also deficient of the yeast nutrients as these pectin compounds having been removed. I macerate overnight and this helps to release the pectin compounds. And it softens the tannins and it can be a good thing with some apples. The beauty of it is that the cider will ferment very slowly and

it will stop short of being fully dry.' She has some Kingston Black which has stopped at a Specific Gravity of 1040 and is very slowly fermenting still and beautifully sweet, and when it goes on a bit further she will bottle it. And that is real skill – knowing when to bottle it.

Some people used to use chalk when keeving, or you can get it in solution. Calcium salts help the precipitation of the pectin. Rose uses calcium chloride. 'That is the most usual one or calcium carbonate … very cheap to buy. Makes about 1,000 litres, doesn't all work, you need cold weather otherwise the fermentation starts before the brown head forms and it all churns up and falls to the bottom. The truth is that people prefer to drink a cider that is just a little bit sweet. They will say they prefer a dry cider; the ladies in particular go for a sweeter. It is the Holy Grail: if you can make a cider which is naturally sweet you've got a winner. I have seen that time and time again.'

Rose acknowledges that she has learned a lot from Andrew Lea, whose name has cropped up several times when I've talking to people. I heard Andrew talk at Putley in spring 2007. Rose is

Opposite. A cottage industry.
Above. The end of the day.

Andrew's number one disciple. 'He is the expert.' Andrew did his PhD at Long Ashton when it was still functioning as England's leading cider research institute. And after years of advising the industry on how to make safe but boring cider he moved to Oxfordshire and planted an orchard of his own and went native using natural yeasts. He then monitored every batch of cider he made until he understood what was going on, and many of his results are on his website (www.cider.org.uk). Many of the small, high-quality cidermakers have taken inspiration from his experiments and now know how to use and allow wild natural yeasts to improve their ciders rather than knocking them on the head with sodium metabisulphite and introducing a very good but very predictable wine yeast.

Another of Rose's idols is Jean Nowell of Lyne Down near Much Marcle. Rose did a bit of cider-making with her and she would love to think that she could emulate what Jean did in Dorset, inspiring other people to start cidermaking with quality in mind. 'Of course she started James Marsden off, she has her cider boys. Interestingly enough I have a few cider boys who come up here. We hope to get a mobile cider press going this autumn … I want to keep going as long as possible, but it is good to see others carrying on the tradition.'

Rose is very generous in her praise for books and people who have inspired her. 'I often think of your phrase, "Cider: the forgotten miracle". It is often a miracle that it comes the way it does! And all this inspires people to have a go and reawaken their interest in what is only on their doorsteps. I love the Common Ground *Book of Orchards*, with all the James Ravilious photographs … very evocative, Miss Betty's orchard. James Ravilious was a famous photographer and son of the war artist Eric Ravilious. Miss Betty was a determined orchard owner in Somerset.

'I have met lots of wonderful people since I've been making cider. In this village we have reintroduced two of the old traditions to go with cider, the May Queen and the Wassail. I was inspired by the picture of Lustleigh's May Queen in the Common Ground *Book of Orchards*, and I went down there to have a look and was enthralled. We have now had our own ceremony for the last four years. The May Queen presides over the maypole dancing. I made a throne out of an old rocking chair and hazel twigs round it and a lady in the village decorates it with flowers. This chair is like a sedan chair, it has poles and we have the Bourne River Morris Men to perform the ceremony. They carry her through the apple blossom to the bottom of the orchard where there is a level area of grass. They sit her there; then she is crowned the May Queen by the Squire of the Morris Men. The children then dance round the maypole and the Morris Men dance a sequence of their own. Then we have barbecue and cider tasting. It is a jolly social occasion.

'In January we find some little girl to become the apple maiden and carry out the wassail ceremony in the orchard. She puts the cider-soaked toast in the tree. We then sing wassail songs and finish with the traditional firing of shotguns. Then back at the cottage we have the mulled cider with appley eats and sing more wassails accompanied by our local musicians, the Bulbarrow Band. Colin, a great guy with a glorious tenor voice always treats us to 'Linden Lea', whilst we put the ashen faggots on the fire and pass round the cider. We've only got a small place so it gets rather crammed, but it is such a happy thing to do in the bleakness of January. I love the way it gets people together and it is good for the community. It was how people enjoyed each other's company before television came along.'

With her background in electronic engineering Rose is constantly inventing new ways of doing things or adapting equipment from other industries. Her big tanks for holding the cider actually came from a cheese factory in Crewkerne, Somerset. She thinks that more women are drinking cider now, which is a good thing. 'They want quality rather than quantity.'

And Rose is certainly providing quality cider. It just shows that even in a remote part of Dorset anything is possible, and she is keen to help others start off cidermaking and learn as she did: and in so doing keep the traditions alive.

PART TWO: *Gazetteer*

CHANNEL ISLANDS

The Channel Islands were at one time an important stepping stone between France and England, whether for smuggled brandy, wine, French silk, cider apples, or even cider. There were often very close links with seafaring families on the Cornish, Devon, Dorset and Hampshire coasts. There is even a Guernsey Street on Portland.

The density of orchards on Jersey was at one time very high indeed and in the late seventeenth century this threatened the island's ability to grow enough corn for bread. In 1673 the States passed an Act that forbade the planting of orchards except to replace old ones. So far this is the only known case in the world of a law to prevent the planting of orchards. In 1680 there were not enough barrels on the island to take the cider and many apples simply rotted. Frank Falle in his *History of Jersey* published in 1692, says, 'I do not think there is any country in the World that produces so much cider [proportionately] as Jersey does, not even Normandy itself … We prefer the bitter-sweet to *all* other apples, but the cider requires more time in refining.'

The highly accurate map of Jersey made by the Duke of Richmond in 1795 shows some parishes with more than 40 per cent under orchard. In 1801

Revd Francoise Le Couteur, rector of Grouville, one of the most heavily orchaded parishes in the east, estimated that Jersey produced 30,000–35,000 hogsheads of cider a year, of which 20,000 were consumed annually on the island and the rest exported. So in a good year they could export nearly 810,000 gallons of cider, which from a small island of 24 parishes was extraordinary. This cider would have gone to ports such as London, Portsmouth, Poole, Weymouth, Bridport and Exmouth, even Plymouth. In 1853 Jersey exported 142,240 gallons of cider and 99,715 bushels of apples, and in the following year 89,790 gallons of cider and 179,676 bushels of apples.

Many of the orchards were later grubbed up for the Jersey Royal potato, and during the German Occupation of 1940–45 many of the orchards were cut down to provide firewood and land for cultivation. With the demise of the early potato, the re-planting of orchards has started on a small scale and there are several mother orchards for Jersey varieties on the island at Hamptonne and St John.

Commercial cider-making has also restarted, and for anyone visiting Jersey or Guernsey the cider is worth sampling.

JERSEY

La Mare Vineyards & Distillery

La Mare, an old, well-established farm in the parish of St Mary, was first set up as a vineyard by Robert and Ann Blayney in 1972. There are now 16 acres of vines. They also planted two acres of orchards and started making cider setting up a small distillery to make Jersey apple brandy in 1993. Robert and Ann retired in 1997 and La Mare is now owned by Trevor Owen.

The cider is made from old Jersey cider apples such as Jersey Rouget, Douce Dame and Noir Binet. They have just planted another six acres of English cider apples such as Harry Master's Jersey, Brown's, Michelin, Dabinett and Yarlington Mill. They also get apples from 60 other growers on the island and from the National Trust orchard at Trinity. In 2007 they pressed 11 tons.

They use a 100-year-old copper calvados pot still and a very effective 750-litre computer-controlled Charentes cognac pot still. The chief cidermaker and distiller is Daniel de Carteret. Jersey born and bred, a chef who spent eight years in the wine trade and cut his teeth in New Zealand in Blenheim, Spy Valley and in Otago. Tim Crowley is Managing Director.

La Mare also produces black butter, which is made from apples, spices, liquorice and cider. Grapple, which is 8% fruit wine, made from cider and wine mixed, and was used, so it is said, in the sixteenth century to top up casks of wine that had mysteriously evaporated on the voyages from the south of France and Spain when they just happened to call in at Jersey on their way to England.

Cider: Traditional Jersey medium 6.5% abv; Branchage Premium Table Cider 8% abv; Grapple 8% abv; *méthode traditionelle* 8% abv; cider brandy and apple brandy 40% abv; Jersey Cream Liqueur 17% abv
Outlets: Vineyard shop, St Mary or Maison La Mare, St Helier
Address: La Mare, St Mary JE3 3BA
Telephone: 01534 481178
www.lamarevineyards.com
Maison La Mare, 33 King Street, St Helier, Jersey
Telephone: 01534 733090
Website: www.maisonlamare.com

La Robeline's Cidre dé Jèrri

This is a new cider-making venture in the westerly parish of St Ouen. Started in 2005 by Richard Matlock, who has planted 500 Normandy French cider apple trees from the Pays D'Auge and hopes to get up to 1,000 in a year or two. He also has access to several other orchards on the island in St Lawrence and St Peter. One or two have old Jersey varieties like Capy and Noir Binet. Richard's cider is much more like a Normandy or Breton cidre bouché than an English-style cider. He macerates the apples, keeves and keeps the residual sweetness in the cider. This is pure juice cider fermented with wild yeasts. In his day job Richard is a marine engineer in St Helier, and this stood him in good stead when he brought over his cider-making machinery from Normandy. The mill was 80 years old and the hydraulic press about the same age. He learned cider-making in the Pays D'Auge and is determined to keep the French connection going. His cider was awarded a highly commended at the Royal Bath & West Show in 2007. Currently he produces around 10,000 bottles a year but hopes to increase this to 60,000.

Cider: La Robeline's Cidre dé Jèrri medium dry cidre bouché, bottles 4.5% abv
Outlets: Relish fishmarket, St Helier; Classic Herd Farm Shop and Dunells, St Peter; Farm Fresh Organics, St Lawrence; Home Grown Grouville; Victor Hugo Wines and Corkscrew, St Hellier; also Jersey farmers' markets
Address: Les Petits Robelines, St Ouen, Jersey, JE3 2ET
Telephone: 01534 487883

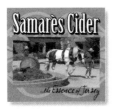

Samarès Cider

Samarès Manor is an elegant and fascinating house with extensive gardens run by Vincent Obbard. The cider comes from Vincent's orchard, which includes varieties such as Kingston Black and Dabinett, as well as Jersey varieties such as Côtard, Tétard, Gros Binet, Noir Binet, Romeril, France, Belle Fille and Douce Dame. The cider is made in true Normandy style by Richard Matlock of St Ouen. Samarès Manor in the parish of St Clement is sheltered yet near to the sea and has a very good climate for cider apples. The 1795 Richmond map shows that almost 40% of the parish was orchards. Vincent has an agricultural museum with cider-making machinery, horse-drawn carriages, a walled herb garden with espaliered pears and apples and a flock of sheep, which is normally found in the orchard.

Cider: Samarès Cider cidre bouché medium sweet, bottle-fermented Normandy method, sparkling 4.5% abv
Outlets: Samarès Manor
Address: Samarès Manor, St Clement, Jersey JE2 6QW
Telephone: 01534 870551
Website: www.samaresmanor.com

GUERNSEY

Cider has been made in Guernsey for many centuries. Between 1834 and 1843 half a million gallons were exported, which is on average more than 50,000 gallons a year. In the same period more than 70,000 bushels of apples were exported. An old cider press dating from 1734 and other equipment can be seen at Saumerez Manor. Cider was made in *le prinseux*, the press house very similar to those in western Normandy, and the apples crushed in a circular trough called *le tour*, with a large round granite wheel often powered by an old but steady horse. Sometimes wooden wheels were used in pairs. Men and oxen were sometimes used as well if horses were not available.

The massive oak presses were called *l'emet* and some had the farmer's initials carved on them, with his wife's and the date. Some are even pre-1700. The beam would be coaxed down on two wooden threads either side, with lots of squeaking and juice pouring out. Often wooden capstan and ropes were used to exert the pressure. They would only crush and press about half a ton of apples a day, so it was a long and laborious job. The pomace was often left to stand in tubs where it would oxidise before being pressed out.

A few traditional Guernsey cider apples are Amrey de Jersey, Barbarie Falla, Barbarie Rillie, Blanc Amrey, Gros Doux de France, Loumet, Messuriers, Petits Doux, Pommes de Normandie, Pommes à Sucre, Romry (also called Romeril), Rouge Amrey and Sur Avoigne. There are only a few of these apple varieties left but the islanders have not lost the taste for cider. Today more than 2 million litres of cider are drunk annually in the Channel Islands.

The Guernsey Cider Company

The tradition of cider-making almost died out in Guernsey but it has been started again commercially by James Meller's family, who planted ten acres of cider orchard on the hillside of the Fauxquets Valley in 1998. The 3,000 trees, which originally came from nurseries in Hereford, are now giving about 60 tons of apples a year and this will rise as the trees mature. The cider company is based in barns at Castel, two miles west of St Peter Port. The cider is 100% pure juice, with no added colours, flavours or sweeteners. James has recently decided to sell draught cider in pubs on the island and this has been a great success.

Cider: Rocquette bottled 6% abv and draught 4.5% abv
Outlets: most supermarkets on Guernsey, 25 pubs on draught and small export orders to Alderney and Scotland
Address: Les Fauxquets de Haut, Rue des Fauxquets, Castel, Guernsey, GY5 7QA
Telephone: 01481 232501
email: jrmeller@cwgsw.net

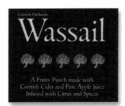

CORNWALL

Cornish Cyder Farm

This is a large cider farm, which is run as a tourist attraction by David Healey. It used to be called The Cornish Scrumpy Co. The company's motto is 'Legless and Smiling'. There is also a distillery and its bond, which is beneath the shop. There are only two small orchards, one with Cornish apples and the other with traditional cider varieties. Unfortunately, no comment was forthcoming about the juice content of their various ciders.

Ciders: Cornish Scrumpy dry and medium sweet, bottled 7.4% abv; Cornish Vintage Cyder bitter sweet 7.4% abv; Cornish Rattler, a cloudy scrumpy derivative, bottled and draught 6% abv
Spirits: Apple Brandy 4-, 5- and 6-year-old 40% abv; Eau de vie 25% abv
Outlets: Farm shop and online. Also available at a wide range of shops and local supermarkets: Sainsbury's, Tesco, Threshers, Bookers cash and carry, Spar, some Asda, Butlins at Minehead
Address: Penhallow, Truro, TR4 9LW
Telephone: 01872 573356
Website: www.thecornishcyderfarm.co.uk

Cornish Orchards

Andy Atkinson lives on a Duchy farm situated between Liskeard and Looe and makes a wide variety of ciders. He uses as many indigenous Cornish apples as he can and over the years has planted several new orchards. He also imports organic cider apples from beyond the River Tamar to see him through till these orchards are in full production. Andy is a purist and will often only use natural yeasts and the very minimum of pasteurisation.

Cider: Draught 5 medium dry, 5-litre 'bag in the box', draught 5.2% abv (also available in 10 and 20 litres upon request); Cornish Black & Gold

Sparkling medium, 50cl bottles 5.8% abv; Cornish Black & Gold Still dry, 50cl bottles 6.2% abv; Veryan strong, wine-like, dry, bottled 7.4% abv; Farmhouse Cider still, medium 1-litre bottles 6% abv; Wassail, mulled cider with spices, 1-litre flagon 5% abv; St Cuby medium, bottle-fermented, sparkling 4.5% abv
Apple juices: Newton Wonder and Old Cornish, Bromell's Medley, Discovery, Ben's Red, Longstem, Tom Putt and Russet, Cox and Bramley, 75cl bottles and 5-litre 'bag in the box'. Also mulled apple juice, summer apple cup and cider vinegar
Outlets: farm shop and online. Many delicatessens and shops in the South west as well as some branches of Waitrose and Booths
Visitor centres: The Eden Project and National Trust, Lost Gardens of Heligan
Address: Westnorth Manor Farm, Duloe, Liskeard, PL14 4PW
Telephone: 01503 269007
Website: www.cornishorchards.co.uk

Haye Farm Cider

Cider has been made here on the farm since the thirteenth century. Colin and Rita Vincent only use apples from their own and neighbouring orchards. They have over 30 different types of apple, some of which are particular to Haye Farm itself. Their cider is of high quality and very traditional, still pressed through straw, using wild yeasts and wooden barrels. St Veep is not far from Lerryn and the Fowey estuary.

Cider: Traditional farm cider, bottled and draught 7% abv
Outlets: Farm gate and barn (open seven days a week). Also Lerryn Stores, Penhaligons off-licence and the Ship Inn, Lerryn
Address: Haye Farm, St Veep, Lerryn, Lostwithiel PL22 0PB
Telephone: 01208 872250

Helford Creek

Down on the Lizard beyond Helston is Helford Creek, run by Jem and Sarah Trewellah on their 55-acre farm called Mudgeon Vean. Jem used to work on oil rigs, and makes the cider; Sarah 'does everything else' and also looks after three holiday cottages on the farm (see link on website). They make their cider with local cider apples, which include Manaccan Primrose and Pig's Snout. They also produce a wide range of apple juices.

Cider: Helford Creek Cider medium, still and sparkling, bottled 5.5–6.5% abv
Apple juice: Orchard-blend apple juices from local Cornish orchards: Treganoon, Downes Apple, Trerose, Poldown, plus Cox, Bramley, Jonagold, Laxton Fortune, Worcester and Russet and two new combinations of apple with raspberry and pear
Outlets: Online; local shops and delicatessens: Gear Farm Shop, Spar at Mawgan and The Stores at Gweek.
Address: Mudgeon Vean, St Martin, Helston, TR12 6DB
Telephone: 01326 231341
Website: www.helfordcreek.co.uk

DEVON

Penpol Cider Farm

Keith Langmaid still makes his cider the old-fashioned way, pressing through straw, with nothing added or taken away, using traditional cider apple varieties. Keith is a very colourful character and sells straight from the cask in the darkened cellar at his old farm.

Cider: Traditional farm cider, draught 7% abv
Outlets: Farm
Address: Middle Penpol Farm, St Veep, Lostwithiel PL22 0NG
Telephone: 01208 872017

Polgoon Aval

John and Kim Coulson run a 13 acre vineyard on the outskirts of Penzance with 13,000 vines. They also have an orchard and have recently produced their first sparkling cider.

Ciders: Polgoon Aval. Sparkling bottle fermented 7% abv
Outlets: Polgoon Orchard and Vineyard, also see website.
Address: Polgoon Vineyard, Rosehill, Penzance, Cornwall TR20 8TE
Telephone: 01736 333946
Website: www.polgoon.co.uk

Ashridge Cider

In South Devon over the last few years, Jason Mitchell has been perfecting the art of making bottle-fermented vintage cider using the *méthode traditionelle*. Each bottle takes two years to reach maturity. Jason took a biology degree, had a sheep and dairy farm, then ran a sawmill and timber yard. In 1997 he moved to Ashridge Farm in South Devon, where he had six acres of orchards. Jason only uses cider apples that come from the South Hams, such as Tremlett's Bitter, Broxwood Foxwhelp, Sweet Coppin, Sercombe's Natural and Brown's Apple. Most of them are traditional Devon varieties, and they all have high levels of tannin and acid, which are essential for a sparkling cider. Up to fifteen varieties are used to give a rich, well-balanced juice. Ashridge Cider won a Three Star Gold Award at the 2007 Great Taste Awards held at Olympia in London. Jason also won First Prize at the Royal Bath & West Show and at the Three Counties Show in 2007.

Cider: Ashridge Brut, a sparkling, bottle-fermented vintage cider 8% abv; Devon Blush sparkling cider with blackberry liqueur 8.5% abv
Outlets: Online shop, Riverford Farm Shops, Dartington Cider Press, Darts Farm, Clyst St George, Exeter, as well as West Country branches of Waitrose in Saltash, Okehampton, Sidmouth and Dorchester. In London, Ashridge is available in Borough Market on the New Forest Cider stand
Address: Ashridge Cider, Barkingdon Farm, Staverton, Totnes, TQ9 6AN
Telephone: 01364 654749 or 07919 992934 (mobile)
Website: www.ashridgecider.co.uk

Bollhayes Cider

Since 1987 Alex Hill has been experimenting with cider-making in the Blackdown Hills. He produces a draught cider and a sparkling bottle-fermented cider with occasional ventures into perry-making. Bollhayes Cider has won first prizes in the Devon County Show Cider Competition in 2001 and 2002, and Supreme Champion at the Bath & West Show in 2006. Alex also runs the highly sucessful business Vigo Ltd, which supplies many cider-makers and wine-makers with modern presses, mills, storage vats and bottling equipment.

Cider: Bollhayes bottle-fermented, dry, sparkling cider 8% abv; Total Eclipse medium, dry, bottle-fermented, sparkling cider 8% abv; Bollhayes perry 8% abv, Bollhayes draught 7% abv
Outlets: Wallace's Farm Shop, Spar Hemyock and Green Valley Cider, Darts Farm, or direct from Vigo Ltd. Also pubs: The Merry Harriers, Clayhidon and The Culm Valley Inn, Culmstock.
For information on cider-making go to www.bollhayes.co.uk
Address: Cider sales through Vigo Ltd, Dunkeswell, Honiton, EX14 4LF
Telephone: 01404 890262
Website: www.vigoltd.com

Brimblecombe's Devon Farmhouse Cider

This farm has one of the oldest cider presses still operating in Devon. Here you have *au naturel* pressing through straw, with a massive old wooden windlass press, using wild yeast of course. It is well worth a visit during pressing. The proprietor, Ron Barter, has been here 14 years; the press is reputedly over 400 years old. Apple varieties include Fair Maid of Devon, Slack-ma-Lasses, Farmer's Glory, Dabinett and Brown's.

Cider: Dry, medium and sweet draught, vintage/farmhouse and rum cask 6% abv
Outlets: Farm gate Easter to October, at other times by arrangement
Address: Farrant's Farm, Dunsford, EX6 7BA
Telephone: 01647 252783

Chucklehead Cider

A few miles east of Bampton lies Shillingford. This is where Michael Dinnage and his wife make cider using apples from his farm and other orchards within six miles.

Cider: Chucklehead Cider draught 7% abv
Outlets: Farm gate by appointment only. Mail order imminent
Address: South Hayne Farm, Shillingford, EX16 9BL
Telephone: 01243 572332
Website: www.chuckleheadcider.co.uk

Countryman Cider

North-west of Tavistock and set above the Tamar valley, two miles from Milton Abbot lies Felldownhead. The fifteenth-century stone barns were once owned by the Lancaster family, who had made cider here from 1858. Countryman Cider is now run by Vernon Shutler, his wife Therese and children Angela and Robert. They have an orchard but also take in other West Country cider apples, many of which come from the Tamar valley area and beyond.

Cider: Dry and medium sweet, bottled or draught 6.5% abv; Gold Label Vintage two years old 7% abv
Outlets: Farm shop as well as Tavistock and Plymouth farmers' markets
Distributors: St Austell Brewery and other wholesalers.
Address: Felldownhead, Milton Abbot, Tavistock, PL19 0QR
Telephone: 01822 870226

Devon Cider Co. Ltd

The Devon Cider Company was founded in 1999, as Devon Contract Packing. In 2001 the company name was changed to the Devon Cider Company. In 2005 it relocated to 10 acre premises on an industrial estate in Tiverton, where it makes a range of own-label ciders for Sainsbury's, Asda, Tesco, Aldi and Lidl, as well as bottling from other cider-makers. It is run by James McIlwraith, Richard Johnson and Guy Birchmore. Devon Cider has orchards at Exbourne and contract growers around Whimple. In certain brands concentrate is used. No specific information on juice content was available though fruit juices such as cranberry, orange and raspberry are added to the Churchwards range.

Cider: Three Hammers White Cider 7.5% abv; Devon Village 5% abv; Churchwards 4.5% abv; Old Moors 4.5% abv
Outlets: Various supermarkets and off-licences.
Address: Howden Road, Tiverton, EX16 5NU
Telephone: 01884 259982

Gray's Farm Cider

Neatly tucked away in the hills between Dunsford and Tedburn St Mary, Ben and Ruth Gray provide a warm welcome to cider connoisseurs. The Gray family has been here since the 1660s, and their long cider barn is well worth seeing. The whole set-up is nineteenth century, though there are now a few hydraulics used at pressing time. Wooden barrels are used, and old standard orchards with a few indigenous varieties from the Halstow area.

Cider: Gray's Cider dry, medium and sweet, draught 6–6.5% abv
Outlets: Farm gate, Darts Farm and Devon County Show
Address: Halstow, Tedburn St Mary, Exeter, EX6 5AN
Telephone: 01647 61236
Website: www.graysdevoncider.co.uk

Green Valley Cyder Ltd

Chris Coles and Nick Pring make their cider at the back of Darts Farm in the Clyst Valley near Topsham. They have a major sales outlet in Darts Farm Village, showcasing a large number of ciders and perries from all over the south-west and beyond. It is their mission to keep traditional cider-making alive using cider apples from old east Devon orchards.

Cider: Devon Farm Cyder bottled and draught 6.8% abv; Stillwood Vintage Cyder still and sparkling, bottled 8.3% abv; Clyst Orchard bottled 8.3% abv; Dragon Tears dry, bottled and carbonated 4.7% abv; St George's Temptation sweet and carbonated 4.7% abv
Outlets: Darts Farm Village, Clyst St George, Exeter, EX3 0QH
Telephone: 01392 876658
email: gvcyder@yahoo.co.uk
www.dartsfarm.co.uk

Killerton Estate Cider

Situated seven miles north-east of Exeter the Killerton estate is able to harvest cider apples from six of its own traditional standard orchards. The 50 different varieties of apple include Killerton Sharp and Killerton Sweet. The cider is made by National Trust wardens and volunteers under the watchful eye of their cider guru, Peter Davies. Cider has been made here since 1990, but was made on a much larger scale in the nineteenth century, when the Aclands owned the estate. The wardens have saved the orchards and planted up the gaps with new trees. They hope to keep the orchards in good condition for wildlife as well as for cider. The cider apples are pressed out by hand on a large old wooden cider press and this can be seen each year on Apple Day in October. Please phone to find out dates.

Cider: Killerton Estate Cider bottled 6% abv
Outlets: Killerton Estate Shop, Buckland Abbey, Knightshayes Court and Arlington Court. For details see National Trust website.
Address: The National Trust (Enterprises) Ltd, Forestry Yard, Killerton Estate, Budlake, near Broadclyst, Exeter, EX5 3LW
Shop number: 01392 881912
For information on the National Trust go to
Website: www.nationaltrust.org.uk

Hancock's Devon Cider

Just a mile or two west of South Molton lies Clapworthy Mill. Five generations of the Hancock family have pressed cider here. The apples are all local. The business is now run by Helen Hancock.

Cider: Sweet, medium, dry, bottled and draught 6–8% abv
Outlets: Farm gate or wholesale only, 20 litres minimum, plus online shop, see website. Also Griffin's Yard, South Molton, Brian Ford's, Barnstaple and many other off-licences in North Devon
Address: Clapworthy Mill, South Molton, EX36 4HX
Telephone: 01769 572678
Website: www.hancockscider.co.uk

Heron Valley Cider

Natasha Bradley and her four sisters, Kirstin, Britta, Danielle and Jasmin, run this South Devon cider farm with a little help from their parents, Stephen and Shirley Bradley, who started Heron Valley in 1997. Natasha wants to keep the cider as natural and organic as possible. She uses such apples as Fair Maid of Devon, Foxwhelp, Pig's Snout, Dabinett, Sheep's Nose and Hangy Down Clusters. Heron Valley is big on apple juice as well.

Cider: Heron Valley organic, sparkling, medium, bottled 6% abv; Farmhouse Cider medium, dry, bottled and draught 6% abv
Outlets: Farm gate, but phone first; online shop, see website; also available in more than 300 pubs, farmshops, delicatessens and restaurants in South Devon.
Address: Crannacombe Farm, Hazelwood, Loddiswell, Kingsbridge, TQ7 4DX
Telephone: 01548 550256
Website: www.heronvalley.co.uk

Luscombe Cider

This organic cider farm lies just above the River Dart between Buckfastleigh and Totnes and is run by Gabriel David. He uses wild yeasts and Devon apples such as Sops in Wine, Tale Sweet, Pig's Snout, Quench, Slack-ma-Girdle and Tom Putt. Luscombe cider also produces apple juice, elderflower, ginger beer and Sicilian lemonade.

Cider: Devon Cider organic, dry 4.8% abv
Outlets: No direct sales but available througout the UK
Address: Dean Court, Lower Dean, Buckfastleigh, TQ11 0LP
Telephone: 01364 643036
Website: www.luscombe.co.uk

Lyme Bay Winery

Located at Shute, near the Axe valley, and run by Nigel Howard, the business started out in 1995 as the Lyme Bay Cider Company but was diverted into wine and all sorts of other drink-related enterprises. Jack Rattenbury cider (named after a dedicated smuggler who lived 1778–1844) was awarded a Gold at the Taste of the West Awards 2007. was a dedicated smuggler. The winery also produces a very wide range of country wines and liqueurs.

Cider: Jack Rattenbury Scrumpy still, medium, bottled 6% abv; Jack Rattenbury Vintage still, dry and medium, bottled and flagons 7.4% abv; Lyme Bay Sparkling Cider dry and medium, bottled 6% abv
Outlets: Winery Shop in Shute and many national outlets
Address: The Lyme Bay Winery, Shute, near Axminster, EX13 7PW
Telephone: 01297 551355
Website: www.lymebaywinery.co.uk

Mill Top Cider

Mill Top Cider is run by Richard Merrin, who started planting apple trees in 1998. He is based at Combeinteignhead, a mile or two east of Newton Abbot, which at one time was a heavy-duty cider town. He also uses apples from old orchards around Stoke and Combe. As well as making cider he also sells apple juice and ginger beer.

Cider: Mill Top Cider bottled 5.5–6% abv; Sweet Annie Cider (made from Dabinett and Michelin) bottled 6.8% abv; Martin Jenny bottled 6% abv
Outlets: Farm shop and online. Available in Teignmouth and local pubs.
Address: Combeinteignhead, Newton Abbot, TQ12 4RE
Telephone: 01626 873030
Website: www.milltop.co.uk

Ostler's Cider Mill

Ostler's cider farm is set in the valley of the Yeo, a tributary of the Taw at Goodleigh just outside Barnstaple. Cider has been made here for centuries and is run by Peter Hartnoll, who can trace his cider-making ancestors back to 1530. Ostler's use cider apples from their own four-acre orchard with 1,200 cider apple trees. He also makes unpasteurised cider vinegar and sells his own blended honey. No chemicals are used and the pure cider apple juice makes a rough, traditional cider. There is also a good wassail.

Cider: Ostler's Traditional dry, bottled and draught 6.5% abv; Ostler's Vintage dry, bottled and draught 6.5%
Outlets: farm gate and online shop and local off licences. Atlantic Village in Bideford and Griffin's Yard, South Molton. Please ring first.
Address: Eastacott Lane, Northleigh Hill, Goodleigh, EX32 7NF
Telephone: 01271 321241
Website: www.ostlerscidermill.co.uk

Palmershayes Cider

Run by Aubrey Greenslade, this cider farm is a mile or two west of Tiverton, with the River Exe down the road. The cider is to be found at the back of the barns. Somewhat rustic. Ring the bell.

Cider: Scrumpy dry, medium and sweet, bottled or draught 6% abv
Outlets: Farm gate and local off-licences
Address: Palmershayes Farm, Calverleigh, Tiverton, EX16 8BA
Telephone: 01884 254579

RealDrink Ltd

Paul Gadd and Rebecca Jack run this small but high-quality drinks company from the village of Stoke Gabriel, set on the River Dart between Totnes and Dartmouth. Paul and Rebecca use apples from old, well-established orchards in the South Hams, which are traditional and unsprayed. These orchards are identified on the label. They have also won a Great Taste Award 2008.

Cider: Real Cider still, bottled 6% abv; Real Natural Sparkling Cider bottled, Normandy method 5% abv
Cider Brandy: Real Cider Brandy 40% abv. This is the first cider brandy to be produced commercially from Devon cider apples.
Outlets: farm gate, online shop (see website), local outlets and some National Trust shops in South Devon.
Address: Elmcroft, Broad Path, Stoke Gabriel, TQ9 6RW
Telephone: 01803 782217
Website: www.realdrink.co.uk

Sandford Orchards

Barny and Marie Butterfield have been making cider commercially since 2002. They use apples from the Sandford area north of Crediton. The cider is made in a very traditional way, pressing through straw. They use local Devon apples such as Tremlett's Bitter, Sweet Alford, Northwood, Kirton Fair, Ellis Bitter, Pig's Snout, Sheep's Nose, Filbarrel, Sugarbush. Kirton is the old name for Crediton, which was once a cathedral city.

Cider: Vintage Cider aged in rum casks, bottled 8% abv; Old Kirton is pressed through oaten straw and thatching straw on an old wooden press aged in oak with very wild yeasts, bottled and draught 6% abv; Traditional Farmhouse dry, bottled and draught 6.5% abv

Outlets: Online shop, Crediton Farmers' Market, Crediton Food Fayre, Bridge Stores, Bow, Darts Farm Village, Topsham Regency News and Wines in Teignmouth. Pubs include Rose and Crown in Sandford and Three Little Pigs in Crediton

Address: Sandford Orchards, Crediton, EX17 2BP

Telephone: 01363 777822

Website: www.sandfordorchards.co.uk

West Lake Cider

George Travis moved down to North Devon from Lancashire and bought a derelict farm with an old orchard between Hatherleigh and Holsworthy. He started making cider in 1997 and buys in cider apples from local orchards including Black Torrington and Whimple. West Lake ciders have won awards at Taste of the West and The Great Taste Awards in 2007. He also makes a wide range of apple juices and cider vinegar. George is ably helped in all aspects of the business by Linda Davies.

Cider: West Lake dry and medium, still, bottled 6.5% abv; West Lake Organic medium, dry, sparkling, bottled 6.5% abv; West Lake Premium medium, sparkling 6.5% abv; West Lake Cider Anglais (Normandy style with Dabinett) 4.5% abv; single variety Dabinett, Yarlington Mill and Kingston Black 6.5% abv

Outlets: Farmers' Markets at Tavistock, Okehampton and Bideford, as well as Darts Farm Village and a good range of delicatessens in Devon, a farm shop near Penzance and an organic delicatessen in West Hampstead. Collection at farm by arrangement only.

Address: West Lake Farm, Chilla, Beaworthy, EX21 5XF

Telephone: 01409 221991

Website: www.westlakefarm.com

Winkleigh Cider Company

Many people will have heard of Inch's Cider, which was formed by Sam Inch after the First World War. Inch's Cider continued to grow until one day it caught the eye of somebody in Bulmers, who bought it for £23.3 million. Inevitably there were redundancies, and production was moved away in 1998. At that point David Bridgman, the chief cider-maker, bought part of the Inch's site and set up a company with his wife, Margaret and brother, Graham. They kept the tradition of cider-making in Winkleigh alive and still use cider apples from many of the small local orchards.

Cider: Scrumpy medium dry and medium sweet, draught 7.5% abv; Autumn Devon Scrumpy sparkling 7.4% abv; Sam's Cider dry, medium and sweet 6% abv; Poundhouse dry, medium and sweet, sparkling 6% abv

Outlets: Shop at Western Barn as well as many other outlets in Devon. Please phone for mail order.

Address: Western Barn, Hatherleigh Road, Winkleigh, EX19 8AP

Telephone: 01837 83560

Website: www.winkleighcider.com

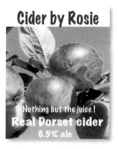

DORSET

Wiscombe Cider

Just a few miles from Honiton and not too far from Beer in East Devon lies Wiscombe Park, home to one of East Devon's more colourful characters. Tim Chichester is a horse-drawn-cider fanatic and has his own methods of making cider. A pair of horses go round and round the granite troughed mill in a clockwise direction to crush the apples. The pomace is then shovelled on to the press and pressed out between straw. Some of the apples come from Wiscombe Park, the rest from local farms. He uses varieties such as Tom Putt, Dabinett and Michelin. The cider is matured in 110-gallon barrels, which are steam-cleaned with his ancient steam engine. He also has a mobile donkey-driven mill, which he takes to shows.

Cider: Wiscombe Suicider medium, draught 8% abv; Merrymaker draught 6% abv
Outlets: Various festivals, the Hare and Hounds near Honiton and other local pubs. Otter Brewery takes his cider to many local shows and events.
Address: Wiscombe Park, Southleigh, Colyton, EX24 6JG
Telephone: 07976 585465

Yearlstone Vineyard

Just a few miles south of Tiverton, at a bend in the Rive Exe, lies Bickleigh, and there, after you have gone up a narrow steep lane above the village, you will reach Yearlstone Vineyard, where you get a fantastic view overlooking the cricket pitch. The Vineyard is run by Roger and Juliet White, who came here in 1991. Their main work is producing wine, but in a good year they also produce bottle-fermented cider. They have 15 varieties of cider apple in their orchard. There is a good café with a fantastic view.

Cider: Cyder Fizz bottle-fermented, sparkling, dry 8% abv
Outlets: Yearlstone Vineyard shop
Address: Yearlstone Vineyard, Bickleigh, EX16 8RL
Telephone: 01884 855700
Website: www.yearlstone.co.uk

Ye Olde Cider Bar

This is one of the last cider houses left in the country. Cider houses were once very common and were often used as informal meeting places, like the cider clubs of West Dorset. Ye Olde Cider Bar was established as a cider house around 1880 and has been run by Richard Knibbs since 1982. He serves 14 varieties of draught cider and some bottled. A visit to the cider bar is an education, particularly for the youth of Newton Abbot. Some of its 'graduates' from Seale Hayne agricultural college are now making some very respectable ciders and perries.

Cider: 14 different varieties (order a taxi home first)
Address: 99 East Street, Newton Abbot, TQ12 2LD
Telephone: 01626 354221

Castle's Cider

Malcolm Castle is the archetypal red-cheeked farmer. His cider is as dry as his wit. The press dates back to the 1850s and the cellar is at least 250 years old. Malcolm also keeps bees, sells honey and is often seen at farmers' markets. He is helped by his wife, Sylvia Creed-Castle, a noted local historian.

Cider: Castle's Dorset Cider bottled and draught 7% abv
Outlets: Farmers' markets in Crewkerne, Bridport, Dorchester, Poundbury and Weymouth.
Address: Crabb's Bluntshay Farm, Whitchurch Canonicorum, DT6 6RN
Telephone: 01297 489064

Cider by Rosie

Rose Grant has made it her mission to revive Dorset's cider traditions in the small village of Winterbourne Houghton, which is about six miles from Blandford. She has her own orchards and also buys in cider apples. She is a dedicated cider-maker and supplies a wide variety of pubs.

Rose won first prize at Putley in Herefordshire for her medium cider in 2007, so to celebrate she has planted 20 more apple trees: mostly Dabinett and Chisel Jersey.

Cider: Medium dry, draught 6.5% abv; single variety keeved Dabinett and Porter's Perfection 5.4% abv
Outlets: available in 15 Dorset pubs and 3 off-licences
Address: Michaelmas Cottage, Winterbourne Houghton, DT11 OPE
Telephone: 01258 880543
Website: www.ciderbyrosie.com

Mill House Cider Museum

Run by the dynamic Penny Whatmoor, this family-run museum and nursery are well worth a visit. This is a wonderful place with 42 old, majestic wooden cider presses and mills, some of which are eighteenth century, collected by Penny's father, Derek. There are scratters galore and some interesting mugs, flagons and cider flutes. Penny runs a shop, which sells ciders from Devon, Somerset and Herefordforshire. They also make some of their own cider and have demonstration days.

Cider: Large variety of bottled and draught; some perry and cider brandy
Outlets: Farm shop and museum
Address: Mill House Cider, Owermoigne, near Dorchester, DT2 8HZ
Telephone: 01305 852220
Website: www.millhousecider.com

Netherbury Cider

Simon and Amanda Mehigan have made cider since 2000. Netherbury is an idyllic village just south of Beaminster in West Dorset. And it is one of the few Dorset villages that has a continuous tradition of cider making following on from two local families of cider makers, Oliver's and Warren's. Simon now has one of Hubert Warren's Dabinett orchards. Other apples that Simon uses are Brown's and Porter's Perfection. Simon has just planted a new perry orchard, which is the first large-scale orchard to be planted in Dorset for many years.

Cider: Netherbury Cider bottled 6.5% (draught on demand)
Outlets: Framptons Butchers and Le Vieux Four French Bakery, Beaminster, Washingpool Farm Shop, Bridport, Majestic Wines, Dorchester, and various local restaurants: The Riverside Restaurant, West Bay; The Bridge House Hotel, Beaminster; Broad Street Restaurant, Lyme Regis.
Telephone: 01308 488757
Website: www.netherburycider.com

Bridle's Cider and Perry

Just outside Shaftesbury in Stour Row at the foot of Duncliffe Hill, Bo Rutter has been making cider since 1995 and perry since 1997. He has his own orchard with Kingston Black, Yarlington Mill, Stembridge Clusters Fillbarrel, Frederick, Bulmer's Norman, Tremlett's Bitter, Brown Snout, as well as one or two unidentified but heavy cropping cider trees. The perry pear trees Bo planted himself include Thorn, Moorcroft, Green Horse and Winnal's Longdon. Bo is a small but dedicated producer who is reviving the cider tradition in North Dorset.

Cider: Bridle's Vintage Cider bottled, still 8% abv
Perry: Bridle's Perry bottled, still 8% abv
Outlets: Abbey Stores, Salisbury
Address: The Cowshed, Stour Row, Shaftesbury, SP7 0QW
Telephone: 01747 852320

GLOUCESTERSHIRE

Brains Cider

David Brain's family has been making cider for more than a hundred years at Littledean, just north of Cinderford, right in the heart of the Forest of Dean. They use only their own apples, which include such varieties as Foxwhelp, Vilberie and Yarlington Mill.

Cider: Dry, draught 5–6% abv
Outlets: Farm gate (phone first on 07887 678209)
Address: The Orchards, Edge Hills, Littledean, GL14 3LQ
Telephone: 01594 822416

Brook Apple Farm Cider & Perry

Robert Cook makes cider at Scrubditch Farm, North Cerney and before that he made cider at Rencomb. The pomace goes straight to the rare breed Gloucester Old Spots and Berkshire pigs on the farm. Robert is a semi-retired gardener who works two days a week and has been producing cider for at least ten years. The cider fruit comes from a number of sources in Gloucestershire, Herefordshire and even Wiltshire. Robert learned his cider and perry making from Jean Nowell of Lyne Down. He belongs to the Three Counties Cider and Perry Association.

Cider: Scrubditch medium, bottled and draught 8% abv; Brook Apple Blend medium 7% abv; Brook Apple Blend Perry 7.5% abv; single variety Kingston Black, Yarlington Mill, Dabinett, Brown's
Outlets: Farm gate (phone first), Cheltenham and Cirencester farmers' markets
Address: 24 Rendcomb, Cirencester, GL7 7HF
Telephone: 01285 831479

Crooked End Farm Organics

Pope Hill Orchard is shared between four friends in the Forest of Dean, who bought the 12-acre organic orchard in 2000. One of the key cider makers is David Norman, and although he has recently sold Crooked End Organic Farm to the new owners, Anya and Barry, he still makes the cider and it is sold through the farm shop. The orchard is about 150 years old and has a very good mixture of perry pear trees, Black Worcesters, Rock, Taynton Squash and Blakeney Red, as well as a nice range of cider apples. The cider is made with natural yeasts and is stored in oak hogsheads.

Cider: Crooked End Farm, bottled and draught 6–7% abv
Perry: Crooked End Farm, bottled and draught 6–7% abv
Outlets: Crooked End Farm Shop
Address: Crooked End Farm Shop, Ruardean, GL17 9XF
Telephone: Anya and Barry Makin-Terry 01594 544482. Dave and Morag Norman 01452 830986

Day's Cottage Apple Juice and Cider Co.

David Kaspar and Helen Brent-Smith live on a farm at Brookthorpe between Gloucester and Stroud. Some of their orchards have been in Helen's family for more than 200 years, so it is no surprise that they are keen on saving old Gloucestershire varieties of cider apple and perry pear and are very active members of the Gloucestershire Orchard Group. They have planted more than 100 varieties in a museum orchard at Brentland's Farm. David does a lot of grafting and has a small nursery. They sell apple juice and also make single variety cider and perry, which are fermented in oak barrels. These varieties may vary each year and depend upon the season and the crop.

Cider: Foxwhelp and Kingston Black, draught and bottled 7% abv
Perry: Blakeney Red, Malvern Hills, Brown Bess, draught and bottled 7.5% abv
Outlets: Farm gate (phone first), Stroud and Bristol farmers' markets
Address: Day's Cottage, Upton Lane, Brookthorpe, GL4 0UT
Telephone: 01452 813602 or 07774 816282
Website: www.applejuice.care4free.net

Hartland's Cider and Perry

Dereck Hartland is the third generation to make cider and perry. Tirley is close to the River Severn and the village on the opposite bank is, appropriately enough, called Apperley. The cider and perry are kept in oak barrels. Dereck won the much-coveted CAMRA Gold award in 2003 and again in 2007 for his perry.

Cider: Hartland's dry and sweet, draught 6% abv
Perry: Hartland's dry and sweet, draught 5.5% abv
Outlets: Farm gate and various festivals
Address: Tirley Villa, Tirley, Gloucester, GL19 4HA
Telephone: 01452 780480

Harechurch Cider

At least four generations of Steve Bursom's family have made cider on the Herefordshire/ Gloucestershire borders and at present are making cider in the Forest of Dean. Only local cider apples and perry pears are used. Foxwhelp, Kingston Black, Yarlington Mill, Stoke Red. 100% pure juice is used with natural yeasts and oak casks.

Cider: Dry, bottle-conditioned and draught 6.5–7.5% abv; bottle-fermented sparkling 7–8% abv
Perry: Dry bottle-conditioned and draught 6.5% abv; bottle-fermented sparkling 7–8% abv; medium draught 6% abv
Outlets: Shop Sunday 10–11 a.m., farm gate (phone first)
Address: White Lodge, Springfields, Drybrook, GL17 9BW
Telephone: 01594 541738

Hayles Fruit Farm

Near Hailes Abbey north-east of Cheltenham, the fruit farm is run by the Harrell family, but was planted by Lord Sudeley more than 100 years ago. The apple juice and cider are made from dessert apples.

Cider: Badger's Bottom dry and medium, bottled 7% abv
Outlets: Farm shop
Address: Hailes, Winchcombe, GL54 5PB
Telephone: 01242 602123
Website: www.hayles-fruit-farm.co.uk

Minchew's Real Cyder and Perry

Kevin Minchew is a real aficionado of cider and perry and will always surprise you with his knowledge and depth of interest and the single-variety ciders and perries he makes. Kevin also keeps some older maturing ciders, which are available upon request.

Cider: Isabel's Orchard, Stoke Red, Kingston Black, Yarlington Mill and Dabinett 7.7% abv
Perry: Blakeney Red, Malvern Hills and blends 6–8%
Outlets: Tewkesbury Farmers' Market, Orchard Hive and Vine on line. See Kevin's website for other outlets. Visitors strictly by appointment.
Address: Rose Cottage, Aston Cross, Bredon Road, Tewkesbury, GL20 8HX
Telephone: 0797 403 4331
Website: www.minchews.co.uk

Orchard's Cider & Perry Co.

Run by Keith Orchard in Brockweir on the River Wye, a mile or two above Tintern Abbey. This is an idyllic spot to be cider making and Keith produces a wide range of cider and perry.

Cider: Wye Valley Cider bottles and flagons 6.6% abv; Farmhouse Cider bottles 6.7% abv; single variety Kingston Black, Dabinett 6% abv; Orchard Mist bottle-fermented, sparkling 8% abv
Perry: Cannock Perry from Little Dean 5.3% abv, Blakeney Red 6.4% abv, Gloucestershire medium, dry 4.8% abv
Outlets: Brockweir Village Shop, Bristol Slow Food Market, and Yewgreen Farm by appointment only.
Address: Yewgreen Farm, Brockweir, near Chepstow, NP16 7PH
Telephone: 01291 689536
Website: www.orchardsciderandperry.com

Prinknash Abbey Enterprises

Set in Prinknash Park just north of Painswick, the Abbey is an ancient site that had links to Gloucester and was given to the Benedictines in the eleventh century. There were vineyards attached to the abbey. No doubt perry was also made here in the years following the dissolution. Certainly perry was made here after the Second World War, but sadly the old trees slowly succumbed to storms. These were replaced by cider-apple trees from Long Ashton and it is the apples from these that are made into cider. The cider making is superintended by Brother Giles. The monks started selling the cider in 1996 and so what was once just their private tipple can now be bought over the counter in the shop. Their perry is still an in-house drink. Some of the known varieties are Moorcroft, Brown Bessy, Red Blackberry and Brett pears.

Cider: Prinknash Cider dry, medium and sweet, bottled 6% abv
Outlets: Abbey Gift Shop
Address: Prinknash Abbey, Cranham, GL4 8EX.
Telephone: Abbey 01452 812455
Gift Shop 01452 812066
Website: www.prinknashabbey.org

Severn Sider Cider

The village of Awre is on a great horseshoe bend of the River Severn below Newnham. Nick Bull's father started making cider and perry here in the 1950s. Awre has three distinct varieties within its parish, the Hagloe Crab, the Box Kernel, a bitter-sweet that Nick saved from extinction, and the Blakeney Red. When it came to seeing in the new millenium they made a special batch of cider for the village party. It was so succesful that Nick's son, Tom, and a friend, James McCrindle, have carried it on and have gone commercial, in their spare time when they are not working in a local quarry. The labels are woodcuts by a local artist Steve Hislop.

Cider: Dry, still and sparkling 6–7% abv; single variety Box Kernel, Dabinett, Brown Snout, Morgan Sweet
Perry: Dry, still, mostly Blakeney Red
Outlets: More than 30 local outlets
Address: The Old Vicarage, Awre, Newnham, GL14 1EL
Telephone: 01594 510282
Website: www.severncider.com

HEREFORDSHIRE

Tiddley Pommes

Pete Smithies and his family make cider at Priding Farm, not far from the banks of the Severn where Jasper Eli once lived. Not many cider makers get their obituary in the *Independent*, but Jasper did; he had tattoos all over his body. Pete worked with Jasper and still has the cider fruit from Wick Court, an old, moated farmhouse down the road.

Cider and Perry: Tiddley Pommes cider and perry, draught 9% abv
Outlets: Farm gate (if visiting please phone first)
Address: Priding Farm, 39 Passage Road, Saul, GL2 7LB
Telephone: 07748 253834 or 01452 740114 (Pete)

Ashgrove Farm

Overlooking the beautiful and winding Lugg valley, this 70-acre organic farm is run by Rod and Rosie Hawnt. They have two traditional, certified organic orchards, which date back at least 70 years. The apples from these orchards include Bulmer's Norman, Michelin, Tanner's Red, Sherringtons, Kingston Black, Foxwhelp, Brown Snout and Yarlington Mill. They started making cider in 2002. The rest of their fruit goes to Westons. On the farm they also keep pedigree Hereford cattle from Westwood bloodlines as well as Ryeland sheep. Rosie is very keen on archaeology and historical research into orchards.

Cider: Orchard Bull dry, still, bottled 7% abv; Orchard Ram draught and bottled 6.2% abv
Outlets: Canon Pyne stores and other local farmshops and local pubs
Address: Ashgrove Farm, Marden, Hereford, HR1 3EY
Telephone: 01568 797867
Website: www.hawnt.co.uk

Brook Farm Cider

In 1998 Peter Keam revived the art of cider making in this north Herefordshire village not a stone's throw from the Slow Food town of Ludlow. Peter uses such varieties as Broxwood Foxwhelp, Yarlington Mill, Porter's Perfection, Stoke Red, Harry Master's Jersey, Brown Snout, Dabinett, White Norman and Chisel Jersey, plus several more whose identity has yet to be determined. The perry pears come from an old orchard about ten miles east of Wigmore.

Cider: Brook Farm dry and medium, draught and bottled, still and carbonated 6–8% abv
Perry: Brook Farm dry and medium, bottled 6–7% abv
Outlets: Farm gate, Ludlow Food Centre, Marches Little Beer Shop
Address: Brook Farm, Wigmore, HR6 9UJ
Telephone: 01568 770562
Website: www.brookfarmcider.co.uk

Bulmers

The company was founded in Hereford in 1887 by Percy Bulmer. He made 4,000 gallons that first year and now Bulmers is the country's largest cider maker. It has 2,500 acres of its own orchards, 6,500 acres under contract and 1,500 acres of new planting. Bulmers also has its own nursery, which has been in operation since 1926. Around 90,000 tons of apples are pressed annually. However, over the years the company has had to import apple concentrate from Europe and beyond. Bulmers as a family business was bought out by the brewers Scottish and Newcastle in July 2003. Scrumpy Jack was originally produced by Symonds of Stoke Lacey and in 1988 was sold to Bulmers. In January 2008 Bulmers announced that they were building a new site for processing cider apples at Ledbury with Universal Beverages Ltd and Q Group. This will create a half-a-million hectolitre bulk cider facility and the building of a new fruit processing mill with eleven Bucher presses that can handle 15,000 tons of fruit a week. The juice content and formula for Bulmers brands will no doubt still remain a closely guarded secret.

Cider: Strongbow 5.3% abv packaged, 4.5% abv draught; Bulmers Original 4.5% abv; Woodpecker 3.5% abv, 4% abv draught; Scrumpy Jack 6% abv, 5.2% abv draught. Bulmers also produce White Lightning 7.5%, Strongbow Sirrus 5% and Pear Cider 4.5%abv
Outlets: Worldwide
Address: Plough Lane, Hereford, HR4 0LE
Telephone: 01432 352000
Website: www.bulmer.com

Butford Organics

Situated just north of the village of Bodenham in the Lugg Valley, this organic smallholding is run by Janet and Martin Harris. Before settling here in 1999 Martin was a consulting actuary in Leeds. Like many small producers he started out by studying cider making with Peter Mitchell at Hindlip college, and then perfected the techniques of producing sparkling cider in Normandy. For a while the couple raised rare breed pigs, Oxford Sandy and Blacks, and they also have Black Rock hens. They now concentrate on cider but have also started making organic apple juice.

Cider: Ganymede organic, dry, sparkling, bottled 6% abv; Thebe organic, medium, sparkling, bottled 5% abv; Aurora medium, sparkling bottled 5% abv, organic and non-organic
Perry: Draught dry, medium dry 6–7% abv
Outlets: Farm shop, Ludlow Farmers' Market and local food fairs
Address: Bowley Lane, Bodenham, HR1 3LG
Telephone: 01568 797195
Website: www.butfordorganics.co.uk

Cider Museum and King Offa Distillery

Run by the Hereford Museum Trust in the middle of Hereford this is a real gem and should be visited by anyone interested in the history and culture of cider. The Charitable Trust was founded in 1973 by Bertram Bulmer and opened to the public in 1981. Its aim is to preserve the history of cider making not just of Herefordshire, but worldwide. The museum houses not just cider presses and scratters but artefacts such as the *Herefordshire Pomona* and many eighteenth-century cider flutes. Here you can see the Bulmers' panelled board room, the Pomagne 'champagne cider' cellars and come right up to date with an excellent interactive website of oral recordings about orchards and cider from local people. It also holds a rich archive of written material. Every year the Cider Museum runs the International Cider and Perry Competition, which is now very prestigious. It also houses the King Offa Distillery, which consists of a 1905 Normandy pot still. The cider is double-distilled and the spirit is aged for at least five years in oak casks to produce Hereford Cider Brandy. The King Offa distillery was given its licence in 1984, the first licence for cider brandy to be issued for over 200 years, a landmark in the cider world.

Cider and Perry: A very wide range of bottled ciders and perries
Cider Brandy: 10-year-old, 5-year-old 40% abv; aperitif 18% abv and liquer 25% abv
Outlets: Museum shop
Address: 21 Ryelands Street, Hereford, HR4 0LW
Telephone: 01432 354207
Website: www.cidermuseum.co.uk

Dragon Orchard and Once Upon a Tree

This is wonderful 22-acre traditional orchard near Ledbury run by Norman and Ann Stanier. The fruit farm has been in the family since 1926. What Norman and Ann have developed is a unique system of crop sharing where people buy annual 'shares' in the orchard and its produce. Norman and Anne wanted to reach customers directly and more than that, to involve them in the whole orchard process, where they visit as a group on set weekends during the year. Dragon Orchard Cropsharers is an exciting way of re-establishing links between producers and consumers. In the autumn they take home a generous share of the orchard produce. This is a form of community-supported agriculture whereby the grower and consumers share the rewards and responsibilities of farming. Here you can plant trees, share in the fruit and there is even an outdoor theatre. Dragon Orchard have paired up with Simon Day of Once Upon a Tree to make their cider and apple juice.

Once Upon a Tree is round the corner from Dragon Orchard, in Putley Green. This is run by Simon Day whose father, Tom Day, was vineyard manager at the Three Choirs Vineyard back in 1975, when Three Choirs was just half an acre ... This is a very good example of a cider maker with wine-making knowledge working in cooperation with an orchard owner. Simon's wife, Hannah, is a garden designer and it was through her work that they met

Norman and Ann Stanier. The cider is made with Dabinett, Ellis Bitter and Brown's Apple. Simon also makes three varieties of apple juice: Brown's, Russet and Bramley.

Cider: Dragon Orchard dry, bottled 7.5% abv (first batch ready April 2008)
Outlets: Dragon Orchard by appointment and local farm shops
Address: Dragon Orchard, Dragon House, Putley, Ledbury, HR8 2RG
Telephone: 01531 670071
Website: www.dragonorchard.co.uk
Address: Once Upon A Tree Ltd, 1 Putley Green, Putley, Ledbury, HR8 2QN
Telephone: 01531 660668

Dunkertons Cider and Perry

Run by Susie and Ivor Dunkerton, this family firm makes cider near Pembridge. They have 38 acres of orchards and make around 50,000 gallons, helped by their cider maker Rob West. They are organic and their cider is made without resort to chemical sprays, colourings or flavourings. The organic perry is made from perry pears such as Merrylegs, Red Horse, Moorcroft, Painted Lady and Thorn.

Cider: Dry, medium sweet and sweet, still, bottled 7% abv; Premium organic, bottled 8% abv; Black Fox 7% abv; single variety Kingston Black, Breakwell's Seedling, Court Royal 8% abv
Perry: Organic, bottled 7.5% abv
Outlets: Farm shop, Orchard, Hive and Vine, Waitrose, Sainsbury's and EH Booth
Address: Cider Mill, Luntley, Pembridge, near Leominster, HR6 9ED
Telephone: 01544 388653
Website: www.dunkertons.co.uk

Great Oak Cider and Apple Co.

Brian Jones used to do contract orcharding for other people and bought ten acres of bush orchard. He has now sold the orchard on but buys back the fruit that he wants for cider making. It is a small-scale operation: no sales available but visitors are welcome by appointment to come round for a chat and sampling.

Cider: House Vat draught 7% abv
Address: Roughmoor, Eardisley HR3 6PR
Telephone: 01544 327400

Gregg's Pit Cider and Perry

Run by James Marsden, Gregg's Pit is a magnificent example of an eighteenth-century smallholder's plot, complete with cottage, marl pit and indigenous perry pear trees named after the property and its original owner, who dug the marl to help with the pointing of St Bartholomew's Church down the road in the village of Much Marcle. James and his partner Helen Woodman make first-rate cider and perry from their own perry pears and cider fruit. James is meticulous about hygiene and has an impressive collection of stainless steel vats in his wooden cider house. He specialises in sparkling bottle fermented and Normandy method. This is artisan cider and perry making at its very best.

Cider: 2007 Vintage – Brown Snout, Chisel Jersey and Dabinett (Normandy method); Brown's Apple and Ellis Bitter and Kingston Black (single variety)
Perry: Thorn (single variety); Gregg's Pit, Aylton Red and Blakeney Brandy: single variety (Normandy method) Butt and Oldfield
Outlets: Farm gate by appointment
Address: Gregg's Pit, Much Marcle HR8 2NL
Telephone: 01531 660687
Website: www.greggs-pit.co.uk

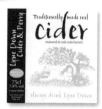

Gwatkin Cider Co. Ltd

Set a mile or two up upstream from the old church at Abbey Dore, Dennis Gwatkin's cider farm is well placed in the middle of Golden Valley. The farm is run as a family business and apart from cider and perry it also produces beef, lamb and pork, butchered on the farm. The soils are rich clays, which are good for fruit trees. There are 15 acres of orchard. Fruit is also bought in from surrounding farms and even from Gloucestershire. Dennis started making cider and perry commercially in 1991 and now makes around 20,000 gallons, concentrating on single varieties. It is all made using natural yeasts and matured in oak vats. Dennis has won many prizes from CAMRA and the Hereford Cider Museum for his cider and perry, and in 2008 his perry won first prize at the Bath & West show.

Cider: Single-variety Foxwhelp, Yarlington Mill, Stoke Red bottled and draught 7.5%
Perry: Blakeney Red, Thorn, Oldfield bottled and draught
Outlets: Farm shop, many local drink outlets and the Wye Valley Brewery
Address: Moorhampton Park Farm, Abbey Dore, HR2 0AL
Telephone: 01981 550258

Hellens Perry

This was once the home of Charles Radcliffe Cooke, the MP for 'Hereford and cider' who did so much in the late nineteenth and early twentieth centuries to get cider recognised as a fine drink in the Houses of Parliament. The Hellens is a Jacobean house open to visitors. The avenue of perry pear trees leading up to the house was planted in 1710. There is even a variety called Hellen's Early. A wonderful exhibition is held here each autumn as part of the Big Apple event. The sixteenth-century Great Barn is filled with hundreds of different varieties of cider apples and perry pears on display. Nick Stephens, who is a manager at Hellen's Manor, started making perry here in 2004, using an old circular trough which was powered by four men: a clear case of dedication.

Perry: Hellens Perry bottled, still 6% abv
Outlets: Hellens Manor
Address: Hellens Manor, Much Marcle, Ledbury, Herefordshire HR8 2LY
Telephone: 01531 660504
Website: www.hellensmanor.com

Henney's Cider Co. Ltd

This is a pure juice cider made by Mike Henney in conjunction with Wyre Croft Farm at Bishop's Frome. Unlike many other large cider makers, Henney's does not add fermenting sugars to the fresh juice or use concentrate. This means that the declared alcohol of 6% can be achieved with the minimum of dilution, or none at all.

Cider: Frome Valley Dry bottled 6% abv; Frome Valley Medium bottled 6% abv; Apple Blossom bottled 6% abv; Frome Valley Sweet bottled 6% abv
Outlets: Supermarkets; no visitors please at the farm
Address: Willow Cottage, Filly Brook, Bishop's Frome, WR6 5BY
Website: www.henneys.co.uk

Lyne Down

A mile or two out of Much Marcle, Lyne Down is run by Mark Catlin. It was originally started by Edgar Davies, then run by Jean Nowell for a good number of years. Mark bought it from the Westlakes. He uses mainly fruit from his own orchards and from local farmers.

Cider: Roaring Meg bottled 5.2% abv; single-variety Kingston Black, Yarlington Mill and Stoke Red Katy and Brown's 7% abv; oak, whisky and rum matured 7.3% abv; Cider brandy liqueur 25% abv
Perry: bottled 6% abv
Outlets: Farm shop; for local outlets visit website
Address: Lyne Down Farm, Much Marcle, HR8 2NT
Telephone: 07756 108501
Website: www.lynedowncider.co.uk

Malvern Magic

Rob Uren has been making cider for a good number of years and has been pruning and grafting just as long. Slightly nomadic, Rob worked for five seasons making cider at Burrow Hill in Somerset and is now based in Herefordshire. He looks after many acres of standard orchards. Rob is very keen to preserve old varieties.

Cider: Kingston Black dry, draught 7% abv; Knotted Kernel, Strawberry Norman and White Beech, Brown's Apple dry cider 7% abv
Perry: New Meadow Perry draught 7% abv
Outlets: Visitors welcome but no direct sales.
Address: Lower House Farm, Swinmore, Trumpet, HR8 2SJ
Telephone: 07771 904127

Newton Court Cidery

Newton Court is a very pleasant farmyard lying just off the main road south of Leominster. Paul Stephens has 15 acres of orchard and makes organic cider and perry with his father Tom. He is keen on bottle-fermented and Normandy-method ciders and perries and has won many prizes. Paul's grandfather, Jack, also made cider and Paul still has his small cider horn. His favourite pear is Winnal's Longdon, and he has access to a lot of them.

Cider: Dry, medium, sweet, bottled and draught 7% abv
Perry: Dry, medium, sweet, bottled and draught 7% abv
Cider/perry: Bottle-fermented sparkling 3–7% abv
Address: Newton, near Leominster, HR6 0PF
Telephone: 01568 611721
Website:
www.ciderroute.co.uk/site/meet/newtonCourt.html

Oliver's Cider and Perry

Tom Oliver is one of perry's fiercest champions in Herefordshire and from his family's old hop farm at Ocle Pychard he experiments with any pear, seeing what the fruit will give him. Tom has tracked down several rare varieties of perry pear including the Coppy, and he has the fruit from the last surviving mature tree. Tom is passionate about what he does and his enthusiasm for promotiong the very individual taste of perry is infectious. Tom is a keen producer of bottle-fermented sparkling perry and his cider is not bad either. He is a founder member of the Three Counties Slow Food Presidium for artisan perry, and he has won many prizes for his perry.

Cider: Vintage Cider bottled and draught 8.2% abv; Yarlington Mill bottled 6.5% abv; Dabinett 8.4% abv; Shezam 6.5% abv; method traditional dry 7.5–8% abv; bottle conditioned 6–7% abv, medium 5.5–6% abv
Perry: Dry perry bottled and draught 7.9% abv; Coppy 8.2% abv; Blakeney Red 6.9% abv; Rabbit Foot & Toby Time 6.7% abv; Oldfield 5.6% abv; method traditional and bottle conditioned 7–7.5 % abv
Outlets: Farm shop, Hop Pocket, Orchard, Hive and Vine, Three Horseshoes at Little Cowarne
Address: The Old Hop Kilns, Moorhouse Farm, Ocle Pychard, HR1 3QZ
Telephone: 01432 820569 or 07768 732026 (mobile)
Website: www.theolivers.org.uk

Orgasmic Cider Company

This is a family-run business owned by Steve and Claire Layton, Steve's brother Andrew Layton and his wife Gill. They have 12 acres of old standard orchard in conversion to organic and 70 acres of bush orchards, which are under contract to Bulmers. They make single-variety ciders.

Cider: Single-variety Brown Snout bottled 8.3% abv and Yarlington Mill 6.4% abv
Perry: Dry perry 6% abv
Outlets: Farm shop and local health food shops and pubs
Address: Great Parton, Eardisley, Hereford, HR3 6NX
Telephone: 01544 327244

Rathays Old Goat Cider

Graham Blackmore was once a government scientist and with his wife Jenny started making cider in 1999 on their smallholding. Their house was built in the 1960s by Peter Prior of Bulmers and has two acres of orchards with eighty-five full standard cider trees and one or two perry trees, varieties such as Bulmer's Norman, Tremlett's Bitter, Michelin, Yarlington Mill, Ball's Seedling, Foxwhelp x Medaille d'Or, Brown's, Thorn, Aiguille Gris, Vilberie. Apples are milled at Wigmore, and a no-nonsense cider is produced with natural wild yeasts and three or four rackings. They also keep 30 Angora goats. Graham is proud of the fact that he is an honorary member of the Hell's Angels gang The Outlaws of England. They like his cider …

Cider: Old Goat Dry 7.5% abv
Perry: Single-variety Blakeney Red and Painted Lady 7.5% abv
Outlets: Shows via wholesalers, Jon Hallam, Merrylegs, Jon Lewis local Hop Pocket, Legges of Bromyard. Small Beer
Address: Rathays, Sutton St Nicholas, Hereford, HR1 3AY
Telephone: 01432 880936

Ross-on-Wye Cider and Perry Co. Ltd

Mike Johnson's farm is at Peterstow. He has been making cider here since about 1985, but his grandfather made cider here before him. Most of the sixty-five acres on the farm are down to orchard. Some are commercial fruit that goes into Hereford, but the rest of the fruit he turns into cider and perry. He enjoys experimenting with single varieties and then makes up certain blends that work for him. His cider cellar is very cool in summer. Once a month he holds a music event that raises money for Third World charities. Broome Farm is also run as a Guest House by Mike's sister Hilary and her husband John: B&B with cream teas and a restaurant. It is an ideal place to stay if you like orchards, cider and perry.

Cider: Sparkling medium dry 6% abv; Old Orchard medium still 5% abv; Foxwhelp Bitter Sharp still 5% abv; dry cider fermented in a whisky cask 7% abv; naturally conditioned farmhouse 7% abv; single variety Kingston Black 7% abv; Harry Masters fermented in a whisky cask 7.4% abv; Sweet Knotted Kernel 7% abv
Perry: Naturally Conditioned Farmhouse 6% abv; Aylton Red dry still 5 % abv; medium dry still 6.5% abv; New Season dry 6.5 abv; Single Variety Gin 6% abv; fermented in a rum barrel medium dry 7% abv
Outlets: Farm gate, Orchard Hive and Vine, Middle Farm Firle, Truffles Roos on Wye, King's Head Hotel in Ross, The Harp, Hoarwithy, White Lion, Wilton.
Address: Broome Farm, Peterstow, Ross-on-Wye, HR9 6LA
Telephone: 01989 567232
Website: www.rosscider.com

Tillington Hills

This cider is made from cider apples grown on the Co-op's farms at Tillington, about five miles north-west of Hereford. They have 300 acres of orchard and grow such varieties as Tillington Ladies Finger, Bulmer's Norman, Yarlington Mill and Nottingham Colonel. This cider was first produced in 2005 and is made for them by Knights. Unlike some large producers they label their bottles with a full list of ingredients and the process of cider making involved.

Cider: Tillington Hills Premium Dry Reserve bottled, carbonated 6% abv
Outlets: Co-Op stores
Telephone: 0800 0686727
Website: www.coop.co.uk

SOMERSET

H. Weston & Sons

Westons are based in the village of Much Marcle and employ around 120 people. The firm's chairman is Helen Thomas, the great-granddaughter of Henry Weston, who founded the company in 1880. It is still a family firm and two of Helen's brothers, Tim and Henry Weston, are active in the business. The main cider maker is Jonathan Blair, who used to work for Bulmers. The company presses 12,000 tons of fruit a year and produces 3.5 million gallons of cider. Increasingly it is turning to organic orchards for fruit. Perry is also important. The works are open to the public and there are frequent visitor tours. There is a shop and the Scrumpy House Restaurant. Westons' ciders and perries are exported to 20 different countries.

Cider: Organic Vintage 7.3% abv; Old Rosie Scrumpy 7.3% abv; Premium Organic Cider 6.5% abv; Bounds Brand Scrumpy 4.8% abv. There are many other ciders (see website)
Perry: Country Perry still 4.5% abv; Original Perry 4.5%; Perry 7.4%
Outlets: Farm shop, many supermarkets and delicatessens
Address: The Bounds, Much Marcle, Ledbury, HR8 2NQ
Telephone: 01531 660233
Website: www.westons-cider.co.uk

Ashill Cider

Ashill is just off the main road between Ilminster and Taunton. Three generations of the House family have made cider here. Clifford House used to have a gaily painted wagon with cider barrels beside the A358 but the local council told him to take it away despite the fact that the council still uses the picture of this wagon as part of its tourist publicity, and the photograph is available as one of their postcards.

Cider: Draught 6–7% abv
Outlets: Farm gate
Address: Ashhill Farm, Ashill, Ilminster, TA19 9NE
Telephone: 01823 480513

Barrington Court Cider

Barrington Court was built in 1560 and was one of the early acquisitions of the National Trust in 1907. Cider making at Barrington ceased at this point, but the house still has a walled kitchen garden and ten acres of orchard with more than 60 varieties of apple. The last family that lived here were the Lyles. Some cider was made for them in the 1960s to a special recipe. The cider apples were also used for a good number of years by Burrow Hill Cider Farm, a mile or two up the road. The recent National Trust venture into cider making was started in autumn 2006 by the restaurant manager, Helen McDonald. A blend of ten varieties of cider apple was used, and made 300 gallons. Helen is a chef and has always used apples, and now relishes the challenge of making cider once more on the estate. The cider is made on a 200-year-old press, and this can be seen by the public on Apple Day each year. Apple juice is also made.

Cider: Barrington Court Phoenix, draught and bottled, dry, still 6.8–7.5%
Outlets: Barrington Court and Montacute House restaurants
Address: Barrington Court, Barrington, near Ilminster, TA19 0NQ
Telephone: 01460 243129
Website: www.nationaltrust.org.uk

Bridge Farm Cider

Nigel Stewart has been making cider since 1988, first at Sandford Orcas just north of Sherborne and now at East Chinnock in the rolling hills between Crewkerne and Yeovil. You can see his orchard right beside the main road. All the apples are local and harvested by him. Nigel makes farmhouse cider and has experimented for a number of years with bottle-fermented cider and perry, which is only available in good vintage years. He also sells apple juice, cider cakes and preserves. as well as heritage potatoes. Nigel is often seen at farmers' markets.

Cider: Bottled and draught, dry, medium and sweet 6% abv; bottle-fermented sparkling 7% abv; single-variety Brown's Apple 5.5–6% abv; Kingston Black, Porter's Perfection and Dabinett 6.5–7% abv

Perry: Bottle-fermented 6.5% abv

Cider Brandy: Bridge Farm Cider Brandy is well on its way, distilled by the Somerset Cider Brandy Company 42% abv

Outlets: Farm shop and farmers' markets at Bridport, Poundbury, Sherborne; occasionally Blandford and Weymouth. Local delicatessens and shops, including River Cottage Stores, Axminster

Address: Bridge Farm, East Chinnock, Yeovil, BA22 9EA

Telephone: 01935 862387

Burrow Hill Cider

This is an old farm on the edge of the grade one South Petherton soils. Julian Temperley has been here since 1972. His orchards stretch as far as the eye can see, and he has more orchards at Over Stratton, 150 acres in all. More than 40 varieties of cider apple are used, including Burrow Hill Early and Somerset Royal. Julian is very keen on cider apples that originated in South Somerset. Harry Master's Jersey is named after the miller at Yarlingon Mill. Chisel Jersey comes from the Martock area, Dabinett from Mr Dabinett of Mid Lambrook down the road, Stembridge Jersey, from Stembridge, Coat Jersey, from Coat. They are all very local to Burrow Hill, which is why the cider is so distinctive. The cider is matured in oak vats and barrels.

One of Julian's most interesting products is sparkling bottle-fermented cider. He has a small, dark cellar, which is full of bottles in racks, and these bottles get turned at the appropriate time, just as in a champagne cellar in France – secondary fermentation, riddling and degorgement. Julian makes two varieties, the clear, dry, crisp taste from Stoke Red, full of tannins and the slightly more fruity Kingston Black. Jilly Goolden once said: "this has got muscles, this has got brawn. It has got a hairy chest. I think that it is gorgeous".

Cider: Bottle-fermented sparkling, Stoke Red and Kingston Black 8% abv; Burrow Hill Farm-pressed, sparkling, medium dry, bottled 6.5% abv; Burrow Hill still, bottled (flagons) 6.5% abv; Burrow Hill draught from oak cask 6.5% abv

Cider Brandy: Alchemy 3-year-old, 5-year-old, 10-year-old, 15-year-old, all 42% abv; Shipwreck cider brandy matured in oak barrels from MSC *Napoli* cask strength c.43% abv (varies with each barrel); Eau-de-vie 40% abv; Kingston Black Aperitif 18% abv; Cider Brandy and Kingston Black apple juice like a Pineau de Charentes; Pomona 20% abv

Outlets: Farm shop and mail order online. Waitrose stocks Pomona; Booths stock 3-year-old Cider Brandy; Tesco 5-year-old Kingston Black Aperitif and Burrow Hill Farm-Pressed cider. Other outlets include Fortnum & Mason, Harrods, Sally Clarke's, A. Gold in London and many other upmarket delicatessens and farm shops, Avery's of Bristol, Vineyards in Sherborne. County Stores in Taunton, Turnbulls in Shaftesbury, Perry's, Sheppy's, New Forest Cider

Address: Pass Vale Farm, Burrow Hill, Kingsbury Episcopi, Martock TA12 6BU

Telephone: 01460 240782

Website: www.ciderbrandy.co.uk

Chestnut Farm Cider

This is the home of the Bennets, a family-run farm business near Burnham-on-Sea. Old-style farmhouse cider. Viv Bennet, like his father, has won many prizes at the Bath and West with his special brew.

Cider: Dry, medium draught 6.5% abv
Outlets: Farm gate and local agricultural shows
Address: Chestnut Farm, Edithmead, TA9 4HB
Telephone: 01278 785376

Cider Farm Lakes

Near Berrow and a mile inland from Brean Beach and the salt air is Dobunni Farm, where Ian Gibson has made cider since 1987. He has seven acres of orchards containing Yarlington Mill, Chisel Jersey, Dabinett and Michelin. This is also a Somerset Wildlife Conservation Area, with fishing lakes among the orchards. There is a conference centre and a well-stocked farm shop.

Cider: Old Dobbie draught 6% abv
Outlets: Farm shop
Address: Dobunni Farm, Wick Road, Lympsham BS24 0HA
Telephone: 01278 751401
Website: www.ciderfarmlakes.co.uk

Crossman's Prime Farmhouse Cider

A few miles out of Weston-Super-Mare on the way to Congresbury is Mayfield Farm in the village of Hewish. This is the home of Ben Crossman, who started making cider in 1987. Ben uses many local apples and is very traditional. All his apples come from standard orchards apart from one bush orchard, which he planted with Tremlett's Bitter, Improved Dabinett, Sweet Coppin, Stembridge Jersey and Harry Master's Jersey.

Cider: Home Orchard Special draught 7–7.5% abv; dry, medium, sweet draught 6% abv; single-variety Dabinett and Tremlett's Bitter 7% abv
Outlets: farm gate
Address: Mayfield Farm, Hewish, Weston-Super-Mare, BS24 6RQ
Telephone: 01934 833174 or 07770 531621 (mobile)
Website: www.ciderpunk.com

Ermie and Gertie's

Tucked right in the middle of Pitney between Langport and Somerton, this family-run business was established in 2000 when Ian Sinclair took over six acres of mature orchard. Ian makes a blend of cider but has found that single-variety ciders are very popular, and these will vary from year to year. Other cider apples come from local orchards. Ian also makes apple juice, Guernsey ice cream and fruit sorbets.

Cider: Dry and medium dry bottled and flagon 7% abv; cider finished in whisky and rum casks bottles 7% abv; single-variety Dabinett, Harry Master's Jersey, Sweet Coppin, Lambrook Pippin and Yarlington Mill 7% abv
Outlets: Pitney Farm Shop; Home Farm Shop Kingweston; Paxton & Whitfield, London and Bath; Waitrose local branches – Gillingham, Dorchester, Bath, Bristol, Portishead; and local National Trust properties. Farm gate by appointment.
Address: Pitney House, Pitney, Langport, TA10 9AR
Telephone: 01458 252308
Website: www.ermieandgertie.com

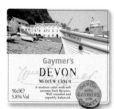

Gaymer Cider Company

Formerly known as Matthew Clark, this firm is made up of well-known cider companies that have been bought up or merged over the years: names such as Coates, Whiteways, Gaymer's, Showerings and Taunton Cider. In turn Matthew Clark Cider was rebranded as part of the Constellation Wine group. The cider wing is now called the Gaymer Cider Company, which is a throwback to a well-known Norfolk cider company founded in the eighteenth century. The company has more than 2,000 acres of orchard and buys in apples from many others. About 30,000 tons of cider apples are pressed annually. Much of this juice is then concentrated on site, which allows the company to make cider all the year round. This is the home of Babycham, launched in 1953 by Francis Showering, as well as Dry Blackthorn, Addlestones and Gaymer's Original. Like many other large-scale cider makers, Gaymer's could not reveal the juice content of their ciders. For discerning cider drinkers, however, there are Orchard Reserve ciders made with 100% cider fruit from specific cider orchards. These orchards include Stewley, near Hatch Beauchamp, Newton's Vale at the foot of the Quantock Hills and Stonesbrook on the banks of the River Brue near West Lydford. They are all lightly carbonated, well balanced and have some real tannin in there. In 2005 Stewley Orchard won the Waitrose Best Environmental Practice award. They also now produce a new range of bottled Somerset and Devon ciders as well as a pear cider.

Cider: Dry Blackthorn 5% abv; Addlestones 4.8–5.2% abv; Gaymer's Original 4.5% abv; Taunton Traditional 5.3% abv; Diamond White 8.4% abv; Olde English 4.5% abv; Special Vat 6% abv; Natch 5.2% abv; and K 8.5% abv; Single orchard Stewley medium dry 6.8% abv; Newton's Vale medium 6.8% abv; Stonesbrook dry 6.1% abv
Perry: Babycham 6% abv
Outlets: Most national supermarket chains
Address: Kilver Street, Shepton Mallet, BA4 5ND
Telephone: 01749 334000
Website: www.cbrands.eu.com

Hecks Farmhouse Cider

Hecks is based in the town of Street, famous for Clarks shoes and its lack of pubs. Glastonbury is only a mile away. They make cider and perry and run a farm shop. John Hecks and his two sons, Andrew and Chris, use a variety of presses: old wooden ones, a hydraulic one and a belt press. As a family they have been making cider since 1840 and specialise in more than 20 single varieties. They even make several varieties of perry. In 2006 they won the CAMRA National Gold award for their Kingston Black Cider. Hecks also make a wide range of apple juices.

Cider: Dry, medium, sweet, bottled and draught 6.5% abv; single variety bottled Kingston Black, Dabinett, Yarlington Mill, Vilberie, Sweet Alford, Brown's, Fair Maid of Devon, Dunkerton's Late Sweet, Porter's Perfection, Hangdown, Morgan Sweet, Improved Dove 7% abv
Perry: Hendre Huffcap, Moorcroft, Blackeney Red 6.5% abv, and others such as Gin, Judge Amphlett and Green Horse depending on the season
Outlets: Farm shop, many local shops and the English Farm Cider Centre, Firle, Sussex
Address: 9–11 Middle Leigh, Street, BA16 0LB
Telephone: 01458 442367
Website: www.hecksfarmhousecider.co.uk

Henry's Farmhouse Cider

Cider making was started here by Harold Pring's grandfather in 1912, when the canal at the bottom of the orchard was still in use. Old-style cider making, wild yeasts, oak barrels. Now run by Mrs Pring, there is also a touring caravan site where you can park up in the orchards.

Cider: Draught, dry 6–7% abv
Outlets: Farm gate
Address: Tanpits farm, Dyer's Lane, Bathpool, Taunton, TA2 8BZ
Telephone: 01823 270663

Naish's Cider

Frank and Harold Naish made cider here for many, many years. Their family has been here for over 200 years. Harold died in 2003 but Frank is now 84 and still carries on with help from Paul Chant of Midsomer Norton. The orchards are very fine and have many unusual varieties, including Glastonbury Port Wine, Pennard Bitter and 20 unrecorded species as well as one of their very own, called Naish's Apple. Frank and Paul blend apples to produce true traditional dry cider using wild yeasts and matured in 120-gallon pipe barrels.

Cider: Naish's natural dry, still draught 7% abv
Outlets: Wholesale only, two locations, phone first
Address: Frank Naish, Piltown Farm, West Pennard, Glastonbury, BA6 8NQ
Paul Chant, Rhybridge Farm, Midsomer Norton, BA3 2QQ
Telephone: 01761 417636 (Paul); 01749 890260 (Frank)

Orchard Pig Cider

Andrew Quinlan and Neil MacDonald started making cider in 2003 and use cider apples such as Vilberie, Stembridge Jersey, Dunkerton's Late and Yarlington Mill from their orchards at Coxbridge. The dessert apples they use come from West Bradley orchards. They also keep Gloucester Old Spots and are obsessed with gammon and ham.

Cider: Dry and medium, bottled and draught 6.5% abv; sparkling medium 6.5% abv
Outlets: Online shop and a wide range of 130 stores not just in the West Country but from Elgin to Cardiff and Essex. See website.
Address: West Bradley Orchard, West Bradley, Glastonbury, BA6 8L
Telephone: 01458 851222
Website: www.orchardpig.co.uk

The Original Cider Company (formerly Broadoak Cider Co.)

Run by Brian Brunt near Clutton in North Somerset, this medium/large-scale cider farm produces a wide range of cider products.

Cider: Broadoak Vintage 4.5% abv; Broadoak dry, medium, sweet 6% abv; Kingston Black 7.5% abv; Old Bristolian 8.4% abv; Pheasant Plucker 6% abv; Moonshine 6.4% abv; Broaoak keg dry 5% abv; Rustic Gold 6% abv; Megawhite 7.5% abv; Classic Gold 6% abv
Perry: Pear cider 5.3% abv; draught perry 7.5% abv
Outlets: National, Ireland and Canary Islands
Address: Blackberry Hill, Clutton, BS39 5QQ
Telephone: 01275 333154

Parson's Choice

The small village of West Lyng is in the heart of the Somerset Levels on the main road from Taunton to Glastonbury and runs along a small ridge that separates Curry Moor from Northmoor. A mile or two further on beyond East Lyng lies Athelney, which is where King Alfred lay low with his Athels while fighting the Danes in the ninth century, hence the name, which means Isle of Athels. Jeanette and her father Phil Dolding have made cider here since 1988. They have their own orchards and also buy apples from the neighbouring villages of North Curry and Burrowbridge. Jeanette is one of the few hands-on women working on cider presses in Somerset. They use wild yeasts.

Cider: Parson's Choice, dry, medium and sweet draught 6.5% abv
Outlets: Farm shop
Address: Parsonage Farm, West Lyng, Taunton, TA3 5AP
Telephone: 01823 490978

Pennard Cider

Dr Hugh Tripp has been making organic cider and wine for more than 20 years. Everything is highly organic here and within a few miles of Glastonbury Tor, the Vale of Avalon is spread out far below. There are few concessions to modernity: true, an old red Massey Ferguson tractor is employed to help with the crushing, but everything else is manual. Wild yeasts are used. All apples come from certified organic orchards. Hugh also makes a wide range of wines, liqueurs and apple juices.

Cider: Pennard Organic Dry draught 6–7% abv
Outlets: Farm shop and Slow Food market in Bristol
Address: Avalon Vineyard, The Drove, East Pennard, Shepton Mallet, BA4 6UA
Telephone: 01749 860393
Website: www.pennardorganicwines.co.uk

Perry's Cider Mills

Set amidst rolling hills, Dowlish Wake lies two miles south of Ilminster. The Perry family have been in Dowlish Wake since the seventeenth century but it was actually one of their uncles, William Churchill, the village black-smith, who started making cider here in 1921. The business is now run by the fourth generation, George Perry. There is a standard orchard and George's father, John Perry, has a large bush orchard down the road. Dabinett, Porter's Perfection and Yarlington Mill are some of the apples they use. The Perrys have stuck to their guns and believe very much in the ethos of high-quality, traditional farmhouse cider. They have also over the years diversified into single varieties.

Cider: Traditional Farmhouse dry, medium, sweet, bottled and draught 6% abv; Vintage dry, medium and sweet, bottled and draught 6% abv; Hogshead dry, lightly sparkling blend 6% abv; single variety Dabinett, Morgan Sweet, Somerset Redstreak 6% abv
Outlets: Farm shop
Address: Perry's Cider Mills, Dowlish Wake, Ilminster, TA19 0NY
Telephone: 01460 55195
Website: www.perryscider.co.uk.

Quality English Cider

Keith Goverd worked at Long Ashton Research Station for 20 years as a microbiologist. He now makes cider, perry and apple juice and is also one of the leading lights in Bath Farmers' Market. He is a consultant and pomol-ogist for cider makers and has given advice to many people over the years. He makes over 100 varieties of apple juice and also specialises in cider vinegar. He works with many types of soft fruit, such as plum, quince, straw-berry and cherry. He is working on a book identifying many Cornish varieties of apple (*The Cornish Pomona*).

Cider: Dry, medium dry 6.5% abv and low alcohol
Perry: Blend of pure perry pear 6.5% abv
Outlets: Bath Farmers' Market
Address: K.G. Consultants, The Bailiff's Cottage, The Green, Compton Dando, Pensford, Bristol, BS39 4LE
Telephone: 01761 490624

Rich's Farmhouse Cider

Jan Rich's father, Gordon Rich, started making cider here in 1954 and the business has grown a little since then. The cider farm is at Watchfield near Highbridge and is set on the Somerset Levels and Moors. Jan is helped by her cousin Martin Rich, who is the chief cider maker. In 2000 they planted a ten-acre orchard, which is now starting to bear fruit. Other apples come from Burrowbridge and Street. Jan has just enlarged her shop and opened a new restaurant serving locally produced food and daily specials.

Cider: Rich's Vintage medium and dry, bottled 7.2% abv; Rich's Farmhouse still, dry, medium and sweet, draught 6% abv; Legbender bottled, draught 6% abv

Outlets: Farm shop and online, the Legbender Cider shop, Cheddar Gorge; Red Lion Inn Draycott; The Original Cheese Company, Cheddar; The Apple Cider Company; Welsh Back; Bristol Docks; Puxton farm shop; Weston-Super-mare; Fox and Hounds Warminster; Lamb and Fountain Frome; Seymour Arms Witham Friary; King's Head Cannington; Rock House Inn Dulverton; Crossways Inn West Huntspill.

Address: Mill Farm, Watchfield, near Highbridge, TA9 4RD
Telephone: 01278 783651
Website: www.richscider.co.uk

Sheppy's Cider

David and Louisa Sheppy's cider farm is at Bradford-on-Tone, which is between Taunton and Wellington. The Sheppy family moved here in 1917 and farmed 317 acres. Today the cider farm is much larger and there are 42 acres of orchard, large oak vats and a state-of-the-art bottling line. Sheppy's still make traditional cider with varieties such as Hangdown, Dove, Yarlington Mill, Dabinett and Kingston Black, but they also have a very succesful line in single varieties as well as Brown's apple juice. They have a rural life museum, a tea room and guided tours.

Cider: Gold Medal Vintage dry, medium and sweet, bottled 7.5% abv; Goldfinch dry and Bullfinch medium, sparkling, bottled 7% abv; Farmhouse Draught and Oakwood, bottled 6% abv; Organic bottled 7% abv; Cider with Honey bottled 5.4% abv; single variety Dabinett 7.2% abv, Tremlett's Bitter 7.2% abv, Kingston Black 7.2% abv; Taylor's Gold 6% abv, all bottled

Outlets: Farm shop, online shop, many local shops and delicatessens as well as supermarkets: Waitrose nationally, Tesco, Sainsbury's and Asda regionally, and Booths

Address: Three Bridges, Bradford-on-Tone, Taunton, TA4 1ER
Telephone: 01823 461233
Website: www.sheppyscider.com

Thatchers Cider

Sandford is near Churchill in North Somerset. John Thatcher's family started making cider in 1904 and recently celebrated their centenary. There are 180 acres of orchards that produce around 2,000 tons of apples – about a quarter of their requirement. The company is run by Martin Thatcher. This is a state-of-the-art factory that relies on computers, a few buttons and a concentrated regime which produces more than 3 million gallons of cider a year. The ciders include such brands as Wurzel Me, White Magic, Scrumpy Jug, Mendip Scrumpy and Old Rascal. Thatcher's single-variety ciders are now only made from dessert apples, such as Cox, Katy and Spartan, which is disappointing for real cider drinkers, though there is talk of reintroducing Dabinett again. Thatchers also make perry from conference pears as well as 'pear cider'. Unfortuntately Thatchers were not prepared to discuss the juice content of their ciders, although their apples are all fresh pressed.

Cider: Wurzel Me 4.8% abv, Gold 4.8% abv; Mendip Scrumpy 6% abv; Old Rascal 6% abv; White Magic 7.5% abv; Scrumpy Jug 6.0% abv; all bottled; Draught Cheddar Valley 6% abv; Gold 4.8% abv; Heritage 4.9% abv; Old Rascal 6% abv; Traditional, unfiltered, uncarbonated. 6% abv; single variety Cox 5.3% abv; Katy 7.4% abv; Spartan 5.2% abv; all bottled

Speciality ciders: Vintage 7.4% abv, oak matured 5.2% abv

Perry: Perry Conference pears bottled 7.4% abv; Pear Cider bottled 4.5% abv

Outlets: Farm shop and supermarkets
Address: Myrtle Farm, Sandford, Winscombe, B525 SRA
Telephone: 01934 822862
Website: www.thatcherscider.co.uk

Torre Cider

Torre Cider is situated on a lane near Cleeve Abbey in Washford between Minehead and Watchet in West Somerset and is run by Jill Gillman. The cider farm was set up in 1989 and produces ciders mainly for the tourist market. The cider apples used are Kingston Black, Yarlington Mill, Dabinett, Sweet Coppin, Somerset Redstreak and Harry Master's Jersey from their own and surrounding orchards. There is a farm shop selling cheese, jams, pickles and honey.

Cider: Bottled and draught Sheep Stagger 7.4% abv; Tornado 8.4% abv; Farmhouse 6.5% abv
Outlets: Farm shop and other local shops.
Address: Washford, Watchet, TA23 0LA
Telephone: 01984 640004
Website: www.torrecider.com

Tricky Cider

Alistair Brice and Steve Watkins have been making cider commercially since 2005. Alistair is a builder and Steve is a carpenter. The cider apples come from the Blackdowns, mostly Dabinetts, which give a strong complex cider with good colour. They also have a mobile cider bar which they take round shows and festivals.

Cider: Tricky dry, draught 7% abv
Outlets: Farm gate and the Culm Valley Inn, Culmstock.
Address: The Bakery, Churchinford, TA3 7RF
Telephone: 01823 602782
Website: www.trickycider.com

West Croft Cider

Nestling under the hillside of Brent Knoll, not too far from the sea, West Croft Farm is a good location for a cider farm. John Harris's grandfather first made cider here but it fell into abeyance until John started making cider again in 1993. He has won many prizes, including the Gold award in the 2007 CAMRA awards. He has his own orchard and the apples from one or two others at North Curry and Burrowbridge. He is not a great fan of sulphur and prefers natural yeasts. He does an early Morgan Sweet Cider which can be very good indeed. His cider vinegar is used by Mark Hix at The Ivy in London. John Harris also has a large Wassail on the third Saturday in January every year.

Cider: Janet's Jungle Juice dry and medium, draught 7% abv; Morgan Sweet draught 6% abv (only available early in the season)
Outlets: Farm gate or online www.ciderpunk.com Merrylegs, RCH Brewery and John Hallam.
Address: West Croft Farm, Brent Knoll, Highbridge, TA9 4BE
Telephone: 01278 760762/760259
Website: www.burnham-on-sea.co.uk/west_croft_cider and www.ciderpunk.com

Wilkins Farmhouse Cider

Roger Wilkins's grandfather came here in 1917 and started making cider. Roger has continued the art and from his farm at Mudgeley near Wedmore he has good views of Glastonbury Tor out across the Somerset Levels and moors. Roger is an old-school, unreformed cider maker: no bottles here or single varieties, just farmhouse cider and farmhouse cheese. The farm is down a narrow, dead end lane where you will find an informal cider club – there are newspapers and chairs and always someone to chat to. Roger has his own small music festival in the summer.

Cider: Wilkins farmhouse dry, medium and sweet, draught 6.2% abv
Outlets: Farm gate
Address: Land's End Farm, Mudgley, Wedmore, BS28 4TU
Telephone: 01934 712385

WALES

The renaissance of Welsh cider perhaps deserves its own book, but a selection of cider makers mainly from Monmouthshire and Glamorgan are included here as cider and perry was often made on farms in these regions within living memory. The valleys of the Wye and Usk provide good microclimates similar to parts of Herefordshire and there are also large orchards here producing cider fruit under contract to Bulmers. There are also many old perry pear trees still standing, which implies that there was once a thriving perry tradition, particularly in Monmouthshire. Committed volunteers have sought to identify and catalogue these varieties before they keel over.

Blaengawney Cider

Andy and Annie Hallett have been making cider since 2002. Most of the fruit comes from ex-Bulmers and ex Westons orchards in Monmouthshire. Andy, who is a mechanical engineer by trade, has worked for the last 20 years in the food industry and is looking to plant up his own orchard with traditional Welsh varieties like Pethyre and Frederick as well as with Ellis Bitter. The farm is about 6 miles west of Pontypool and at 1,000 ft is one of the highest cider farms in Wales. He has also experimented successfully with keeving and hopes one day to make perry. In 2008 they won the Pewterers Cup at the Royal Bath and West and got a Bronze award from CAMRA.

Cider: Blindfold; dry, still 8% abv; The True Welshman bottled 6.7% abv; Heartbreaker dry 7.5–8% abv; Full Fat finished in a rum barrel 8% abv
Outlets: Wholesale only. Pubs: the Fox and Hounds, Risca, Clytha Arms near Abergavenny and The Carne Arms, Llysworney.
Address: Blaengawney Farm, Mynedd Maen, Hafodyrynys, Crumlin, Newport, Gwent NP11 5AY
Telephone: 01495 244691
Website: www.blaengawneyfarm.co.uk

Bragdy Brodyr

Four Brothers cider and perry are made by Richard Williams, a teacher, and his elder brother, Allan, as well as Chris and Lynn, who lend a hand at pressing time. They started cider making in 2002 and then progressed to perry – a new venture for Glamorgan. Their apples come from Monmouth and the perry pears from around Leominster. The variety is unknown but gives very good results. They won Gold and Bronze awards with their medium/sweet perry in 2007 in the Welsh Festival. They only make a small amount but they savour it and drink the perry like wine with a meal at the table.

Cider: Goldrush and Satisfaction draught 6–8% abv
Perry: Silver Lady sweet 3–4% abv
Outlets: Clytha Arms Welsh Cider Festival
Address: Glynneath, Glamorgan SA11 5AF
Telephone: 01639 720693

C J's Cider

Situated a few miles north of Raglan, John Watkin's family has made cider since 2004. They have two acres of Michelin orchard and previously supplied fruit to Bulmers, but when the price dropped they started to make cider commercially.

Cider: Draught only 7.5–8%
Outlets: Welsh Cider Festival and through Jon Hallam (see p.239)
Address: Bottom Farm, Penhors, Raglan, Usk, Monmouthshire, NP15 2DE
Telephone: 01600 780216

Clytha Arms

Just off the A40 and set close to the
River Usk a few miles east of
Abergavenny, the Clytha Arms is the
setting for the Welsh Cider Festival, held
every year at Whitsun. This pub is run
by Andrew and Bev Canning, who have
also been making perry in small
quantities at the Clytha Arms since
2001. They use the pears from the
garden and from a local orchard, with
perry pear trees reputedly up to 400
years old. Andrew told me that many of
the old men talked about perry being
made here on the farms before the
Second World War and some until the
1950s. Perry also used to be made at
Usk College, where it was pressed by
the students.

Perry: Clytha Dry bottle conditioned 6% abv
Outlets: Clytha Arms only
Address: Clytha Arms, Abergavenny,
Monmouthshire, NP7 9BW
Telephone: 01873 840206
Website: www.welshcider.co.uk/prod-clytha

Gwyynt y Ddraig Cider and Perry

Otherwise known as the Welsh Cider
and Perry Company, this is run by Bill
George and Andrew Gronow at Llest
farm, which is in East Glamorgan at
Llantwit Fardre, between Pontypridd
and Llantrisant. They started making
cider in 2000 and by 2004 they had
won a CAMRA Gold medal for their
cider and in 2005 a Gold for their perry.
They also won Champion Cider and
Perry of Wales 2005. Their cider apples
are 70 per cent Welsh and come mainly
from Monmouthshire. The perry pears
come from Monmouthshire as well.
Between the ages of ten and seventeen
Andy grew up round Sandford and
Ilminster in Somerset, so his taste for
cider began at an early age. Gwyynt y
Ddraig is the largest cider maker in
Wales. In 2008 he won two second
prizes – one at Hereford Museum
International Competiton and the other
at The Big Apple Putley Trials.

Cider: Bottled: Orchard Gold medium, oak conditioned 4.9% abv; Gold Medal 7% abv; Black Dragon
medium, oak conditioned 6.5% abv; draught:
Kingston Black, Haymaker, Yarlington Mill, Dabinett,
dry farmhouse cider, Barnstormer, Dog Dancer and
Fiery Fox 5.5–7.2% abv
Perry: Draught: Malvern Hills Perry, Blakeney Red,
Red and Green Longdon, Two Trees Perry approx.
5.5% abv
Outlets: Online shop, Old Swan, Llantwit Major,
Plough and Harrow in Monknash, and many pubs
including Brains and Wetherspoons in Wales, as
well as Tesco, Waitrose and Asda
Address: Llest Farm, Llantwit Fardre, Pontypridd,
Glamorgan CF38 2PW
Telephone: 07791 066240 or 07791 066257
Website: www.gwyntcider.com

Ralph's Cider and Perry

Six miles over the Welsh border from
Herefordshire lies Ralph Owen's farm
at 850 feet above sea level. Encouraged
by his grandfather, Ralph started
making cider after the hot summer of
1976 and hasn't looked back. After a
spell in Anglesey as a farm manager for
Bertram Bulmer he moved to Badland
Farm in 1986, where there was a
neglected orchard with White Norman
cider trees, and he has planted up the
gaps ever since. Dabinett and Brown
Snout do well. He has also planted
Thorn for perry. Ralph has won many
Gold awards at the Welsh Cider and
Perry Festival. In 2005 he was overall
champion at Putley Cider trials and
won a national Gold medal at the
Reading CAMRA Festival. In 2007 he
was perry champion at the Hereford
International cider competition. On his
50-acre farm he keeps suckler cows and
a flock of 130 ewes. In 2008 they won
two second prizes at the Bath and West
and a Gold at the Great Taste Awards for
their Yarlington Mill.

Cider: Ralph's dry, medium and sweet, bottled and
draught 6-8% abv
Perry: Ralph's dry, medium and sweet, bottled and
draught 6% abv
Outlets: Farm gate and online sales as well as food
and drink festivals in Wales
Address: Old Badland Farm, New Radnor LD8 2TG.
Telephone: 01544 350304
Website: www.ralphscider.co.uk

Seidr Dai

Dave and Fiona Matthews started making cider in 2000 using only Welsh hand-picked fruit from traditional, unsprayed and unfertilised orchards. They are purists and use no water, sugar or added yeast, allowing nature to take its course. Wherever possible, Seidr Dai uses rare and endangered Welsh varieties of cider apple and perry pear. In June 2001 Dave founded the Welsh Cider Society and has an impressive range of single-variety ciders and parries, which are testament to the varieties that were once grown in Wales. One of his aims is to save, identify and propagate these 'rare breeds' of cider apple and perry pear, so that future generations of Welsh cider makers can enjoy their superb flavours. They have founded a museum orchard in north Monmouthshire with ten varieties each of perry pear and cider apple. Dave grew up in Gloucestershire and acquired a taste for experimentation from Kevin Minchew and Mike Broome. The cider is kept in his mother-in-law's old stone garage.

Cider: Berllanderi Blend, Dai's Dry, Gwehelog, Kingston Black, Major Tom and Major Tom II, Monmouthshire Heritage, Raglan's Rarest, Yarlington Mill Blend all 6–7% abv
Perry: Berllanderi Green, Blakeney Red, Burgundy, Crwys Fach, Cwm Green, Gwehelog, Hellen's Early, Little Cross Huffcap, Monmouthshire Burgundy Painted Lady, Panker's Pride, Potato Pear, Rock, Sweet Huffcap, Taynton Squash, Thorn, Tom Thumb all 6–7.5%.abv
Outlets: Only at festivals or wholesale
Address: For events and historical info see
Website: www.welshcider.co.uk

Seidr Mynediad Ysbyty

Jon Hallam is better known as a distributor of cider and perry to festivals and events throughout the country, but he does experiment with cider making in his spare time. These ciders are in short supply and hard to get hold of. Jon has planted trees on both sides of the River Wye. He has a wide knowledge of the cider world and has been distributing craft ciders and perry for more than 25 years.

Cider: Ellis Bitter/Red Vallis 6.5% abv; Ellis' Blend 6.5% abv; Deity Grade 6.5%
Outlets: Wholesale only
Address: 97 Parc Sant Laurens, Cas-Gwent
Telephone: 01291 627242

Springfield Cider

Alan and Jo Wordsworth run a 110-acre farm near Llangovan on the lanes between Trellech and Raglan. They look after an orchard of 25,000 trees planted in 1998/99. The varieties are bitter-sweets such as Ashton Bitter, Dabinett, Ellis Bitter, Major, Michelin and a sharp for apple juice, Brown's Apple. Alan uses only natural yeasts, no added water, sulphites or sugar. In 2007 the couple won several awards at the Welsh National Cider and Perry Festival including the prestigious Gold medal for overall Champion Cider and Silver medal for the bottled Farmhouse Cider. Some of the old perry trees on the farm are Gin and Burgundy. Alan and Jo also keep a fair number of Andalusian horses and Kune Kune pigs.

Cider: Farmhouse bottled and draught 6.8% abv; Old Barn bottled and draught 7.2% abv; Sledgehammer matured bourbon casks 8.2% abv; Red Dragon 7.4% abv
Outlets: Ross Feeds and Irma Fingal-Rock, Monmouth, D & M Watkins Raglan
Address: Springfield Farmhouse, Llangovan, Monmouthshire NP25 4BU
Telephone: 01291 691018 or 07752 030858
Website: www.springfieldcider.co.uk

Troggi

Set between Shirenewton and Llantrisant in Monmouthshire, Troggi was founded in 1984 by Mike Penney. Troggi takes its name from the brook which runs through the Earlswood Valley. Initially Mike used contract milling and pressing based at Usk College but when the equipment fell into disrepair he switched to a contractor based at Llanishen. His own equipment was installed in 1989. A permanent cider house opened in 1995. Troggi specialises in whole juice dry cider and perry, and is developing bottle-conditioned (traditional method) products, some of which are 12 years old. Troggi has also won many prizes and in 2007 won the alcoholic product award from True Taste of Wales for his Old Perry, as well as The Big Apple dry draught perry prize.

Cider: Draught Troggi Cider non-filtered and oak conditioned, 7.1% abv; bottle-conditioned 6.2% abv; Kingston Black 6.1% abv; Yarlington Mill 5.9% abv
Perry: Draught Troggi Perry non-filtered 6.2% abv; Bottled Old Perry 6.4% abv; Kevin's 6.2% abv; Earlswood 6.1%abv
Outlets: Jon Hallam and John Reeke
Occasional outlets: The Boat, Penallt; The Carpenter's Arms, Mynydd Bach, Shirenewton.
Address: Lower House Cottage, Earlswood, Monmouthshire NP16 6RH
Telephone: 01291 650653

Ty Gwyn Cider

Run by Jimmy and Judith McConnel, Ty Gwyn cider is made on their farm in the beautiful Monnow Valley. The orchards were planted by them in the 1960s. For their own cider they use Brown Snout and Vilberie but they also supply other larger cider makers with cider apples and also grow blackcurrants for Ribena. Ty Gwyn Cider is available in several restaurants and gastro pubs. They won a Gold medal at the 2007 Leeds Beer Cider and Perry Festival and a Bronze at the Welsh Cider and Perry Festival.

Cider: Ty Gwyn bottled and draught 6% abv
Outlets: Farm gate, Clytha Arms, Irma Fingal Rock Monmouth; the Bell at Skenfrith and the Felin Fach Griffin near Brecon, and local Waitrose. It can also be found at the Gurnards Head, Zennor near St Ives, Cornwall
Address: Whitehouse, Crossways, Newcastle, Monmouthshire NP25 5NF
Telephone: 01600 750287

W. M. Watkins and Sons – Ty Bryn Cider

Tony Watkins makes cider 5 miles east of Abergavenny. He started making it in about 2003 and has two traditional orchards totalling five acres. Some of the apples still go into Bulmers and the rest they make into cider.

Cider: Oak Barrel dry, traditional, draught 6.5–7% abv; rum and whisky cask cider 8.3% abv; Ty Bryn bottled 6.3% abv
Outlets: Jon Hallam
Address: Upper House, Grosmont, Monmouthshire NP7 8LA
Telephone: 01873 821237

Wernddu Perry

Frank and Leigh Strawford are based a few miles east of Raglan and produce limited quantities of perry from the Potato Pear and Hellen's Early, which are 120 years old. They also collect perry pears from surrounding farms and, when possible, make single-variety perry from Blakeney Red, Gin and Thorn pears. They also have an organic vineyard with more than 2,000 vines, and keep alpacas.

Perry: Wernddu Perry 5.7% abv; Blakeney Red blend 5.5% abv
Outlets: Own winery and Waitrose in Monmouth and Abergavenny
Address: Wernddu Farm, Pen-Y-Clawdd, Monmouth NP25 4BW
Telephone: 01600 740104
Website: www.wernddu-wine.co.uk

WORCESTERSHIRE

Barbourne Cider

Richard Reynolds, who lives in Worcester, has been making cider since 2002. Some of the fruit comes from Tupsley Court, a family orchard near Hereford, which has 30 mature trees that include Foxwhelp, Bulmer's Norman, Vilberie, Sweet Coppin, Yarlington Mill, Brown Snout, White Norman and Ashton Brown Jersey. All the perry pears are from old Worcestershire orchards and are hand-picked. Richard is keen to identify old trees and has managed to find some Judge Amphlett, High Pear and Normand Carosa. Recently his dry cider won second prize at Putley out of 45 entries. He is also a founder-member of the Three Counties and Welsh Marches Slow Food Presidium.

Cider: Barbourne Cider dry, draught 6.5% abv; Foxwhelp Norman 6.3% abv; Yarlington Mill in whisky barrels 7.4 % abv; Somerset Redstreak and Brown's 6.5% abv; Kingston Black Bottle Conditioned Cider 6.5% abv
Perry: Barbourne Perry 4.1% abv; Normand Carosa 6% abv; Bottle-conditioned Perry 6% abv
Outlets: Local shows, Worcester Wines, The Plough in Worcester, Nags Head in Malvern, Wellington in Birmingham (draught), Worcester Arts Workshop
Address: 19 York Place, Worcester, WR1 3DR
Telephone: 01905 27151
Website: www.barbournecider.co.uk

Knight's Cider Co. Ltd

Keith Knight has been making cider for 30 years and his company has grown in size, as has his orchard, which started out at 25 acres and is now 200 acres. Keith's products are made without any apple concentrate, artificial colours, flavours or sweeteners. In 2003 his cider won first prizes at both The Cider Museum, Hereford, and at the Royal Bath & West Show. In 2006 Keith sold the production part of his company to Aston Manor, a large cider maker in Birmingham, but kept the orchards.

Cider: Malvern Gold Medium Reserve bottled 6% abv; Malvern Oak Dry Reserve bottled 6% abv; Knights Traditional Dry, medium sweet, draught 6% abv; Knights Premium Reserve Cider 5.8%, made from bitter-sweet apples.
Outlets: Farm shop. Malvern Oak and Gold: many regional delis and wine bars, Ludlow Food Centre, Orchard Hive and Vine, local Waitrose and Budgens. Knights Premium Reserve at Morrisons and Asda.
Address: Crumpton Oaks Farm, Storridge, Malvern, WR13 5HP
Telephone: 01684 568887
Website: www.knightscider.co.uk

Norbury's Black Bull Cider Co.

Tom Norbury has been making cider at Storridge on the outskirts of Malvern since 1979. All the cider fruit comes Holywell Farm and surrounding farms. He also grows cherries, plums, soft fruit, damsons, makes fruit wine and sells top hats for cavaliers and roundheads. Tom makes about 5,000 gallons of cider.

Cider: Black Bull dry, medium and sweet 7% abv; in rum barrels 9.3% abv
Perry: Dry and medium sweet, sparking dry still 8% abv
Outlets: Farm gate July–October; 16 farmers' markets in the Birmingham, Staffordshire, Worcester area; Ludlow Food Festival; 150 markets a year.
Address: Holywell Farm Buildings, Storridge, near Malvern, WR13 SHD
Telephone: 01886 832206

The Monkey House

This is one of the last cider houses left in the country. Basically a small, thatched, half-timbered cottage, the cider is kept in barrels behind a stable door and is served in jugs, which is how all cider and beer used to be served. The Monkey House, which is the local nickname for the cider house, is situated in Woodmancote near Defford, set back from the A4104. It is run by Graham and Jill Collins, and has been in Jill's family for well over 100 years, handed down from her great-great-grand-parents. The cider that they serve is made specially for them by Westons.

Cider: Woodmancote Dry 6% abv
Opening hours: Sunday 12–4pm, Monday 12–2pm, Tuesday closed, Wednesday 6–10pm, Thursday 12–2pm and 6–10pm, Friday 12–2pm and 6–10pm, Saturday 12–2pm and 6–10pm
Address: The Monkey House, Woodmancote, Defford, WR8 9BW

BERKSHIRE

HAMPSHIRE

Mitchell F & D (Food and Drink)

Peter Mitchell has run courses on cider and perry making for many years and he has helped train or advise many of the producers in this book. He also advises the industry as a consultant across the spectrum. If you are interested in making cider or perry, contact Peter direct. In his spare time he also makes cider and perry from local fruit and is a key member of the Three Counties Perry Presidium.

Cider: Mitchell's dry, bottled 6% abv
Perry: Mitchell's bottle-fermented perry 6% abv
Outlets: Products still in research and development, but will be available at local shows in 2009
Address: 74 Holloway, Pershore, WR10 1HP
Telephone: 01386 552324
Website: www.tasteandexplore.com
www.mitchell-food-drink.co.uk
www.cider-academy.co.uk

Tardebigge Cider

Set near the Tardebigge flight of locks on the Birmingham to Worcester canal, Steve Cooper found a derelict farmhouse and very wisely planted an orchard in 1995, which now supplies him with cider fruit. He has been making cider since 1999. Steve collects old vehicles as a hobby and has a travelling lorry he takes around as part of his cider roadshow. He has 100 cider trees and access to more fruit locally.

Cider: Dry, medium, sweet, bottle-conditioned and draught 6.5% abv
Outlets: Farm gate and at local agricultural shows and school fêtes
Address: Tutnall Mount, Tutnall, Bromsgrove, B60 1NB
Telephone: 01527 877946
Website: www.tardebiggecider.co.uk

Lambourn Valley Cider Company

Roy Bailey has been making cider since 1995 in the village of Great Shefford, north east of Hungerford. Roy is technically retired and cider and perry making is a self-financing hobby. Roy's cider making is in abeyance for the moment but he is the sales wing for a cider consortium with Rick Wyatt of Wyatt's Cider and Nick Edwards of Ciderniks. Roy is still continuing to make perry with pears from two old trees. This will no longer be draught but bottle-fermented. He also produces cider vinegar and perry vinegar.

Perry: Old Berkshire Perry bottle-fermented 6% abv
Outlets: Sheepdrove Organic Farm, outdoor shows: White Horse Show, Uffington, Coleshill Organic Food Festival, The Walled Garden, Basingtoke
Address: The Malt House, Great Shefford, Hungerford, RG17 7ED
Telephone: 01488 648441
Website: www.lambournvalleycider.co.uk

New Forest Cider

Based at Burley in the New Forest, Barry Topp has been making cider since 1988. Barry does things in style: on special weekends he makes cider with a steam-driven press; and he has a thatched mobile scrumpy wagon, which he takes to shows. He also sells at Borough Market in London. Barry's cider apples come from Hampshire and Somerset. He has also been making Normandy method bottle-fermented cider.

Cider: Kingston Black 7.5% abv; Snake Catcher dry, medium and sweet, draught and bottled 7.4% abv; New Forest Farmhouse Blend 7.4% abv
Perry: New Forest Perry draught and bottled 7% abv
Outlets: Farm shop and Borough Market, London
Address: Littlemead, Pound Lane, Burley, BH24 4ED
Telephone: 01425 403589
Website: www.newforestcider.co.uk

OXFORDSHIRE

Harp Hill Cider

Andrew Lea is a chemist, plant biochemist and food scientist who did his PhD at Long Ashton Research Station in the 1970s but like so many of its other employees now has to earn a living by other means in the food and drinks industry. Andrew is passionate about passing on his knowledge and experience of making craft cider. His website is an excellent introduction to the chemistry and microbiology of cider making and has been a great source of information to would-be cider makers. Andrew helped on a research project for the Food Standards Agency (FSA) on assessing chemical markers for the establishment of juice content in ciders. The results of this work can be reached on his website called FSA PROJECT Q01057. Andrew Lea has his own orchard and makes cider regularly and monitors it carefully. He is a great believer in natural yeasts and allowing nature to do the best it can. The apples he uses are: Broxwood (bitter-sharp), Foxwhelp (bitter-sharp), Harry Master's Jersey (bitter-sweet) Kingston Black (bitter-sharp), Stoke Red (bitter-sharp), Frederick (sharp), Sweet Coppin (sweet), Dabinett (bitter-sweet), Crimson King (sharp), Yarlington Mill (bitter sweet), LeBret (sweet), Medaille d'Or (bitter-sweet)

Cider: Harp Hill Cider bottled 7.4% abv
Outlets: Occasional local events.
Address: www.harphill.co.uk
Website: www.cider.org.uk

Upton Cider Company

The fruit for this cider company comes from a ten-acre cider orchard planted in 1970 by Taunton Cider for Stan Lynch. There are nine varieties of cider apple, including Dabinett, Yarlington Mill and Michelin. Back then, the fruit was going to Taunton Cider but Stan had his own ideas and started to make cider in 1983 and slowly went 'organic'. He stopped chemical spraying in 1989. The Upton Cider Company is now run by Valerie Fitchett, assisted by her husband Robert. But Stan still does some of the tractor driving in the orchards and advises on the cider making and quality. The cider was a winner in 2004 and 2005 of CAMRA's overall awards for cider.

Cider: Upton dry, medium and sweet, draught 7% abv
Outlets: Farm shop, The Bell at Aldworth and The Retreat at Reading
Address: Upton Fruit Farm, High Street, Upton Didcot, OX11 9JE
Telephone: 01235 850808
Website: www.uptoncider.co.uk

SHROPSHIRE

Mahorall Farm Cider

Mahorall is a small 150-acre family farm situated on the southern slopes of Clee Hill, near Ludlow in South Shropshire. It is run by Peter King-Turner and his son Chris. Peter came here in 1969 and milked cows until 1992. He started making cider in 1998 on a 200-year-old press. It came from the next village, where it had been the communal press. As demand for their cider has grown they have now graduated to a hydraulic press. They use no chemicals, no colourings, just natural yeasts and oak barrels.

Cider: Medium Sweet Carbonated Cider 6.5% abv; Dry Still Cider and Carbonated 6.5% abv
Outlets: Farm gate (phone first); Little Beer Shop, Ludlow; Crown Country Inn, Munslow, The Sun Inn, Corvedale; The Food Centre, Ludlow' The Clive Arms, The Crown at Hopton Bank; food fairs in Ludlow, Nantwich, Attingham and Shrewsbury
Address: Mahorall Farm, Nash, Ludlow, S78 3AH
Telephone: 01584 890296
Website: www.farmcider.co.uk

CIDER MUSEUMS AND HISTORICAL COLLECTIONS

The Cider Museum, Hereford

This important museum was founded in 1973 by Bertram Bulmer and set up as an Independent Charitable Trust to preserve the history of cider and perry making not just in Herefordshire but nationally. Here they have a large display of old wooden cider presses, a fine set of eighteenth-century fluted cider and perry glasses, several fine illustrated *Herefordshire Pomonas*, the King Offa cider brandy distillery as well as many other important cider and perry artefacts. One significant new addition is the oral history archive, which has been compiled from new and old recordings. There is also a shop and a new research archive and library.

Address: 21 Ryelands Street, Hereford, Herefordshire, HR4 0LW
Telephone: 01432 354207
Website: www.cidermuseum.co.uk

Somerset Rural Life Museum, Glastonbury

Here they have a medieval tithe barn, which once belonged to Glastonbury Abbey, a large wooden cider press and many other cider artefacts, as well as an archive room with many other cider-related photographs. They also have an orchard with Somerset cider trees and have demonstration cider making during the autumn within sight of Glastonbury Tor, as well as a wassail in January.

Address: Abbey Farm, Chilkwell Street, Glastonbury, Somerset BA6 8DB
Telephone: 01458 831197
Website: www.somerset.gov.uk/somerset/ culturecommunity/museums/somersetmuseums/ somersetrurallife/

Mill House Cider Museum, Owermoigne

Run by the dynamic Penny Whatmoor, this family-run museum is well worth a visit, with 42 old, wooden cider presses and mills, some of which are eighteenth-century, and other artefacts such as scratters, mugs, flagons and cider flutes. Penny runs a shop, which sells ciders from Devon, Somerset and Hereford. They also make some of their own cider and have demonstration days. Well worth making the detour. Not far from Lulworth Cove.

Address: Mill House Cider, Owermoigne, near Dorchester Dorset DT2 8HZ
Telephone: 01305 852220
Website: www.millhousecider.com

The Shambles, Newent

This Victorian Village has cider equipment and a good selection of ciders and perries in its shop.

Address: Church Street, Newent, Gloucestershire GL18 1PP
Telephone: 01531 822144
Website: www.shamblesnewent.co.uk

Many cider makers also have their own small museums and these can be very interesting, for example:

Sheppy's

Address: Three Bridges, Bradford on Tone, Taunton, Somerset TA4 1ER
Telephone: 01823 461233
Website: www.sheppyscider.com

Perry's

Address: Dowlish Wake, Ilminster, Somerset TA19 0NY
Telephone: 01460 55195
Website: www.perryscider.co.uk

Rich's

Address: Watchfield, near Highbridge, Somerset TA9 4RD
Telephone: 01278 783651
Website: www.richscider.co.uk

Westons

Address:
Telephone:
Website: www.westons.co.uk

Many county and town museums in the West Country have their own cider sections with presses, jugs and cider mugs, such as those in Taunton, Tiverton, Chard, Honiton, Exeter and Helston.

The Big Apple Association

Runs a series of events each year in Herefordshire around Much Marcle. In the spring there are the famous Putley Cider trials and in the autumn they organise a whole series of Apple Day events, which take place in the surrounding villages of Aylton, Little Marcle, Much Marcle, Munsley, Pixley, Putley and Woolhope. The exhibition in the Tithe Barn at The Hellens is excellent for helping to identify local cider apples and perry pears.

Website: www.bigapple.org.uk

CAMRA (Campaign for Real Ale)

Although CAMRA started out as a real ale lobby, it has for many years now campaigned for 'real cider' and 'real perry' and has a lot of information on its website. It produces a *Good Cider Guide*, which is revised every two or three years, as well as holding national cider and perry competitions. It has many local branches throughout the country. They also run a Cider & Perry Pub Award every year. CAMRA has not yet managed to turn around the big cider makers in quite the same way that it has forced the big brewers to clean up their act, although one or two are producing pure juice cider again. In the meantime CAMRA supports many small to medium producers of high quality. Strangely enough they do not allow pasteurisation in their definition of cider but will allow artificial sweeteners, i.e. saccharin. CAMRA awards are much coveted by producers.

Website: www.camra.org.uk

Common Ground

Based in Shaftesbury in Dorset this important and ethical organisation has turned Apple Day (21 October) into a national event. They have also produced the *Common Ground Book of Orchards* and *The Apple Source Book* as well as *England in Particular* and *The Community Orchards Handbook* and many other smaller publications. For information on orchards, local apple days, wassails, distinctive varieties of pear and apple, visit their website.

Address: Gold Hill House, 21 High Street, Shaftesbury, Dorset SP7 8JE
Telephone: 01747 850820
Website: www.commonground.org.uk
www.england-in-particular.info

Liz Copas

Liz is very well known in the cider world for her work at Long Ashton Research Station as a pomologist and as a consultant for the National Association of Cider Makers (NACM). She has written a very useful book called *Somerset Pomona*, which helps to identify many Somerset cider apples. She is also engaged in research of Dorset's Lost Orchards and cider apple varieties.

Website: www.lizcopas.com

Cornwall Orchards Group

Since 1990 Cornwall County Council has been supporting the establishment of traditional orchards with local varieties, and commissioned the growing of 40 old varieties traditionally grown in Cornwall. They are looking into linking orchards with the local supply chain.

Address: Colin Hawke, Natural Environment Officer, Cornwall County Council County Hall, Truro, Cornwall, TR1 3AY
email: chawke@cornwall.gov.uk

For Devon Orchard Groups see Orchard Link and Orchards Live on p.247

Gloucestershire Orchard Group

This is a very active group and has all sorts of information on its websites, with a very good section on Gloucestershire apples and pears by Charles Martell and pictures by Juliet Bailey. There are also details of several key museum orchards planted in Gloucestershire, like the Mother Orchard near Cheltenham, Laurel Farm Dymock at Ebworth Ebley, Green Farm, Brentland's Farm and Brookthorpe. It is an excellent example of how orchard knowledge can be grafted on line.

Address: Ann Smith, 109 Orchard Way, Churchdown, Gloucester GL3 2AP
Website:
www.orchard-group.uklinux.net/glos/index.html

Hartpury and Prestperry Orchards

On the Gloucester side of Newent, the village of Hartpury is not only named after a pear (Hardepirige – hard pear tree), it has young perry pear trees planted in the churchyard as well as a fine bee shelter. A few miles down the road is the new Cohort project, the brainchild of Jim Chapman, which has been involved with the planting of over 100 perry pears and 100 varieties of Gloucestershire apple at one of the Prestperry Orchards. The collection has recently been awarded 'National Collection' status by The National Collection of Perry Pears (NCCPG). This is a very good example of one village helping to save the perry and apple heritage of Gloucestershire. The new centre, which will primarily be used for training courses, is being built in the newly planted 25-acre orchard. Members of the public may visit this orchard at any time to see the young trees.

Website: www.hartpuryhistoric.org

K. G. Consultants

Keith Goverd worked at Long Ashton Research Station for 20 years as a microbiologist. He is a consultant and pomologist for cider makers and has given advice to many people over the years. He makes over 100 different varieties of apple juice and also specialises in cider vinegar. He also works with many types of soft fruit, such as plum, quince, strawberry and cherry. At the moment he is working on a book identifying many Cornish varieties of apple, *The Cornish Pomona*.

Address: The Bailiff's Cottage, The Green, Compton Dando, Pensford, Bristol BS39 4LE
Telephone: 01761 490624

Marcher Apple Network

Founded in December 1993, the society for reviving old varieties of apples and pears has grown to around 300 members. Recently they have re-published on CD *The Herefordshire Pomona* and *Vintage Fruit* with 290 descriptions of cider apples and 107 of perry pears. They have also produced a book called *Apples of the Welsh Marches* and on their website there is a tantalising section on Apples in Welsh literature.

Address: Dr Peter Austerfield, Stone Croft, Westhope, Hereford HR4 8BT
Website: www.marcherapple.net

Mitchell F&D Limited / The Cider Academy

With over 25 years of experience in running courses, first at Hindlip College and then at Core Food and Drink at Pershore College, Peter Mitchell founded The Cider Academy in 2003. Peter runs all sorts of cider-making courses as well as acting as a consultant and advisor to many in the industry. He runs courses in Ireland, Jersey, the USA, China and Somerset. Peter is also able to advise on all technical matters about labelling, new product development, tutored tastings, etc.

Address: 74 Holloway, Pershore, Worcestershire WR10 1HP
Telephone: 01386 552324
Website: www.cider-academy.co.uk

National Association of Cider Makers (NACM)

The NACM was founded in 1920 and is a self-appointed governing body of the cider and perry industry in the UK. In the main it represents the views of the larger cider companies and their production methods. The NACM is also a member of the Association of the Cider and Fruit Wine Industries of the European Union (AICV: www.aicv.org) and through this body is able to represent the interests of British cider makers within the European Union.

Website: www.cideruk.com

The National Collection of Perry Pears, Malvern, Worcestershire

The Three Counties Showground at Malvern houses the national collection of perry pears, some 126 trees of 59 varieties. Their aim is to have three trees each of every known variety, and it is believed that there are more to be rediscovered. These trees were planted between 1991 and 1998 and in perry-pear terms are still very young. For a full list of perry-pear trees see the website.

Address: The Showground, Malvern, Worcestershire WR13 6NW
Telephone: 01684 584900
Website: www.orchardgroup.uklinux.net/glos/pears/ncpp.php

National Fruit Collection, Brogdale, Kent

This is an important 150-acre collection with over 2,300 varieties of apple, 550 of pear, 350 of plum and 220 of cherry. In spring the range and variety of blossom is extraordinary, as are the fruits in the autumn. They have regular guided tours as well as access to several leading pomologists.

Address: Brogdale Road, Faversham, Kent ME13 8RZ
Telephone: 01795 535286
Website: www.brogdale.org

National Orchard Forum

The National Orchard Forum was established in autumn 2002 and has a comprehensive website providing contacts for a wide variety of orchard groups all over the country. They have links to many different websites, address current problems and pool useful scientific and orchard knowledge in their newsletters.

Website: www.nat-orchard-forum.org.uk

Orchard Link, South Devon

Based around Totnes this cooperative helps to preserve orchards, press fruit and put orchard owners in touch with cider producers.

Contact: Trudy Turrell, PO BOX 109, Totnes, Devon TQ9 5XR
Website: www.orchardlink.org.uk

Orchards Live, North Devon

Founded in 1991 as Save our Orchards, this North Devon group now has over 200 orchard enthusiasts on its books and organises all sorts of events, including Apple Day with the Royal Horticultural Society at Rosemoor.

Address: Michael Gee (Chairman), Varley Cottage, Prixford, Barnstaple, Devon EX31 4DX
Website: www.orchardslive.org.uk

Pershore College, Worcestershire

This college runs courses on cider making, cider-fruit growing, juice production, analysis, etc., and offers a wide range of services including commercial bottling, which has proved very useful to small producers, not just in the Three Counties but in Wales and Oxfordshire. The course can be three-day or single-day units. They also make their own cider and perry here.

For more information contact Richard Toft Warwickshire College, Avonbank, Pershore, Worcestershire WR10 3JP
Telephone: 01386 552 443
email: rtoft@warkscol.ac.uk
Website: www.warkscol.ac.uk/pershore

Shropshire Apple Trust

Based in Coalbrookdale beside the Severn, this is a constituted community trust that works to raise awareness of the importance of traditional orchards. Two of the founder members of the Shropshire Apple Trust have written an excellent book called *Real Cidermaking on a Small Scale* (Michael Pooley & John Lomax).

Address: Michael Pooley, 41 Church Hill, Ironbridge, Telford, Shropshire TF8 7PZ
Telephone: 01952 433632
Website: www.shropshireappletrust.co.uk

Somerset Apple Project 2004–2005

This was a large-scale project which involved taking children from five Somerset schools into orchards at different times of year and getting them to write poetry and make sketches and drawings. The project was run by James Crowden and Kate Lynch and could be replicated anywhere in the country. It provided a useful framework for using orchards as an educational opportunity, but made links with cider makers, grafters and beekeepers.

Website: www.somersetapples.org.uk

Somerset County Council Countryside Group & Somerset Orchard Group

For advice on planting new standard orchards and council grants. Over 20,000 trees have been planted in this scheme since 1987. Also available: a DVD on Somerset Orchards, price £10, p&p free.

Address: County Hall, Taunton, Somerset TA1 4DY
Telephone: contact Phil Stone or Rose Wickes 01823 355617
email: PRStone@somerset.gov.uk

Somerset Orchards Ltd

A co-operative founded in 2004 of small cider orchard owners to find new markets for their apples. Their first venture is to produce single variety cider apple juice.

Contact: Rosie Inge
Telephone: 01749 670070
Website: www.somersetorchards.co.uk

South West of England Cider Association (SWECA)

Formed in 1937 as the Association of Somerset Cidermakers, in 1967 it became the Somerset and Devon Cidermakers Association, then in 1974 Avon was added, and, finally, in 1983 took its present name. It exists to promote the interests of those engaged in the cider-making industry in the south-west of England. Membership is open to bona fide cider makers, who make for sale not less than 1,000 gallons per annum.

Address: Contact Bob Chaplin, Gaymers, Kilver Street, Shepton Mallet, Somerset BA4 5ND
Telephone: 01749 334000
Website: www.cbrands.eu.com
www.intellectbooks.com/on_line/heritage/cider/makers/exec.htm

Symondsbury Apple Project

Run by Kim and Dave Squirrell, this project has undertaken research into Dorset's lost apple varieties and has looked into the ways in which orchards can be researched through public records, tithe maps and early Ordnance Survey maps.

Address: Treewise Co-operative Ltd, The Office, The Old Post Office, Symondsbury, Dorset DT6 6EZ
Website: www.appleproject.org.uk

Three Counties Cider and Perry Association

The Three Counties are Worcestershire, Herefordshire and Gloucestershire. The Association was founded in 1993, has some 60 members and represents their interests. Their intention is to improve the image and quality of farmhouse cider and perry. They meet several times a year and are particularly active during the Cider and Perry trials at Putley as well as during Apple Day events.

Website: www.thethreecountiesciderandperry association.co.uk

Three Counties Perry

This is another interesting group of producers who have achieved Slow Food Presidium status with Three Counties Perry. This is a major first for the perry world and pioneered by Tom Oliver, Peter Mitchell and John Fleming from Slow Food Ludlow.

Website:
www.threecountiesperry.co.uk/producers.html

Tidnor Wood Orchard Trust, Herefordshire

Based a few miles to the east of Hereford, Tidnor Wood Orchard Trust has around 24 acres of orchard, which form a living museum collection of cider-apple trees. It has been recognised as a National Collection and is in the process of conversion to organic status with the Soil Association. The fruit is currently under contract to Westons. Visitors on Open Days only.

Website: henrymay@tidnorwood.org.uk
www.tidnorwood.org.uk

UK Cider

A very comprehensive website loaded with all sorts of useful information including 200+ UK cider makers, 950 cider pubs and even 350 cider makers in France. The organisation is also keen on campaigning for the rights of small and real cider makers, often instigated by Andy Roberts. Of particular interest are the wholesalers who act as middle men between the cider makers and the publicans, or those putting on shows and festivals. Also has a good on-line bookshop for cider books, etc.

Website: www.ukcider.co.uk

Welsh Perry and Cider Society/Cymdeithas Perai a Seidr Cymru

When the Welsh Cider Society was started in 1991 by Dave and Fiona Matthews there were only 5 members and represents their members: now there are 36 members and represents their cider makers and 140 other members, i.e. dedicated consumers. There is a lot of other information on the website about Monmouth perry varieties and Welsh cider makers.

Website: www.welshcider.co.uk

The Wittenham Hill Portal, Oxfordshire

Run by Andrew Lea, this website is an excellent introduction to the chemistry and microbiology of cider making and has been a great source of information to would-be cider makers.

Website: www.harphill.co.uk
www.cider.org.uk

Worcestershire Orchard Workers

Set up in 1998 as the Worcestershire Traditional Orchards Forum to encourage the conservation and enhancement of traditional orchards, the Worcestershire Orchard Workers is run by Wade Muggleton, Countryside Officer at Worcestershire County Council.

Address: Wade Muggleton, The Countryside Centre, Wildwood Drive, Worcester WR5 2LG
Telephone: 01905 766493
Email: wmuggleton@worcestershire.gov.uk

To test cider and meet cidermakers, also visit various county shows:

Royal Cornwall Show

Royal Bath and West Show

Devon Show

Three Counties Show, Malvern

… and numerous food and drink festivals.

Bibliography

Anderson, H.M., Lenton, J.R. and Shewry, P.R. *One Hundred Years of Science in Support of Agriculture 1903–2003* (Long Ashton Research Station)

Atherton, Ian *Ambition and Failure in Stuart England. The Career of John Scudamore* (Manchester University Press 1999)

Austen, Ralph *Treatise of Fruit Trees and The Spiritual use of an Orchard* (1653 and 1657)

Beale, John *Herefordshire Orchards: A Pattern for all England,* 1656

Browning, Frank *Apples* (North Point Press 1998)

CAMRA Good Cider Guide (Campaign for Real Ale, 2005)

Charley, Vernon *The Principles and Practice of Cider Making* (Leonard Hill Ltd, 1949). A translation of *La Ciderie,* 3rd edition, 1928 describing the French methods of cider production.

Chapman, Jim *Champagne and May Hill* (unpublished article 2001)

Common Ground Book of Orchards (Common Ground 2000)

Common Ground Apple Games and Customs (Common Ground 1994)

Common Ground Apple Source Book (Hodder & Stoughton 2007)

Common Ground England in Particular (Hodder & Stoughton 2006)

Common Ground Orchards A Guide to Local Distinctiveness 1989

Copas, Liz *A Somerset Pomona – the cider apples of Somerset* (Dovecote Press 2001 and Grenadier Publishing 2006)

Crowden, James *Cider. the Forgotten Miracle* (Cyder Press 2 1999)

Crowden, James *Somerset Cider and Apple Juice. a Guide* (Somerset County Council 2002)

Crowden, James *Bottling it up* (Bristol University 2002 and Petits Propos Culinaires 2003)

Crowden, James *Apples* (Country Life 2001)

Digby, Sir Kenelm *The Closet Opened* (1669; reprinted Prospect Books 1997)

Evelyn, John *Sylva, Pomona* and *Aphorisms on Cider* (John Beale et al. Royal Society, 1664)

French, Roger *The History and Virtues of Cyder* (Robert Hale 1982)

Foot, Mark *Cider's Story Rough and Smooth* (published privately 1999)

Gayre, G.R. *Wassail in Mazers of Mead* (Phillimore 1948)

Godfrey, Eleanor *The Development of English Glassmaking 1560–1640* (Clarendon Press 1975)

Haines Richard, *Aphorisms on the New Way of Improving Cider* (1684)

Hills, Margaret *Cider Vinegar* (Sheldon 1997)

Hinton, David *The Sheppy's* (Rocket Publishing 2000)

Juniper, Barrie and Mabberley, David *The Story of the Apple* (Timber Press 2006)

Knight, Thomas *A Treatise on the Culture of the Apple and Pear and the manufacture of Cider and Perry* (Proctor, Ludlow 1808)

Latimer, Jonathan *Orchards: Through the Eyes of an Artist* (Langford Press 2005)

Lea, Andrew and Piggot, John *Fermented Beverage Production* (Springer 2003)

Legg, Philippa and Binding, Hilary *Somerset Cider* (Somerset Books 1986)

Luckwill and Pollard editors *Perry Pears* (Long Ashton Research Station Bristol University 1963)

Mac, Fiona *Cider in the Three Counties* (Logaston Press 2003)

Marcher Apple Network *Apples of the Welsh Marches* (Oldlands Press 2002)

Marcher Apple Network *The Herefordshire Pomona 1885* on CD, ed. Richard Wheeler (2005)

Marcher Apple Network *Vintage Fruit* on CD, ed. Richard Wheeler (2007)

Morgan, Joan and Richards, Alison *The New Book of Apples* (Ebury Press rev. ed. 2002)

Oxford Dictionary of National Biography (Oxford 2004) for details on Robert Mansell, Sir Kenelm Digby, Ralph Austen, Sir Paul Neile and John Scudamore

Petersonn, R.T. *Sir Kenelm Digby* (Jonathan Cape 1956)

Phillips John *Cyder a Poem* (H. Hills, Blackfriars 1708)

Pollard, A. and Beech, F.W. *Cider Making* (Hart-Davis, 1957)

Pooley, Michael and Lomax, John *Real Cidermaking on a Small Scale* (Nexus Special Interests 1999)

Proulx, Annie and Nichols, Lew *Cider* (Storey Publishing 3rd edn 2003)

Quinion, Michael *A Drink for its Time* (Museum of Cider, Hereford 1979)

Quinion, Michael *Cidermaking* (Shire Publications 1997)

Radcliffe Cooke, C.W. *A Book about Cider and Perry* (London 1898)

Royal Society Archives and Registers for 1662 and 1663

Royal Society biographies of past Fellows

Russell, James *Man-Made Eden* (Redcliffe Press 2007)

Spiers Virginia and Martin, Mary *Burcombes, Queenies and Collogetts* (West Brendon 1996)

Stafford, Hugh *A Treatise on Cyder making* (1759)

Stevens Charles and Lieubault John, *Maison Rustique,* translated 1600

Stewards Accounts of John Scudamore for the year 1632 transcribed by FC Morgan with notes (MS in the Cathedral Library, Hereford)

Umpelby, Roger and Copas, Liz *Growing Cider Apples: a guide to good orchard practice* (NACM 2002)

Wallace, T. and Marsh, R.W. (ed.) *Science and Fruit – Long Ashton Research Station 1903–1953* (Bristol University)

Ward, Ruth *A Harvest of Apples* (Sage Press 1997)

Watson, Ben *Cider, Hard and Sweet: History, Traditions and Making Your Own* (1999)

Whiteway, E.V.M. *Whiteway's Cider A Company History* (David & Charles 1990)

Wilkinson L.P. *Bulmers. A Century of Cidermaking* (David & Charles 1987)

Williams-Davies, John *Cider Making in Wales* (The Welsh Folk Museum. 1984)

Williams, Ray (ed.) *Cider and Apple Juice Growing and Processing* (Long Ashton/Bristol University 1988)

Wilson C. Anne (ed.) *Liquid Nourishment* (Food and Society Series, vol. 5. Edinburgh University Press, 1993)

Worlidge, John *Vinetum Brittanicum or Treatise on Cider* (London 1678)

Index